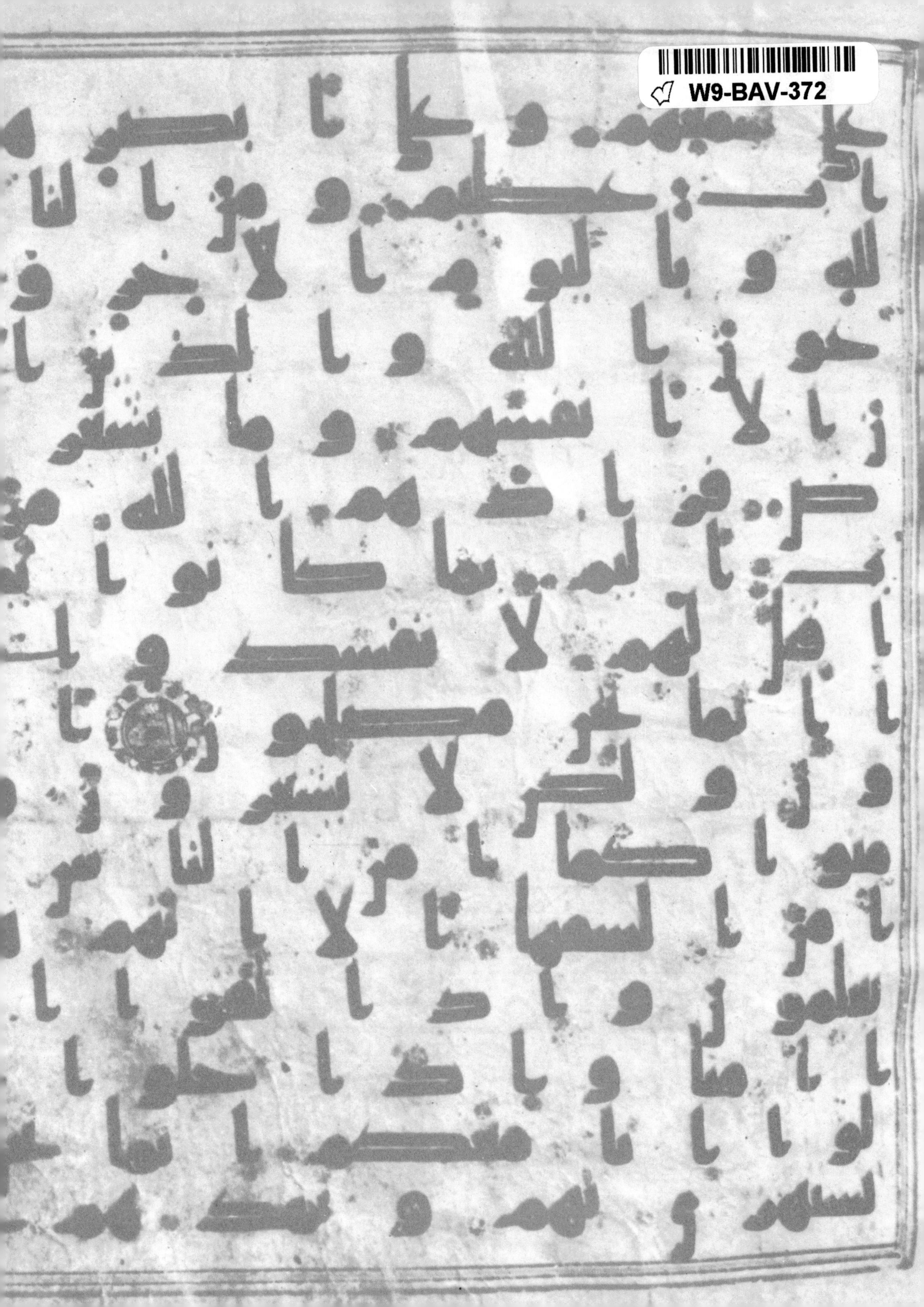

MECCA THE BLESSED
MADINAH THE RADIANT

General Editors: Elizabeth and Paul Elek   *Production: Stanley Freeman*

ERRATA

The publisher would like to point out that, as indicated in the list of text illustrations, the tailpiece decorations in this volume come from a 19th century book and show examples of local and other craftsmanship found in Mecca at that period. Their inclusion does not indicate that the objects are either made or in use today.

page 13 "page 206" should read "page 210".
page 140 In line 24 "astrologers" should read "astrologer".
page 159 The caption here, and in the list of text illustrations, should read: "Islamic miniature of about the fourteenth century showing an angel carrying a taper. *(Topkapu Museum)*".
page 166 In line 42 "mosque" should read "Zamzam Pavilion".
page 213 In note 32 from line 9 omit: XXVII, 53.
page 214 In note 42 from line 11 omit: XII, 213.
Throughout, *Mir'at i-Mekke* should read *Mirat i-Mekke.*

MECCA THE BLESSED
MADINAH THE RADIANT

Text Emel Esin Photographs by Haluk Doganbey

Crown Publishers, Inc., New York

Istituto Geografico De Agostini S. p. A. - Novara 1963
Printed in Italy

TABLES OF CONTENTS

Through the kind recommendation of 'Abd al-Rahman 'Azzam Pasha, to whom I am deeply obliged, I was privileged to be granted a permit to travel and to take photographs in the Hijaz by His Majesty the King of Saudi Arabia. I beg His Majesty and Their Royal Highnesses Prince and Princess Faysal to accept my profound gratitude for the gracious hospitality with which I was honoured in the Hijaz.

I am most grateful for the kindness shown to me during my visit to Saudi Arabia by the Sheikh al-Qazzaz of Mecca, by the officials of the Department of Press, by Mr A. Birden, the Turkish Minister to Saudi Arabia and by the members of the Legation, by Mr and Mrs Amroussy and many other friends.

A special acknowledgement is due to Professor Necati Lugal of the Faculty of Theology of the University of Ankara for his kind guidance in the interpretation and translation of Arabic texts, and to Professor M. Hamidullah for his patience and generosity in the painstaking correction of my text. I should like to thank Dr Ibrahim Artik, Professor Adnan Erzi and Dr O. Rescher for helping me in the choice of reference works, Professor R. B. Serjeant of the University of London for his kind advice, and the directors and curators of the Topkapu Museum, the Türk ve Islam Eserleri Müzesi and the Eski Sark Eserleri Müzesi in Istanbul; the Palestine Archaeological Museum; the Museum of Islamic Art and the Sharif Sabri Pasha Collection in Cairo; the Musée du Louvre, Paris; the British Museum and the Victoria and Albert Museum, London; the Aleppo Museum and the Baghdad Museum, for their kind permission to reproduce photographs of objects in their collections.

I am particularly indebted to Mrs Tamara Talbot Rice who introduced me to Paul Elek Productions Ltd., to Mr and Mrs Paul Elek who encouraged my endeavours, and to Miss Ann Lee who patiently corrected my English.

Mr Haluk Doganbey the photographer was a most helpful and able collaborator in this work. Our Linhof cameras gave excellent results despite the particularly difficult climatic conditions under which we were working.

EMEL ESIN

LIST OF ILLUSTRATIONS

14. ‘Uuj (Og), according to Islamic legend the illegitimate son of Adam’s daughter ‘Anaq: a Turkish book-painting, from a manuscript written in 991 A. H. (1583 A. D.) for the Ottoman Sultan Murad III and illustrated by an unknown painter. *(Colour)* *(Museum of Turkish and Islamic Art, Istanbul)*
15. An angel bringing the ram, as Abraham is about to sacrifice Ishmael: a Turkish book-painting. *(Colour)* *(Museum of Turkish and Islamic Art, Istanbul)*
16. Noah’s Ark sailing round the site of the Ka‘bah, submerged beneath the Flood: a Turkish book-painting. *(Colour)* *(Museum of Turkish and Islamic Art, Istanbul)*
17. A South Arabian limestone idol. *(Museum of the Ancient Orient, Istanbul)*
18. The head of a colossal statue in red sandstone, *circa* 700 B. C., from Madain Salih in the north of the Hijaz. *(Museum of the Ancient Orient, Istanbul)*
19. An onyx stele, dating from about the beginning of the Christian era, with a camel-rider and bearing an inscription in archaic South Arabian characters. *(Louvre, Paris)*
20. Alabaster slab, carved in a design of bull-heads and grapevines and bearing an archaic South Arabian inscription, dating from about the first century B. C. *(Museum of the Ancient Orient, Istanbul)*
21. The Yemenite army, led by Abrahah, invading Mecca and being destroyed by pebbles thrown by a flock of birds: a Turkish book-painting. *(Colour)* *(Topkapu Museum, Istanbul)*
22. ‘Abd al-Muttalib, in Abrahah’s camp, whispering the name of his grandson Muhammad, as yet unborn, into the ear of an elephant, as it kneels in token of respect: a Turkish book-painting. *(Colour)* *(Topkapu Museum, Istanbul)*
23. The Qorashi merchant Muttalib and his nephew, the young archer ‘Abd al-Muttalib, arriving in Mecca: a Turkish book-painting. *(Colour)* *(Topkapu Museum, Istanbul)*
24. Abrahah’s elephants, charging upon the Ka‘bah: a Turkish book-painting. *(Colour)* *(Topkapu Museum, Istanbul)*
25. The newly-born Muhammad, in his mother’s arms, is shown to his grandfather ‘Abd al-Muttalib and to the wondering Meccans: a Turkish book-painting. *(Colour)* *(Topkapu Museum, Istanbul)*
26. An alabaster head of a youth or girl, from Southern Arabia, dating from about the beginning of the Christian era. *(Museum of the Ancient Orient, Istanbul)*
27. A bronze horse, bearing an archaic South Arabian inscription. *(Museum of the Ancient Orient, Istanbul)*
28. Stone bas-relief of two heads, with a South Arabian inscription. *(Louvre, Paris)*
29. Stone stele from South Arabia, showing several human figures and camels, and dating from about the beginning of the Christian era. *(Louvre, Paris)*
30. Muhammad’s marriage to Khadijah: a Turkish book-painting. *(Colour)* *(Topkapu Museum, Istanbul)*
31. The young Muhammad, on a caravan expedition to Syria, being served a meal by Christian monks: a Turkish book-painting. *(Colour)* *(Topkapu Museum, Istanbul)*

32. Muhammad meeting a monotheist shepherd: an eighteenth-century Turkish book-painting, by Seyyid Suleyman Kasim Pasha. *(Colour)* *(Museum of Turkish and Islamic Art, Istanbul)*
33. Muhammad pacifying a giant reptile: a Turkish book-painting. *(Colour)* *(Museum of Turkish and Islamic Art, Istanbul)*
34. Muhammad hearing the complaint of a doe: a Turkish book-painting. *(Colour)* *(Museum of Turkish and Islamic Art, Istanbul)*
35. A desert plant, near Mount Hira.
36. Boulders on Mount Hira.
37. The desert round Mecca, seen from Mount Hira.
38. View from within the cave on Mount Hira.
39. Muhammad hearing a voice and seeing a vision, as he is on Mount Hira: a Turkish book-painting. *(Colour)* *(Topkapu Museum, Istanbul)*
40. Muhammad's vision of ascension: a Turkish book-painting. *(Colour)* *(Museum of Turkish and Islamic Art, Istanbul)*
41. The ruins of Nabatu (Petra), the rock-hewn city of the Nabateans in Arabia Petraea.
42. A calcite gravestone of about the second century A. D., probably from Qataban in Southern Arabia, showing a young woman holding cornstalks, together with an inscription of the name "Aban". *(British Museum, London)*
43. Two plaster heads from the 'Omayyad palace at Khirbat al-Mafjar near Jericho. *(Palestine Archaeological Museum)*
44. Stone head from the 'Omayyad palace at Khirbat al-Mafjar. *(Palestine Archaeological Museum)*
45. Muhammad, leading the Moslems' prayer at the Ka'bah, is attacked by the pagan Qorashi Abu Jahl, who attempts to crush him under a rock: a Turkish book-painting. *(Colour)* *(Topkapu Museum, Istanbul)*
46. Muhammad prays alone in the Ka'bah: a Turkish book-painting. *(Colour)* *(Topkapu Museum, Istanbul)*
47. The oratory at 'Aqabah, near Mecca. *(Colour)*
48. A plaster statue of the 'Omayyad period, representing a man wearing a loin-cloth. *(Palestine Archaeological Museum)*
49. Polychrome plaster statue of the 'Omayyad period, representing a dancer holding a posy. *(Palestine Archaeological Museum)*
50. Head of a plaster statue of the 'Omayyad period. *(Palestine Archaeological Museum)*
51. Madinah in Ottoman times: a Turkish book-painting by Osman Yumni, dated 1323 A. H. *(Colour)* *(Arif Hikmet Library, Madinah)*
52. The early Moslems building the Apostle's original mosque in Madinah: a Turkish book-painting. *(Colour)* *(Museum of Turkish and Islamic Art, Istanbul)*
53. Muhammad preaching on his bench in the Madinah mosque: a Turkish book-painting, possibly sixteenth century. *(Colour)* *(Sharif Sabri Collection, Cairo)*
54. The Archangel Gabriel inspires Muhammad: a Turkish book-painting. *(Colour)* *(Museum of Turkish and Islamic Art, Istanbul)*
55. The Apostle praying for rain before the battle of Badr: a Turkish book-painting. *(Colour)* *(Museum of Turkish and Islamic Art, Istanbul)*

56. Muhammad pledging his daughter Fatimah to her cousin 'Ali in marriage: a Turkish book-painting. *(Colour)* *(Museum of Turkish and Islamic Art, Istanbul)*
57. A Mameluk period Egyptian pulpit in carved wood inlaid with ivory. *(Victoria and Albert Museum, London)*
58. Persian *mihrab* in blue ceramic of the Selçuk period, *circa* 700 A. H. (1300 A. D.) *(Victoria and Albert Museum, London)*
59. An undated monument erected at a site in Quba where Fatimah, Muhammad's daughter, is said to have stayed overnight on her journey from Mecca to Madinah.
60. The mosque at Quba, near Madinah, where Muhammad built the first Islamic house of worship.
61. Zaynab, Muhammad's elder daughter, escaping from Mecca to Madinah: a Turkish book-painting. *(Colour)* *(Museum of Turkish and Islamic Art, Istanbul)*
62. The Meccan women prepare to mutilate the corpses of the fallen Moslems at the battle of Ohod: a Turkish book-painting. *(Colour)* *(Museum of Turkish and Islamic Art, Istanbul)*
63. Muhammad tries to persuade the Moslems to await the attack of the pagan Meccans within Madinah, instead of meeting them at Ohod: a Turkish book-painting. *(Colour)* *(Topkapu Museum, Istanbul)*
64. Qoran III, 199 is revealed to Muhammad during a battle: a Turkish book-painting. *(Colour)* *(Museum of Turkish and Islamic Art, Istanbul)*
65. Plaster bust of the 'Omayyad period, representing a warrior. *(Palestine Archaeological Museum)*
66. Undated tombstone on the battlefield of Badr.
67. The oratory built on the site near Madinah where the expansion of Islam was prophesied to Muhammad, in Qoran XLVIII, 1.
68. The site in the plain of 'Arafat where Muhammad prayed on his farewell pilgrimage.
69. Muhammad delivering his last sermon: a Turkish book-painting. *(Colour)* *(Museum of Turkish and Islamic Art, Istanbul)*
70. The angel of death asking permission to take Muhammad's life: a Turkish book-painting. *(Colour)* *(Topkapu Museum, Istanbul)*
71. The inner gate of the pavilion of the Holy Mantle at the Topkapu Palace in Istanbul.
72. A golden casket in which the Apostle's mantle was kept during the reign of the Sultan Murad III. *(Topkapu Museum, Istanbul)*
73. Part of the iron and brass-work railing which surrounds Muhammad's mausoleum within the Madinah mosque.
74. The " Green Dome " above Muhammad's mausoleum, built in 1277 A. H. (1860 A. D.) *(Colour)*
75. The southern porticoes of the Madinah mosque. *(Colour)*
76. A Persian *mihrab* made in tiles, from Kashan, *circa* 1300 A. D. *(Colour)* *(Victoria and Albert Museum, London)*
77. A Syrian mosque lamp in glass, dating from the Mameluk period. *(Colour)* *(Victoria and Albert Museum, London)*

110. Courtyard of the mosque at al-Khaif, near Mecca. (*Colour*)
111. Exterior of the al-Khaif mosque. (*Colour*)
112. A mosque on the way to the 'Arafat plain. (*Colour*)
113. The Ka'bah, before evening service. (*Colour*)

Jacket Illustrations:

Front: Interior of the Apostle's Mosque in Madinah, taken from the north. The grey marble porticoes were renovated and extended by the Saudi government during 1948-55. The southern arcades in rose-coloured stone, which indicate the site of the Apostle's original mosque, date from the Turkish rebuilding in 1860.

Back: Muhammad riding at the head of his disciples to Badr, where the small Moslem force was to meet the pagan Meccan army in battle.

End-papers:

Front: Verses 7-15, Chapter II of a Qoran in Kufic script – one of those attributed to the caliphs 'Othman and 'Ali.

Back: Turkish lithograph representing the Ka'bah in Ottoman times, reproduced from E. Sabri's *Mir'at i-Mekke*, Istanbul 1301 A. H.

Binding brass:

Calligraphic composition in Arabic Thuluth script. The words are the credo of Islam: " There is none to worship but God." The artist is Kämil Efendi (1862-1941), the last head-calligrapher of the Ottoman court. (*Reproduced by kind permission of his son, Prof. Sheref Akdik.*)

The book-paintings in illustrations nos. 21, 22, 23, 24, 25, 31, 39, 45, 46 and 70 come from the same manuscript as that in illustration no. 1; nos. 15, 16 and 40 come from the same manuscript as no. 14; nos. 33, 34, 52, 54, 55, 56, 61, 62, 63, 64 and 69 come from the same manuscript as no. 32, and are by Seyyid Suleyman Kasim Pasha.

All illustrations marked with an asterisk in the captions are Turkish book-paintings. The sizes given refer to the size of the page on which the painting appears in the original manuscript.

Although the accepted date of the Hegira is 622 A.D., Anno Hegira (A.H.) dates are not necessarily 622 years less than A.D. dates, owing to a discrepancy between the Julian calendar and that used by the Moslem world.

ILLUSTRATIONS IN THE TEXT

The reconstructions of the Ka'bah on pages 24 and 46 are by Shaikh Tahir al-Kurdi of Mecca, reproduced after A. al-Saba'i, *Tarikh Makkah*, published 1952. Reproduced by permission of the Press Department of Saudi Arabia. The tail-pieces of pp. 42, 47, 66, 74, 79, 91, 104, 117, 139, 152, 170, and 193 are drawings of objects of everyday use in Mecca in the nineteenth century. The drawings, by P.W.M. Trap, are reproduced from *Bilder-Atlas Mekka* by Dr. C. Snouck Hurgronje, The Hague, 1888. The illustrations on pp. 36, 175 and 206 are from the same work.

In compiling the maps, reference was made to *The Atlas of Islamic History* published by Princeton University Press. The spellings of place-names used in the Atlas were retained in the maps.

ACKNOWLEDGEMENTS

The Publishers are indebted to the following museums and photographers for permission to show many of the paintings, objects and scenes shown in this volume.

Arif Hikmet Library, Madinah
From the MS *Dalail al-khayrat* (The Ways of Edification), by Osman Yumni, dated 1323 A. H.
Ill. 51, 97
British Museum and Mr. Wim Swaan
Ill. 42
Mrs. Emel Esin
Ill. 41, 66, 88, 105
Musée du Louvre, Paris
Ill. 2, 3, 19, 28, 29
Museum of the Ancient Orient (Eski Sark Eserleri Müzesi), Istanbul
Ill. 4, 5, 10, 11, 12, 13, 17, 18, 20, 26, 27
Museum of Turkish and Islamic Art (Türk ve Islam Eserleri Müzesi), Istanbul
Ill. 104, front end-paper
From MS No. 1973, *Zubdat al-tawarikh* (Epitome of Histories), written in 991 A. H. (1583 A. D.) for the Ottoman Sultan Murad III and illustrated by an unknown painter
Ill. 14 (*fol.* 19), 15 (*fol.* 26), 16 (*fol.* 23), 40 (*fol.* 46)
From an eighteenth century MS copy of Erzeni's life of Muhammad, with paintings by Seyyid Suleyman Kasim Pasha
Ill. 32 (*fol.* 63), 33 (*fol.* 65), 34 (*fol.* 56), 52 (*fol.* 49), 54 (*fol.* 12 b), 55 (*fol.* 239), 56 (*fol.* 26), 61 (*fol.* 313), 62 (*fol.* 438), 64 (*fol.* 257), 69 (*fol.* 459)
Palestine Archaeological Museum.
From 'Omayyad palace, Khirbat al-Mafjar *Ill.* 43, 44, 48, 49, 50, 65
Sharif Sabri Collection, Cairo
Ill. 6, 7, 8, 53
Topkapu Museum, Istanbul
Ill. 72, 83, 84, 85, 90, 91
From a 3-volume MS., No. 1221-23, copied by the calligrapher Ahmed Nur ibn Mustafa from an earlier version of *Sirat al-Nabi* (The Apostle's Biography), a work written in 770 A. H. (1368 A. D.) in Turkish, by Mustafa Dariri Erzeni
Ill. 1 (*vol.* I, *fol.* 214), 21 (*vol.* I, *fol.* 200), 22 (*vol.* I, *fol.* 186), 23 (*vol.* I, *fol.* 82), 24 (*vol.* I, *fol.* 196), 25 (*vol.* I, *fol.* 234), 30 (*vol.* II, *fol.* 30), 31 (*vol.* II, *fol.* 64), 39 (*vol.* II, *fol.* 158), 45 (*vol.* II, *fol.* 366), 46 (*vol.* II, *fol.* 151), 63 (*vol.* III, *fol.* 148), 70 (*vol.* III, *fol.* 408), back of the jacket
Victoria and Albert Museum, London, and Mr. Wim Swaan
Ill. 57, 58, 76, 77, 87, 101

INTRODUCTION

Mecca and Madinah are among the principal religious centres of the world. Ever since the foundation of Islam fourteen centuries ago, Moslem men and women have turned, when they pray, towards the birth-place of their faith. Pilgrims have come each year, from distant countries and in great numbers, to achieve the crowning-point of their lives by visiting the holy cities. This book is an invitation to the reader to wander with the pilgrims in the land of Islam, and to discover for himself both its present and its remote past, far back even to the times before legend gave place to history.

The author has taken care to assure the authenticity of her descriptions of ancient times by consulting as far as possible the earliest Arab sources. For the period of the first civilisations in Arabia, the testimony of archaeology is added to that of the Qoran, to create a picture of the peninsula from the first millennium B. C. to the beginning of Islam. The life of the Prophet Muhammad is seen through the eyes of his contemporaries, as reported by successive generations of chroniclers. Works of pre-Islamic art help the reader to understand the culture to which Muhammad belonged. Then, with the birth of Islamic mysticism, as described in Sufi texts, comes the development of Moslem literature, music and art. For later periods, Ottoman Turkish and modern Arabic works have been used as source material.

The Hijaz is a narrow tract of land about 875 miles long, on the eastern coast of the Red Sea, with the Tropic of Cancer passing through its centre. The Arabic word "Hijaz" means "barrier", and indeed the region's backbone is formed by the chain of the Sarat mountains, which runs parallel to the Red Sea and separates the flat coastal area, called Tihamah, from the lonely highlands of Najd. Between the volcanic peaks of the Sarat there are sandy passes and natural depressions, and in one such basin stands the ancient temple of the Ka'bah, the goal of Moslem pilgrimage.

To make the journey to the Hijaz is often the central aim of a Moslem's lifetime, and to achieve it he will endure hardship and privation, perhaps even walking hundreds of miles to get there. At the beginning of the month of pilgrimage, when he first sets foot on holy ground, he takes his pilgrim's vows and puts on the two lengths of white cloth in which he will approach the House of God, and which will be used as his shroud when he dies. Once within sight of the Ka'bah, he makes the age-old response to the pilgrimage call: "At Thy command, O God, at Thy command." He walks seven times round the temple, the symbol of Man's attachment to God.

Then begins the congregational pilgrimage. A vast crowd (in 1962 it numbered one and a quarter million) gathers in the plain of 'Arafat, a few miles east of Mecca. Slowly it moves in procession towards the Ka'bah. The journey across the parched desert, under the merciless sun, takes two days, for the pilgrims stop at various "stations," to pray, to meditate, or to take part in ceremonies that date from times before the foundation of Islam.

At the close of the Meccan mysteries, as the pilgrim stands at last within the confines of the House of God and joins the immense congregation in a thunderous Gloria, he reaches the consummation of a drama which is an allegory of Man's destiny.

I

ADAM

"AND LO, THY *Lord said unto the angels: 'Verily I shall create a regent in the earth.' They said: 'Wilt Thou create in it one who will work corruption into it and shed blood? And we celebrate Thy praise and extol Thy holiness.' He said: 'Verily, I know what ye know not'.*"

(*Qoran:* II, 30) [1]

In the ninth century A. D. (the third century Anno Hegira, according to the Moslem calendar), Islamic authors recorded a legend which had grown up around this verse.[2] The angels had questioned the will of God, and, in contrition, they sought refuge beneath His Holy Throne. They raised their forefingers to bear witness to the Oneness of God, and wept bitterly as they made a circuit of the Throne (*ill.* 7). The Lord showed them His mercy and peace descended upon their troubled spirits, as they became aware that they were themselves the spiritual and emotional forces which bound the universe to God and would eventually achieve Man's salvation.[3] Below the Throne the angels saw a reflection of it—a ruby ceiling supported by four emerald columns. This vision was of the first temple on earth: the Ka'bah (*ill.* 1).

The legend thus far epitomises the destiny of Man; granted free will to choose between faith and doubt, Man was to abandon faith and therefore to experience the great grief caused by his separation from the Divine Beloved. God would then return to Man in the Throne that Man must build within his own purified heart.[4]

The legend continues with the story of Adam.[5] It is said that he fell from heaven to earth just as the sun was setting. He found himself on the lofty peak of Mount Budh, either in India or Ceylon. Adam was immensely tall; his head, which still wore a wreath of starry leaves (the constellation of Iklil), almost reached the celestial spheres from which he had come. He stood there upon the mountain, motionless, trying to hear the echoes of the angels' singing as they circled round the Holy Throne.

As darkness fell, the angels were so moved by the sight of the enormous creature in silent despair that they prayed it might be taken from them. God heard their prayer and reduced Adam's size until he was in proportion with other creatures on earth. The harmoniously shaped being of superior intelligence, to whom the noble gift of self-expression had been granted (*Qoran:* LV, 3-4), now became a humble "*earthen vessel*" (*Qoran:* XV, 26), "*complete, yet incomplete,*" (*Qoran:* XXII, 5), "*a clod of sensitive flesh,*" (*Qoran:* XXII, 6). As his height diminished, Adam could no longer hear the angels' hymns and told God of the sorrow this gave him. On earth, came the reply: "*Man is nought but what he has striven for*" (*Qoran:* LIII, 39); "*O Man, verily thou strivest upon a hard way towards thy Lord and thou wilt meet Him*" (*Qoran:* LXXXIV, 6).

God urged Adam to seek the Divine Throne on earth. In wonder, Adam looked around him. The dried leaves had fallen from his wreath and fertilised the ground. Where they lay there now grew the aromatic trees of the Indian clime. But Adam could not stay in this sweet-scented land, for he had to fulfil his destiny of toil.

Following God's behest, Adam journeyed northwards as far as Mount Judi in Asia Minor. From there, he turned on a southerly course, crossing Mount Lebanon and the Mount of Olives, to Sinai. At the Red Sea coast, Adam saw in the distance a range of rocky peaks running from north to south along the shore.

Now he entered the arid valleys of the Hijaz, through gorges where tornadoes blew the sand high into the air. At last he stood in a natural basin, immured within a ring of mountains, shiny black pyramids of rock. This, he knew, was the "navel of the earth,"[6] the axis of God's Throne, round which the earth had spun as it came into being. Here in this barren pit, God's mercy would fall like balm upon mankind.

On a small elevation in the midst of the sandy basin there stood a baldaquin, supported on four emerald columns and roofed with a giant ruby. Under the baldaquin, shining so brightly that it illumined the whole valley, lay a pearly white stone, the symbol of Man's soul. The vision was of: "*an arch in which is a lamp, the lamp in glass and the glass like a resplendent star, lit from a blessed tree, an olive neither of the East nor of the West, the oil whereof giveth light, though fire touch it not; light upon light.*' (*Qoran:* XXIV, 35). Adam circumambulated this symbol of his own soul,[7] and then, with stones brought from nearby Mount Hira, he tried to bind it forever to the earth by walling it with strong masonry.

Leaving the holy place where the vision had been vouchsafed to him, Adam journeyed on to the 'Arafat wilderness. Whereas in the Meccan basin the mountains rise oppressively close, at 'Arafat their brown and blue ranges lie some distance away. Meagre shrubs grow here and there, bearing spicy fruits or fragrant mimosa. In the mellow twilight, Adam caught sight of a high heap of boulders in the midst of the plain.[8] He ascended it, and watched the sudden setting of the tropical sun. Then the father of mankind lay prostrate in supplication, and God addressed the souls of future generations that would spring from him, asking them: "*Am I not your Lord?*" They answered: "*Aye, we witness*" (*Qoran:* VII, 172).

In the plain at 'Arafat, Adam found Eve again. He had known her in Paradise, contemplating her with wonder and calling her "My bone, my flesh, my kin" (*ill.* 9), but now he remembered her only faintly. United in loneliness, they started their life on earth together, and as they lit their first domestic fire the eyes of the wild beasts that prowled in the desert glinted fleetingly in the light. The *fahd* (a feline beast of prey) and the hyena were hunting the peaceful camel, the ostrich and the oryx, in the darkness of the Hijaz night.

Death came to Adam in Mecca, at the end of a long life. His pious son Seth buried him in a cave beneath Abu Qubais, the highest mountain of the Meccan area. The luminous white gem-throne was taken from the baldaquin and placed in Adam's grave.

Eve died on the shore of the Red Sea. She had walked to the flat beaches, perhaps watching the intricate branches of coral floating on the pale tropical sea, or looking into the deep pits filled with turquoise-coloured water, where lay the graceful shells shaped like roses, the amber fossils, and the pearl-oysters clinging to the alum banks. Her grave is said to be at Jiddah, on the Red Sea. The pile of stones built upon it was fifty ells long, lending colour to the legend that Adam and Eve, even when diminished in size, were still as tall as palm trees.

THE FLOOD

SETH LIVED on in the Hijaz after his father's death and honoured God's Throne on earth. One day the jewelled vault suddenly ascended to heaven, and Seth realised that the sins committed by his brethren who lived outside the sacred valley had caused Man's vision of God to vanish.

Indeed, Adam's progeny (*ill.* 14) had spread into more fertile regions than the Hijaz, to agricultural lands where they could lead an easy life. Iblis, the Evil Spirit, had insinuated himself among them, teaching them to worship idols. In the lands to the east, the accursed city of Shamsa was built and dedicated to the sun. Cain, the fratricide, and his children were living in the Yemen, and had built a fire temple there. The Evil Spirit fashioned musical instruments for these inhabitants of Arabia Felix; first they had the *nay*, a reed flute, then the drum and the stringed instruments such as the lute, the rebec (*rubab*) and the *tanbur*. On warm nights, the children of Cain would discard the fleece garments inherited from Adam and Eve, and would feast and drink wine to the sound of these instruments. Up in the peaks of the Sarat mountains the God-fearing sons of Seth shepherded their flocks. They looked down upon the clamorous orgies and were tempted by the beauty of Cain's daughters.

1.* Angels decorating the Ka'bah: a Turkish book-painting by Lutfi Abdullah, head painter of the court, or his school; made in 1003 A. H. (1594 A. D.). 15 × 14 cm.

Further south, near Mount Budh, where Adam had arrived on earth, lived the people of Noah. They were dissolute and worshipped idols and the stars. Warned of the deluge to come, Noah built his Ark with the wood of a giant Indian teak. As the torrents of water gushed along the valleys, the Ark was carried upon them to the Meccan basin (*ill.* 16). The site of God's Throne was submerged, and Adam's body floated upon the surface of the water. Noah admonished his companions to refrain from committing any sin while they were in the holy place, while the Ark, of its own volition, sailed seven times round the sunken stone. Then it took a northerly course, towards its resting-place on Mount Judi.[9]

When the floods subsided, shipwrecked humanity started afresh in the land of Babel. The three strains of red, black and white earth that had been used to mould the body of Adam now reappeared in Noah's progeny. Each was now given its own language, and the races separated to dwell in different parts of the world. The issue of Japhet—blond, ruddy-skinned, large-faced, small-eyed —went to live under the cold, starless skies of the north. These were the Turks, the Khazars, the Saqlab, Gog and Magog, who were later to return to the Southern lands as conquerors. The dark-skinned, curly-haired race of Ham populated Africa. Shem's descendants, who had a pleasant appearance and luxuriant hair, became the Arabs, the Nabateans and the tribes of Israel. Known as Semites, they settled between the Yemen and Syria. It was to this race that the gift of prophecy and the holy books were granted.

III

ABRAHAM BUILDS THE KA'BAH

A THOUSAND YEARS after the Flood, two people came walking across the Hijaz desert.[10] The man, tall and elderly, was the Prophet Abraham, born in the land of Babel, the son of Azar and of Nuna of the Semite race. His companion was Hagar, a comely Egyptian girl, carrying in her arms their child Ishmael. She wore a dress with a trailing skirt, in order to efface her footprints on the sand, as she was afraid that Abraham's wife Sarah might pursue them and punish her fugitive maidservant.

Their wanderings brought them at last to a wilderness in which there rose a mound of reddish sand. No one at that time was aware that under the mound there lay the remains of God's Throne on earth, yet it was known as a place of refuge for the oppressed and prayers that were uttered there were answered. Abraham settled Hagar and her child on the mound, under a thorn-tree.

"At that time Mecca was desolate.[11] No one lived there. There was no water. Abraham abandoned the mother and the child in this place. He left them a bag of dates and a leather bottle of water, and went away. Hagar, Mother of Ishmael, ran after him and said: 'O Abraham, whither goest thou, leaving us in this desert? A desert where there is no one and nothing.' She repeated these words, yet Abraham did not turn back. She then asked him: 'Has God commanded this?' Abraham answered: 'It is God's command.' 'Then,' she said, 'He will not let us go to waste.'

"The Mother of Ishmael suckled her child and drank the remaining water. When it was exhausted, the mother and son were thirsty. Hagar looked at her child, who lay writhing and crying on the ground. Unable to bear this sight, she went to the nearest hill, which was al-Safa, and climbed it. She looked down into the valley to see whether anybody was there, and saw no one. She came down from al-Safa, lifted up her long skirt with the determination of one who is preparing to struggle, and set off across the valley to Marwah. She looked to see if there was anyone there and saw no one. And she repeated this seven times.... And when again she climbed upon Marwah, she heard a sound whispering in her own soul: 'Listen.' After this she heard it again, and said: 'Thou whom I hear, if thou canst, bring help.' And lo, there stood an angel beside her, upon the site of the Zamzam well. With his wing the angel struck the ground until the water sprang. And she hurried to dig a well, also filling her bottle meanwhile. And the water hummed forth."[12]

I

Hagar and her child continued to live upon the mound, in loneliness. Then the Jurhum came wandering across the desert. This was an Arabic tribe of Yemenite origin, named after their ancestor who was a son of Qahtan (known in the Bible as Yoqtan), the son of 'Amr, of the race of Shem. The Jurhum came from the north across Mount Kada and made camp in the lower part of the Meccan valley. " They had seen a flying bird, and said: 'This bird is one that circles over water. Surely, according to our reports, there was no water in this valley.' They sent out one or two scouts. These saw the water and returned to give the news. The Jurhum came... and found Ishmael's mother beside the water. They said: 'Wilt thou allow us to camp beside thee?' She said: 'Yes, but you will have no rights over the water.' They had found Ishmael's mother when she was desirous of human company. And they settled and sent messengers to their kindred, and these settled near them until there were amongst them people who built houses. The boy grew up and learnt Arabic from them and became one of them. And they looked at him with admiration..."

In a Qoranic passage, Abraham addresses his son as follows: "*O my son, verily I saw in a dream that I should sacrifice thee. So consider what thou seest.' He said: 'O my father, do as thou art commanded. If God will, thou wilt find me of those who are patient'*." (*Qoran:* XXXVII, 102).

Early Arab historians relate the episode in this way: When Abraham returned to the Hijaz, he told his son to bring a cord and a knife, and to accompany him to Mount Thabir, to the north of the Meccan valley. They were going, he said, to cut and carry back fuel for the hearth. As they started on their way to the mountain, Iblis, in the shape of a man, stood in their way and said to Abraham: " Methinks thou hast seen in a dream the Devil ordering thee to cut thy son's throat." "Away, thou enemy of God," replied Abraham, and stoned him, according to the ancient Semite way of casting out evil. Iblis then turned to Ishmael: " Knowest thou, child, that he thinks that God has ordained that thy throat shall be cut? " The child answered: " May God's will be done." Iblis then rushed to Hagar, saying: " O Mother of Ishmael, he will kill thy son." She said: " Nay, he loves his son." " But he believes that it is God's command," said the Evil Spirit. " Then," said Hagar, " let God's will be done."

Abraham and Ishmael went on to the summit of Mount Thabir. The boy said to his father: " Bind my hands and my feet, to prevent my blood spurting over thee in the death-agony. Sharpen well thy knife so that I may die quickly. Turn me upon my face, with my forehead upon the ground, so as not to see me and not to be moved by love. Give, if thou wilt, my shirt to my mother, to comfort her."

So when they both submitted and he had laid him down upon his forehead, we called out to him: " O Abraham! Thou hast indeed shown the truth of the vision... And we ransomed him with a great sacrifice." (*Qoran:* XXXVII, 103, 107).

Through God's mercy, Abraham's supreme offering was transformed into a ram (*ill.* 15). The animal bounded away down the stony slopes of Mount Thabir, to the Mina gorge, one of the entrances to the Meccan valley. There the Patriarch caught and sacrificed it.

Later, tradition has it, Abraham visited the Hijaz again.[13] Neither Hagar nor Ishmael was on the mound where he had left them, but a strange young Jurhumi woman stood there in the shade of a bower. Nearby there were a few goats in a small enclosure. This was Ri'lah, the daughter of Mudad ibn 'Amr and the wife of Ishmael. Her husband was away hunting. The goats, she said, had been a present to Ishmael from a group of 'Amalik who had camped there. The young woman complained that no crops would grow in the arid Meccan soil, and the goats barely sufficed to assure a living for her and her husband. Hospitably, Ri'lah offered meat and water to Abraham, and as the traveller's hair had been soiled with dust, in true Arabian fashion she washed it for him. Abraham asked her about Hagar; Ri'lah told him that she had died and lay buried in the mound, beneath their feet.

When Ishmael returned, Abraham asked his son's help in a great undertak-

2. An alabaster statue from Mari in Mesopotamia, dating from the third millennium B. C. – some time before the period attributed to Abraham's lifetime by Moslem historians.
Height 52.5 cm.

ing: the construction of God's House. A violent wind (the *sakinah*) carried across the mound a cloud in the shape of a two-headed dragon, writhing in tempestuous contortions. Following the outline of the cloud's shadow, Abraham and Ishmael dug the ground, and beneath the sand they found with awe the ancient site of Adam's temple. A stone came to light which bore the words: " I am the God of Bakkah (the Meccan valley). I have created compassion and love as two of my appellations. Whoever attains these virtues shall meet Me. Whoever cuts away from them is cut away from Me."

And when Abraham and Ishmael raised the foundations of the House, (they said) Our Lord accept from us; verily Thou art the Hearer, the Knower (*Qoran:* II, 127). The foundations were in an irregular, trapezoidal shape, measuring 32 ells on the north-western side, 22 ells on the north-eastern, 37 and 20 on the other opposing sides.

Ishmael carried stones as big as camels on his back, and reached them up to his father who set them in place, using no mortar. As the heat was intense, the old man could lay only one row of stones a day. They needed a stone of exceptional appearance at the eastern corner, to indicate where the circumambulatory rites should begin. Ishmael went to the neighbouring hills to look for such a stone, and while he was gone the gem-throne was miraculously carried from Mount Qubais where it had lain buried since Adam's death. The soft light from the heavenly jewel again illumined the whole of the Meccan area.

When the height of the walls exceeded that of a man, Ishmael brought a rock on which the Patriarch could stand to do his work. His feet left an indelible mark upon the rock. They continued to build until the walls were nine ells high. No roof was made. The building then appeared approximately cubic in shape, and was therefore called " Ka'bah ", the Cube.

Cast out from the society of his time, banished by his father, the priest of astral gods, chased out of the great cities and into the desert by Nimrod and Pharaoh, Abraham had at last found a place in which to build the token of his faith in God, his " *Friend* " (*Qoran:* IV, 125). This humble edifice, constructed by the puny ability of Man, was the only House of God in a pagan world full of monumental temples, towering ziggurats and colossal pyramids. Yet " the Cube " was to change the course of mankind's history.

God said to Abraham:

Associate naught with Me, and purify My House for those who make circuits and stand to pray and bow and prostrate themselves.

And proclaim to mankind the pilgrimage. They will come towards thee on foot and on every lean camel, and through deep passes.

That they may be present at what helps them and remember God's appellation... and perform the circuit around the Ancient House. (*Qoran:* XXII, 26-9)

God has created the Ka'bah the Sacred House standing towards men (V, 97).

In the midst of the forsaken desert, Abraham climbed upon his rock and, turning North, South, East and West, he uttered the call to pilgrimage. From all the seven climes between East and West, those as yet unborn answered: "At Thy command, O God, at Thy command."

In the presence of the Archangel Gabriel, Abraham and Ishmael made the sevenfold circuit of the Ka'bah. They ran seven times between the hills of Safa and Marwah, in commemoration of Hagar's anguish. Then they walked to the plain of 'Arafat, and turned back again towards the Ka'bah, recalling the ordeal of the sacrifice.

As the mysterious rites were performed, Gabriel asked Abraham: " Hast thou penetrated the significance? " [14]

When he left the Hijaz forever, Abraham raised his hands in prayer, and blessed the Meccan valley:

Our Lord, I have settled a part of my offspring in an infertile vale near Thy Sacred House...

Our Lord! And raise up in their midst an Apostle from amongst them who shall recite to them Thy revelations and teach them the Book and the Wisdom and purify them (*Qoran:* XIV, 37; II, 129).

THE DAWN OF HISTORY

In the preceding pages we have moved in the timeless atmosphere of ancient tradition. Now as the dawn of history illumines the cities of Arabia, we can gradually begin to consider Mecca and Yathrib (a pre-Islamic name for Madinah) within the wider ambit of the Peninsula itself.

Archaeological material, inscriptions in ancient languages make their appearance, allowing a certain chronology to be established.

The term "Arab," perhaps meaning "desert dweller," is first encountered in an inscription of the Assyrian king Salmanazar II dated 854 B. C., and it was in common use by ancient authors thereafter.

In the northern part of the Peninsula, supposedly the home of the ancient Semitic races, there were proto-Arab settlements, known variously as Aram, Eber and Khabiru.

According to general Islamic opinion, Abraham and Ishmael lived at the beginning of the second millennium B. C.[15] The descendants of Ishmael are described as "arabicised," in contrast to other tribes which are regarded as pure Arabs.

The 'Amalik (called in the Bible "Amalekites") seem from the works of Moslem historians to have been a people of Arabian stock who had settled in every region of the Peninsula, in Southern Arabia, in Syria-Palestine, in the land of Canaan, and in the Hijaz.

The 'Abil branch of the 'Amalik are said to have founded a city which was in the vicinity of, if not actually in, the present site of Madinah, and which was named after their archon, or chief, Yathrib. It lay in a plain, strewn with black lava and watered by underground springs, which stretched between the ranges of the Sarat mountains. Tame gazelles wandered in the shade of date-palms, mimosa trees and fragrant bushes of deep pink roses. There the kings of the Arqam dynasty reigned over a prosperous and civilised community. But the 'Amalik transgressed the laws of God and retribution followed, first in the form of pestilence, then of Hebrew warriors sent by Moses to subdue them. It was not, however, at this time that the Jews became established in Yathrib. They are said to have sought refuge there later, fleeing perhaps from Nebuchadnezzar or some other pursuer.[16]

Another branch of the 'Amalik, who lived in Mecca, were the cause of a long period of inter-tribal warfare for the custody of the Ka'bah. They launched an attack on the Ishmaelites who guarded the holy place, but as it was sinful to fight there, the latter refused to defend themselves. The 'Amalik drove them out, and for centuries they wandered as nomads in the gorges which lie between the mountains and the coast. Later some branches of the tribe moved away and, as their numbers grew and the available pastureland became insufficient for their needs, took up trading. Other Ishmaelites, Muhammad's ancestors among them, could not bear to leave the vicinity of the Ka'bah, even though they were allowed to visit it only on the occasion of major pilgrimages.

The temple of Mecca had now become Arabia's foremost sanctuary, a place where strife and bloodshed were, in principle, prohibited. The fugitive from enemy pursuit and the hunted beast alike found safety in Bakkah, as the valley round the temple was called. Bushes and trees which grew there were never cut down. In these early days, the Ka'bah stood alone in the valley; the tribesmen's tents

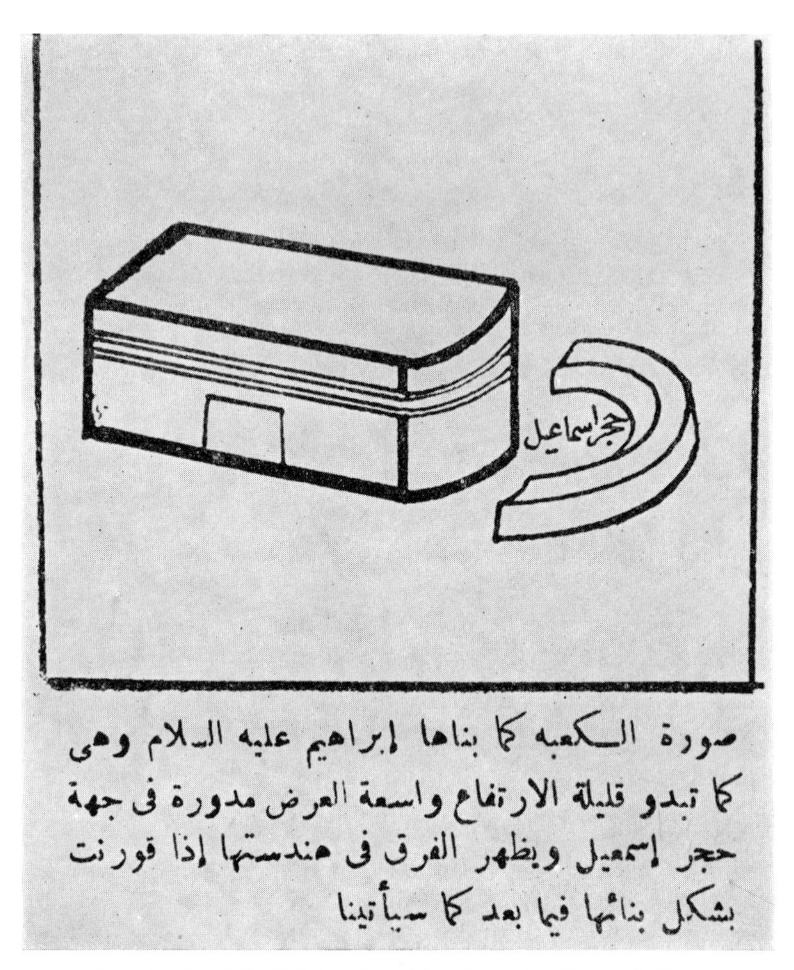

Reconstruction of the Ka'bah as it must have been when Abraham built it.

and cattle-pens, and some cave-dwellings, lay on the slopes of Mount Abu Qubais and the Red Mountain, or else beyond the four gorges which lead out of the Meccan valley. During the daytime, the people would gather around the temple; at night they would return to their tents, leaving the Ka'bah and the valley in solitude.

It will be remembered that when Abraham built the Ka'bah, it stood upon a mound. Since that time, alluvial mud carried down by the flood waters had gradually raised the level of the surrounding plain until the mound disappeared. This meant that the area of the temple itself had to be constantly cleared, and by the 'Amalik period the Ka'bah was standing in the centre of a deep depression.

3. A limestone relief from Mesopotamia, representing a ram; third millennium B. C. Height 33 cm.

4. Bronze sculpture of a horse and rider, bearing an archaic South Arabian inscription. Length 15 cm.

5. A Yemenite limestone relief, showing the façade of a South Arabian temple, c. 700 B. C.

3

4

5

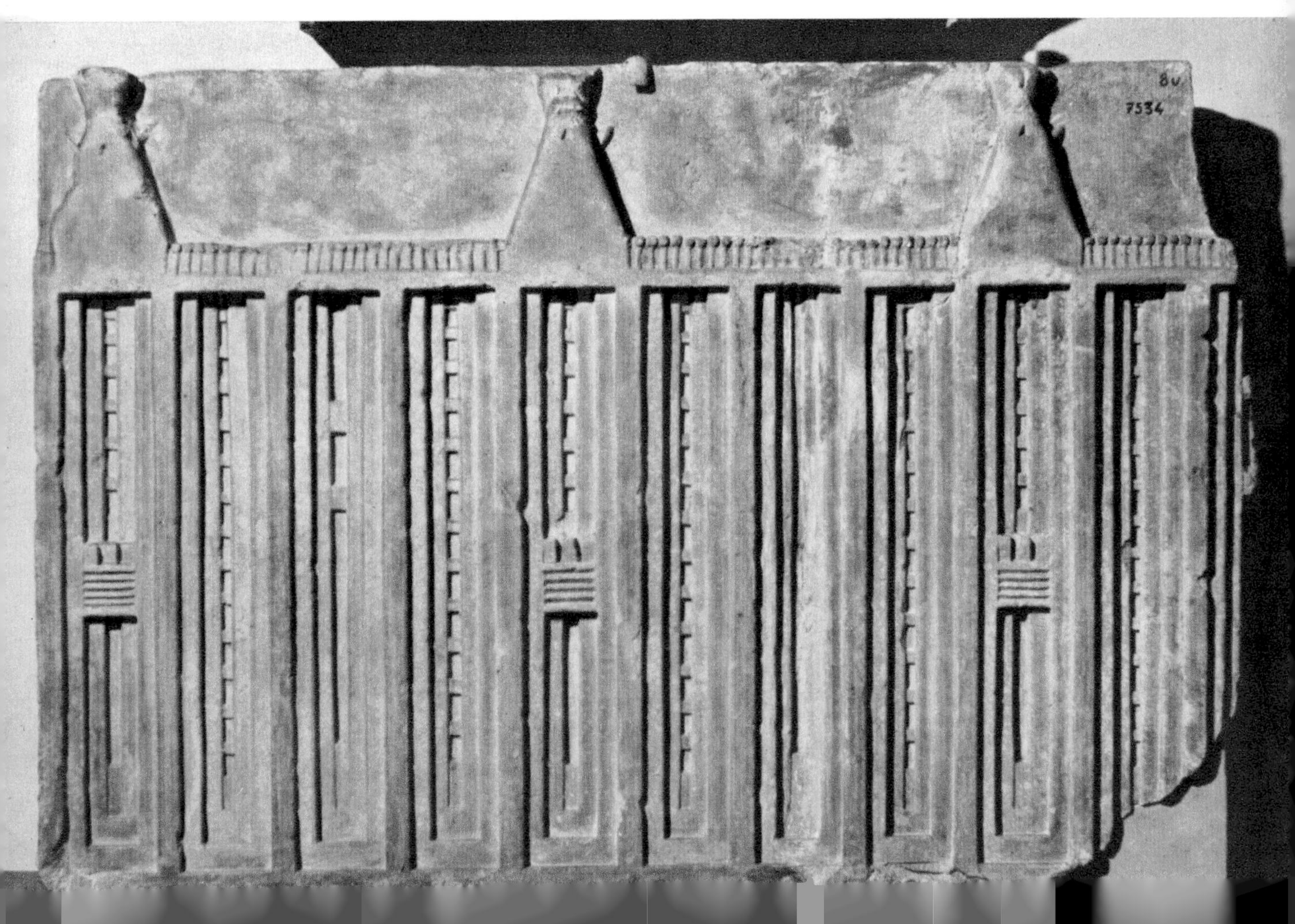

6

7

8

In the winter months, Mecca is lashed by rare but violent rainstorms. After one such storm, torrents of water rushed down the hillsides and along the ravines, filling the basin in which the Ka'bah stood. As a result, the building was undermined and collapsed in ruins. The 'Amalik rebuilt it exactly as it had been before, with profuse decoration in a technique and style unknown to us.[17]

A constant stream of pilgrims and petitioners visited the sanctuary. There is a story in Arab lore of a deputation sent to the Ka'bah by the moon-worshipping people of 'Ad, one of the early Arabian tribes, also mentioned in the Qoran. It is believed that they lived in Southern Arabia, in a "town of pillars" set among sand dunes, which was named Iram after their chief, and was traditionally located a little to the east of Aden. They lived in fortresses and worshipped at high altars set on mountain peaks. As a punishment for their sins, the scourge of a long drought was visited upon the 'Ad, and in their despair they sent a deputation to Mecca to pray for rain.

The members of the delegation were entertained in the dwelling of a Meccan with whom they were in alliance; there they proceeded to engage in a series of drinking bouts enlivened by the singing of slave-girls. After a month of this, the weary host induced his musicians to improvise a song reminding the visitors of the purpose of their journey. Thereupon the head of the deputation went down to the valley and made his supplications for rain at the sanctuary. As he did so, clouds began to form overhead. He singled out one that seemed to him to be heavy with rain, and besought the God of Mecca to send it to his country. His people however were not to escape retribution, for the delegate had chosen a cloud that contained a tornado. For seven days and nights the wind raged across the sand dunes, burying the city and its inhabitants, who lay "*prostrate as if they were the trunks of hollow palm-trees.*" (*Qoran:* LXIX, 7). The deputation was still in Mecca, unaware of the disaster, until a camel-man arrived one moonlit night to tell them of their fellow-tribesmen's terrible fate.[18]

* * *

The Yemenite tribes of Jurhum and Qatura, who had long lived in the Meccan area awaiting their opportunity, succeeded at last in ejecting the 'Amalik from the Hijaz. They divided the Meccan valley between them, along its physical configuration from the north-east to the south-west. As the dynastic leader of the Jurhum, who was called the Mudad, was descended from Ishmael's father-in-law Mudad ibn 'Amr, the Jurhum claimed the right to guard the sacred precincts of the Ka'bah. They occupied the upper part of the valley and Mount Qu'aiqi'an, and exacted a toll from all travellers who entered Mecca through their territory. The rocks of Qu'aiqi'an rang with the martial clatter of their accoutrements; these consisted of swords, spears, leather shields and quivers full of arrows which rattled as they rode along, menacing all who passed their way. The Qatura, who settled in the lower part of the valley, were no less warlike than the Jurhum. They were great horsemen, riding on swift chargers of noble race, probably like those represented in archaic Arab sculpture (*ill.* 4). Pilgrims who came from the direction of the Yemen were forced to pay them dues for right of passage.

It was inevitable that there should be a clash between these two tribes, and at last it came. The Qatura chief was killed and his tribe sustained a humiliating defeat. Yet, in the end, because of the kinship between them, the tribes concluded a peace treaty in an atmosphere of amity, and a feast of celebration was held in a ravine near the city. This place was afterwards known as "the kitchens", in commemoration of the vast amounts of meat which had been prepared there that day.[19]

6.* 'Azra'il, the archangel of death, being made to bear the death-pangs of a mortal. Possibly sixteenth century. 17×9.5 cm.

7.* Angels weeping in sorrow for the sins of mankind. 17×9.5 cm.

8.* The archangel Israil blows the trumpet of resurrection. 17×9.5 cm.

THE ARCHAIC CIVILISATIONS

IT HAS NEVER been possible for archaeologists to make excavations in the holy cities of Islam, but as the regions of Southern Arabia and the northern borders of the Hijaz had close tribal and cultural ties with Mecca and Yathrib, a certain amount of information about the Hijaz can be deduced from such archaeological researches as have been conducted to the south and north of it.

The archaic civilisations of Arabia came into being at the beginning of the first millennium B. C. Stimulated by the great neighbouring centres of civilisation—Assyria, Babylonia, Persia and Egypt—an Arabian art, nonetheless fairly homogeneous and distinctive, made its appearance. A proto-Arabian alphabet was used—cuneiform in the south and cursive in the north—of a type closely allied to the Canaanite alphabets of Syria-Palestine.[20]

In these early times, Arabian architecture took the form of solid masses, after the style of Assyrian buildings. Sculpture was at a monolithic stage; elements of human or animal form were incised or carved in relief on pieces of rock (*ill.* 17). It was not until about the last hundred years B. C. that elaborately sculpted forms appeared.

Many stele-portraits have been found in cemeteries and elsewhere, some of them possibly representing the priest-kings and sibyl-queens who reigned over Southern and Northern Arabia since the seventh and eighth centuries B. C. In the sculpture of this period, the Arabs appear as a finely-built race, moderate in height, with oval faces, large straight noses, small chins and big eyes (*ill.* 28). The pupils, often inserted with black stone or with lapis lazuli, would almost seem to be dilated in religious trance, as in Sumerian heads (*ill.* 26). The significance given to the eyes may have been prompted by the Arab belief that the tremendous spiritual powers attributed to the human being were partly concentrated in the faculty of sight. An evil glance could kill. There is in the Museum of the Ancient Orient in Istanbul a funerary stele with a decorative motif which consists of the incised outline of a pair of eyes (*ill.* 11). This piece is reminiscent of the eye-effigies, dating from 2200 B. C., in the Temple of Brak in Northern Mesopotamia.[21]

The Arabs also had great regard for the power of the spoken word, and on public occasions were wont to express themselves in poetic language. The augur (*kahin*) and the pythoness used a rhythmic form of prose known as *saj*ʿ, in which they would utter incantations and cast paralysing spells upon the enemy. When animated by their familiar spirits, which sometimes came to them in the form of snakes or birds, they would make oracular pronouncements in this medium.[22]

9. Adam and Eve tempted by the Evil Spirit in the form of a serpent, watched by an angel and a peacock: a book-painting, either Central Asian or an Ottoman copy of a Central Asian original.
This is Folio 16 verso of a Persian manuscript dated 987 A. H. (1579 A. D.), by ʿAla al-Din Mansur on the lives of the prophets and of the four orthodox caliphs.
35×24 cm.

10

From the remote past, worship had been offered to one God, Allah, but a multitude of astral deities was also known. Figurative representations of these dating from the first millennium B. C. have come down to us (*ill.* 13, 17). One of the most widely worshipped was the moon, generally represented as male. The crescent moon was a dual deity: in Southern Arabia the waxing crescent was associated with Hubal (Abel), the Shepherd, and the waning moon took on the ominous personality of Kain (Cain), the Blacksmith and Musician. In Nabatea, where the moon rose over the Sarat range, the crescent moon was called "He of Shara," a primeval archetype of Dionysus. The sun was regarded as a female divinity, either the consort or the daughter of the moon, and sometimes alluded to as "She of the Temple." One of the solar personifications, al-Lat, or Ilat, the mother-goddess, was borrowed by the Greeks, who called her Lato. The morning star was worshipped in the person of 'Athtar (Astarte); the god Nakruh was Saturn or Mars, and Manat, a goddess of fate, represented the darkened moon. Besides these and many others, the Arabs had household gods, over which they would pass their hands for luck.[23]

Countless altars, in sandstone, granite or alabaster, bearing stylised representations of ibex, rams and oxen, sometimes in conjunction with crescent moons, testify to the fact that animals were sacrificed to the Arabian gods (*ill.* 13, 20). On an altar in the Museum of the Ancient Orient in Istanbul there is an inscription stating that oxen were immolated upon it on the ninth of the month of Thawr (the Ox).[24] Comparisons have been drawn between some of the ibex figures of Arabia and those which appear in the Achaemenid art of Persia. There is also a curious resemblance between the frequently recurring Arabian motif of a bird of prey carrying off a snake in its beak and claws (*ill.* 12) and the Indo-Scythian and Central Asian garuda and snake theme.[25]

The Southern Arabs considered themselves the descendants of Qahtan (the Biblical Yoqtan). Recent archaeological investigations have shed new light on the disputed dates of the southwards migration of some of the tribes: the Katabanians (called by Pliny the Catabanae), the Ma'in (Mineans), and the inhabitants of Hadramawt (the Chatramotitae), are now thought to have reached Southern Arabia before 1500 B. C., and the Sabeans (named after Sheba, the son of Yoqtan and grandson of Abraham) before 1200 B. C.

From figures cast in bronze, and sculptures in stone and glowing alabaster, it is possible to see how the civilised, graceful Southern Arabians looked. While archaic Greek heads mostly have a mysterious smile on their lips, the Southern Arabians would seem from their expressions to have been somewhat melancholic (*ill.* 10). They wear knee-length waist-wrappers, necklaces, and sometimes the pelts of large felines across their shoulders.

There are some charming feminine heads among the later, more developed sculptures, carved in pale, translucent alabaster (*ill.* 26). The Queen of Sheba and the Shulamite of the Song of Songs could have looked like these. On the softly rounded cheeks there is often a tiny indentation, perhaps indicating a decorative or tribal scar. The chin is faintly dimpled. The pupils of the eyes may be of lapis lazuli, like those of the blue-eyed Arabian pythoness al-Zarqa'. The hair is elaborately curled, as was also the fashion in Egypt at the time, and falls to the nape of the neck.

The air of Southern Arabia was balmy with the exotic perfumes of aromatic plants—the frankincense, myrrh, cassia, balsam and cinnamon—that gave the region its Roman name of Arabia Odorifera. As frankincense was sacred, only the high-born members of the Minean and Sabean tribes could look at it or collect it, and then only as part of a religious rite.

The highly civilised cities of Southern Arabia such as Timna', Karnaw and Marib contained great temples with square pillars, obelisks, fortresses and palaces,

10. Triangular limestone head from an undated South Arabian stele. Height 22 cm.

now buried, like 'Ad, under the sands. The temple to 'Athtar in Timna', one of the most ancient of Southern Arabian monuments, consisted of a central nave with several rows of pillars. The stairways and some of the floors were in russet-red marble, and the walls were niched as though to contain statues.

In the city of Marib, there was an oval building dedicated to the moon. Tall, monolithic pillars supported its peristyle. Its windows were of transparent alabaster, like those in parts of the Yemen today, and its stairway was plated with bronze.

The Museum of the Ancient Orient in Istanbul has a seventh century alabaster relief which shows the complete façade of a Southern Arabian temple. It is divided into narrow panels, surmounted by triangular pediments, and with vertical rows of window-like openings (*ill.* 5).

Even earlier than the first millennium B. C., camel caravans had begun to cross the Arabian deserts, establishing commercial links between areas as remote from each other as India, the Mediterranean, East Africa and the valley of the Euphrates. Merchants, it is thought, regarded the desert routes as less hazardous than the sea, where there was risk of monsoons, as yet unpredictable. The warehouses of Southern Arabia were therefore filled with the merchandise of Indian and Cingalese ships, the gold of Ophir, and the produce of Arabia herself. At certain seasons of the year, long files of camels would set out, laden with precious metals, pearls, ivory, lapis lazuli, tortoise shell, silks and spices.

The perfumes of Arabia were a famous and most valuable commodity; the Arabs believed that it was Höl, the phoenix-god, who caused their perfumes to be transported to the altars of foreign lands. So widely known were they that they were used in the Buddhist shrines of India. Ramses II of Egypt had frankincense burned in the sanctuary of Ammon. The temple in Jerusalem contained a special store-room for scents and spices. The altar to Bel in Babylon was fragrant with Arabian incense. Many tons of frankincense were sent to Darius of Persia. Arabian perfumes were eagerly sought after in Rome.

The caravans (*ill.* 29) started at Sumhuram in Zafar and followed the coast, halting in various towns such as Cana in the kingdom of Hadramawt (now Husn al-Ghurab), until they reached Mawza' in the Yemen, at the south-western corner of the Peninsula. Then the route took a northerly course, through Timna' in Katabah, Marib in Saba, and Karnaw in the land of Ma'in. At Karnaw, the trail forked in two separate directions. One road led to the Persian Gulf, along the latitude of Bahrain; the other followed the west coast on the Red Sea, with halts at Mecca and Yathrib, and went on to Madian, the land of cave-tombs and palm-groves where Moses had lived for a time, then to Aila ('Aqabah) to the port of Gaza, and to Egypt.

Other caravans stopped to water at the oases of Taima, al-Hijr, and Petra, *en route* to the Euphrates valley by way of Tadmur (Palmyra), the city that had been the scene of the meeting batween Bilqis, the Queen of Sheba, and Solomon.[26]

The Arabs who lived on the northern borders of the Hijaz seem to have been a sturdier race than the Southerners. In the Istanbul Museum there are three seventh-century heads of gigantic statues, carved at al-Hijr in the red sandstone of Arabia Petraea. They show gaunt-faced, vigorous men. One of them has, nonetheless, a surprisingly sensitive expression. Another has slightly negroid features, while the third appears to be wearing the typical Arab head-band (*ill.* 17). Judging from the sculptures found in this northern region, the dress of both men and women consisted of a sort of loin-cloth.

The Northern Arabs were hardened warriors, often engaged in fighting against the neighbouring empires, which coveted the spices of Arabia and occasionally annexed the ports at the destinations of her trade routes. In 880 B. C., the Arabs fought against the Assyrians, along the Upper Euphrates. Between 738 and

732 B. C., Tiglat-Pilesar III of Assyria occupied the port of Gaza and the land of Musri (Madian and the Northern Hijaz), after defeating Zabiba, the queen and high priestess of the Kedar Arabs. He also vanquished another Arabian queen, Samsi, who offered him white camels as a tribute. Sargon and Assurbanipal made war against the Yemen. Nabonidus (555-539) spent some time in Arabia, in his hunting pavilion at Taima'. Arab troops joined with the armies of Cyrus in the defeat of Babylon.

The early Islamic historian Tabari recounts an episode which probably refers to Nebuchadnezzar II, at the time that he deported the Jews. The king was angered, not only by the Jews, but also by the Arabs of Babylonia, living in the region of Hira and al-Anbar. He had the Arabs confined in their cities, and prepared to massacre them. An Ishmaelite, ʻAdnan and his son Maʻadd had journeyed from Mecca to Babylonia, and therefore were condemned along with the rest. The Arabs first pleaded for mercy, then fought desperately until nearly all were killed. ʻAdnan lay dead, but Maʻadd escaped and returned to Mecca. It was from his progeniture that Muhammad was later to be born.

In the frontier area between the Hijaz and Syria-Palestine, it is still possible to see the ruins of long-dead Arabian towns, some of them dating from between 1000 and 100 B. C. This region, the heart of Arabia Petraea, is a bleak and stony wilderness, broken by the sombre basalt peaks of the Sarat mountains. Black pebbles shine like silver under the merciless sun. Nabatu (Petra), the capital of Arabia Petraea, was created amid towering cliffs of red sandstone (*ill.* 41). Ornamental façades were carved in its stone walls, covering dwelling-places, temples, or tombs. The high altars were reached by means of steps cut in the vertical precipices of coral-coloured rock. As well as the moon ("He of Shara"), al-Lat and other Arabian gods were worshipped here in early times, in the shape of monolithic idols. It is possible that the Nabateans set their tombs within the rock-face partly because of the uncanny sound effects that could be obtained there. If, for instance, one stood in the opening of the façade hiding a funeral cave and called, perhaps the name of the dead person, an eerie echo would answer. This may in turn have had some connection with the fact that in Arab mythology a departed soul was likened to an echoing bird.

The kingdom of the Nabateans extended from Damascus in the north to the Hijaz in the south. Some of their coins have been found, bearing portraits of their kings and queens. Their inscriptions were in a cursive writing, from which the Arabic alphabet was later developed.

Al-Hijr (known to Pliny as Egra) was yet another important centre of the Northern Arabs. Various peoples seem to have lived here, either side by side or at successive periods of history. The earliest of these was a Minean colony. Later came the Lihyanites, known to Pliny as the Lechieni. Although the Lihyanites venerated a supreme deity whom they called Allah, they must also have worshipped idols, as a round temple dedicated to Wadd, the god of love and friendship, has been found to have belonged to them. This temple contained a large central tank, perhaps for ritual ablution.

To the west of al-Hijr, in a group of strangely-shaped sandstone hills called Athalith, there are more rows of façades carved in the rock. Over some of the doorways in the stone are reliefs showing a bird of prey carrying a snake in its claws, a motif which, as previously mentioned, was also widely employed in Southern Arabia (*ill.* 12).

At Al-ʻUla, not far from al-Hijr, Thamudic inscriptions have been found. The Thamud, generally identified with the Lihyanites, were believed by Tabari to have been descendants of a certain Lukaym, one of the deputation sent by the tribe of ʻAd to Mecca. Their fate is described in the Qoran as follows: The Thamud, who dwelt in chambers excavated in the rocks, cruelly slaughtered a gentle she-camel which had been entrusted to their care by the Prophet Salih. For this breach of trust and other iniquities they were punished. A cry of anguish was heard in the stone-hewn city, and the Thamud were annihilated in the convulsions of a violent earthquake.[27]

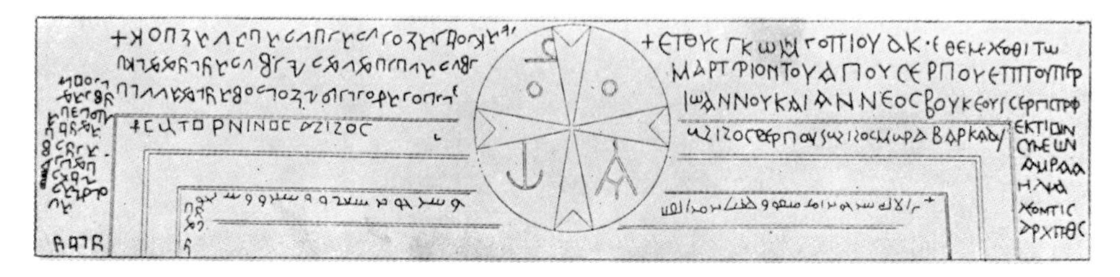

Transcription of an Arab–Greek–Syriac inscription dated 512 A. D.

THE DOWNFALL OF THE JURHUM

UNTIL SUCH TIME as archaeological evidence can provide more substantial information, the history of Mecca during its domination by the Jurhum must remain shrouded in the mist of popular lore. Their rule in the city may well have lasted over a thousand years. It will be remembered that the Jurhum claimed to be closely related, by intermarriage, with the Ishmaelites, and on this they based their claim to be the rightful guardians of the Ka'bah. Perhaps for this reason too, certain Ishmaelites were apparently allowed to live in the sacred valley; some of them were even promoted to high priesthood. One of these was called Iyad; he built a holy tower in Mecca, probably in the style of a ziggurat, where he worshipped God. Another famous Ishmaelite of this period was Nizar, the son, by a Jurhumi woman, of Ma'add, who had fled to Mecca from Nebuchadnezzar's persecution of the Arabs. Nizar in his turn had four sons, to whom he assigned the insignia that were to distinguish the four main branches of the Ishmaelites: the Scarlet Tents, the Black Tents, the Silver-haired, and the Owners of the Dappled Camels. The Scarlet Tents were thereafter proudly displayed on festive or solemn occasions by the branch of Mudar, the forebears of Muhammad.

At the height of their power, the Jurhum became neglectful of their duties as keepers of the Ka'bah. Far from maintaining peace in the sacred precincts, the temple guardians began to steal from the pilgrims the gifts they brought to the sanctuary. Some young men attempted to rob the Ka'bah of its treasure. They posted a guard at each of its four corners, while a fifth tried to climb into the roofless building from above. He, however, was struck dead before he could enter, and the others fled in terror.

A woman called Nailah and her lover Isaf, who had made a tryst within the precincts of the Ka'bah, were turned to stone. The reigning Mudad, who viewed these profanations with indignation and alarm, ordered that the petrified bodies of Nailah and Isaf should be placed as a warning to other potential sinners on the hills of Safa and Marwah, where Hagar had once searched for water. He was afraid that these acts of sacrilege might bring down the judgment of God upon the Jurhum. Indeed, it seemed that his fears were justified, for the waters of the miraculous Zamzam well began to sink, and at length dried up.

The Mudad took the opportunity thus offered, and hid the treasure of the Ka'bah in the empty holy well, hoping thus to save it from would-be marauders. Azraqi, a Meccan historian of the ninth century A. D., relates that a pair of golden gazelles that had stood in the courtyard and some swords that had been presented to the temple as gifts were among the objects that were concealed in the well. Then the Mudad gathered his family together and set out for the desert, to await the final calamity he felt was sure to come.

It came, in the wake of a catastrophe that was happening some distance away, in the land of Saba. The huge Marib Dam, once one of the wonders of the world, was now in a state of decay. Repairs were made piecemeal, but the great edifice continued to crumble. It appears from inscriptions and records that this disintegration, regarded in Arab lore as a portent of Southern Arabia's decline, was taking place somewhere between the fourth century B. C. and the fifth century A. D.

A priestess called Turaifah, allied to the Azd tribe, oracularly foretold the total collapse of the dam and the consequent inundation of Saba. Her tribe and others had accordingly decided to move northwards, to escape this disaster, and the migration probably took place in the last century B. C. When the tribes approached Mecca, they were met by the unwelcoming Jurhum, and a pitched battle ensued. The refugees, with the aid of a group of Ishmaelites, succeeded in defeat-

A piece of the *Kiswah*, the embroidered cover of the Ka'bah.

ing the Jurhum. In accordance with ancient custom, the women were taken into slavery and the warriors were massacred.

The Mudad, whose forebodings had been so amply fulfilled, looked down upon Mecca from his place of concealment on Mount Abu Qubais, and expressed his anguish in these verses:

> Many a woman reciter, her tears flowing abundantly,
> Her eye-sockets reddened from weeping,
> (said): " It is as if there had (never) been from Hajun to Safa,
> A friend or a companion to speak together in the Meccan night."
> And I replied to her, while my heart
> Palpitated within me, as a bird between its wings:
> "Aye, we were its people and we have been exterminated.
>
> . . . .
>
> The eyes pour tears, weeping for a land
> In which is a safe sanctuary and holy stations
> Weeping for the temple where the doves are unharmed,
> Where they live securely. There (dwell) also the sparrows,
> And the wild beasts, untamed.
> And if they leave, they would fain return."

An epidemic began to rage among the members of the victorious tribes, causing them to wonder whether they should remain in the holy city. They consulted a sibyl, who advised them to disperse into other regions. Some tribes therefore returned southwards towards 'Oman and their native land. Others, the progenitors of the later Ghassan dynasty, travelled northwards to Syria. The 'Aws and Khazraj tribes settled in Yathrib, alongside the Jewish tribes of Beni Nadir and Beni Kurayza. Yathrib had now become one of the many agricultural oases on the caravan route from the Hijaz to Syria inhabited by Jewish mercantile communities.

One group of Sabean invaders, the Khuza'ah, stayed in Mecca, where they established, shortly before the Christian era, a powerful state which was to last for about five centuries. Their ruling house, the Luhayy, allied themselves to the family of the Mudad, and all hostility between the various tribes then ceased. For a time, the Khuza'ah allowed their Ishmaelite allies to assume responsibility or the Ka'bah. However, a quarrel arose between the Ishmaelites of the Scarlet Tents and those of the Dappled Camels, and as a result the Khuza'ah took charge of the temple themselves.[28]

THE IDOLS

THE WEALTH and generosity of 'Amr, of the dynasty of Luhayy, were legendary throughout the land. He would feed the pilgrims who came to Mecca on meat from his enormous camel herds, and distribute Yemenite robes to them. He lived in great luxury, spending the summers in the cool highlands on the Yemen border, at Taif, and the winters on the warm Tihamah coast.

Yet this great chief was to go down in history as a man of evil repute. On his trading expeditions, he had become a devotee of the idols that were worshipped in various parts of the Peninsula, and he it was who introduced paganism to Mecca.

A statue of Hubal, carved in precious agate, was sent to him from Hit, an 'Amalik town in the north. The right hand of the statue was broken off during the journey and had to be recast, this time in gold. The statue was placed in the Ka'bah, on top of the treasury well. Hubal was an oracular deity; divinatory arrows marked with various responses were used by those who consulted him. After this, each tribe gradually installed its own idol in the courtyard of the Ka'bah. All the gods known in Arabia, both male and female—Manaf, the sun god, Quzah, who held the rainbow, the eagle-shaped Nasr, Wadd, and particularly al-Lat, Manat and al-'Uzza—now encroached upon Abraham's monotheist temple, together with their hierophants. A piece of silex on which a crown was incised, known as Dhu-al-Khulasah, was placed in the plain near Marwah; two statues designated " the Windmaker " and " the Bird-Eater " were placed on the summits of Safa and Marwah, and the petrified lovers were brought back to the Ka'bah, the scene of their sacrilegious tryst.

Trees and stones were also invested with supernatural significance. An acacia grove on the Tihamah coast was sacred to al-'Uzza, the Arabian Aphrodite. A rock in the highlands of Taif, where a hermit had once given milk to travellers, became a symbol for al-Lat, the mother-goddess.

Litholatry spread even to the Ishmaelites. During the time of their exile, when they could only enter Mecca as pilgrims, they had taken rocks from the holy city back to the desert as souvenirs. These stones were now set in the court of the Ka'bah, along with the other idols.

Some steles and funerary pylons also became objects of worship. In pre-Islamic Arabia, extreme veneration was accorded to the dead, and funeral rites were performed with intense emotion. The mourners wept, scratched their faces and tore their clothes, while they exhorted the spirit not to leave them. Elegies were chanted over the dead body, which lay with its head resting on its arm, as though sleep-

11. Marble tombstone, with carving representing a pair of eyes and an inscription in archaic Arabian characters of the name of the deceased, " Yausil ". 25 × 15 cm.

12. Alabaster altar from Southern Arabia, dating from about the sixth century B. C., with relief showing a bird of prey holding a snake in its claws. Height 36 cm.

13. A limestone incense altar, *c.* 300 B. C., showing an indeterminate figure, flanked by two ibexes and surmounted by a crescent and a disc. Height 40 cm.

11 12

13

14
15

ing. Wine was provided to quench the soul's thirst, and a camel was hamstrung and left to die on the grave. If a monument was then built there, the tomb became a shrine and a sanctuary.

When a man was murdered, the murderer's tribe would apostrophise the victim's spirit: " Leave us— ". The nearest blood relation of the murdered man would vow to seek revenge, dedicating himself to the service of the man's ghost. He would give up all worldly pleasures: the company of his friends and of women, wine, perfume, baths, horse-racing, and jousting for trophies in the desert. Covering his face, he would set off in search of the murderer, looking for him at fairs, on pilgrimages, in all those places where people would gather together. Once he had found the criminal, he would pursue him until they were outside sacred precincts and beyond the range of any hospitality rites. Then the avenger would throw off his disguise, cry aloud the name of the murdered man, and drive his knife into the assassin's heart. He would leave the corpse where it lay, without taking any of its possessions, thus being freed from the vow made to his relative's spirit. Then he would compose a poem, describing the circumstances of the chase and the ultimate combat. All these rites contributed to establish the cult of the dead.

The celebration of Abraham's pilgrimage to Mecca had now become a general festivity, full of heathen ritual. Each year, the date of the pilgrimage was computed anew by a seer, and was always made to coincide with a fair. On the way to Mecca, the pilgrim would attend a series of smaller fairs, reaching the holy city in time for the great culminating ceremony. All the Arab tribes and potentates would send delegations with gifts. The processions of pilgrims were led by hierophants and sybils. Sacred camels, decorated with amulets, carried leather tents which contained the tribes' idols. There were seers, in a state of trance, who chirped, cooed or hissed according to the bird or snake-genie that inspired them. Sorceresses, who were believed to entangle the course of human lives by tying symbolic knots, came with their long hair flying loose behind them, uttering incantations. Musicians clashed their cymbals and tambourines. Behind them streamed the crowd of pilgrims, some of them no doubt wearing 'Amr's gifts of striped Yemenite robes, in the sombre tones of Arabian dyes.

Poets came too, straight from the poetic contest held at the fair of 'Ukaz, near Taif, to chant short *rajaz* verses, in a four-syllable metre said to have been suggested by the camel's pace, or the long odes (*qasidah*), which would begin with homage to some wayward mistress, and continue with stories of adventures in the desert, of hunting the onager, of martial exploits, or lordly carousal. The minstrels would direct bitter satires against their enemies. A soothsayer would select the seven best poetic compositions which would be written out fairly and set on the walls of the Ka'bah.

On the fairgrounds, merchants bought and sold pieces of gold and silver, or the precious ore taken from the mountains of Arabia. They brought slaves from Africa, Persia and Anatolia; tanned leather; senna leaves, balsam, scented woods, oils, perfume and spices; cottons and fine white linen " Coptic " fabrics from Egypt; Chinese silks; and from Bosra finely worked arms, and the grain that was such a precious commodity in the unfertile region of Mecca. Wandering surgeons attended the ailing, replacing with gold broken teeth and noses severed in battle.

14.* 'Uuj (Og), according to Islamic legend the illegitimate son of Adam's daughter 'Anaq.
65×42 cm.

Great quantities of Arabian date wine were drunk, particularly in the course of those ceremonies which had a decidedly bacchanalian flavour. In large tents, singers and dancing girls entertained the pilgrims, while foreign cup-bearers served them Syrian wine. There was much gambling.

15.* An angel bringing the ram, as Abraham is about to sacrifice Ishmael on Mount Thabir.
65×42 cm.

The aristocracy of Mecca, who also formed its religious hierarchy, were busy directing the pilgrimage. As a sign of their rank, they wore long pieces of draped

16.* Noah's Ark sailing round the site of the Ka'bah, submerged beneath the Flood.
65×42 cm.

cloth that swept the ground. They went out to Muzdalifah, a widening of the Meccan pass not far from 'Arafat but still within the sacred purlieus of Mecca; here the high priest of the Ka'bah lit a fire and the Mudar Ishmaelites pitched their scarlet leather tents. The noblemen's guests and allies had the right to join them in their camp. Everyone else, the rank and file of the pilgrims, the common people who lived furthest from the temple, the outlaws and vagabonds who had been cast out of their tribes, the desert Beduin, and all the foreigners who were not guests of the Meccan aristocracy, gathered together on the 'Arafat plain, just outside the consecrated ground. At a given sign, they ran towards the fire at Muzdalifah, where a feast was served to them by the Meccans. Then the crowd continued the rites, offering vociferous homage to each idol, monolith or sacred bush, and hanging necklaces and nose-rings on some of them. They consulted the oracular effigies, and sacrifices were made at the altars and at the pointed leather tents that were erected over tombs. These took the form of libations, gifts of grain and ostrich eggs, sacrificial animals, and occasionally, it is thought, even human victims.

When they approached the Ka'bah itself, the non-Meccans would remove all their garments. Sometimes they would put on a scant piece of clothing, bought or borrowed in Mecca, but more usually they would remain naked. Clapping their hands and whistling, they entered the temple which had formerly been consecrated to the One God and now held three hundred and sixty idols, among them the effigies of the Patriarchs Abraham and Ishmael.[29]

GRAECO-ROMAN INFLUENCES

AT THE CLOSE of the first millennium B. C., Arabian culture, like that of surrounding regions, underwent a change. The great civilisations of the ancient world—Assyria, Babylon, Achaemenid Persia, Egypt of the Pharaohs—were either extinct or fundamentally changed, for now the light of Graeco-Roman culture shone on all sides.

In the wake of Alexander's armies came the pervading influence of Hellenism. The naturalism of Greek figurative art began to seduce the conquered Asians from their own hieratic sculpture. The elegant orders of softly rounded Graeco-Roman columns held a fascination that was to condemn the massive monuments of Asia to oblivion. This infatuation spread to North Africa, to the Near East, even to remote Turkestan.

In the Hijaz, the incursion of the Macedonian conqueror, who is said to have visited Mecca itself, brought no immediate effect. But Greek thought did begin to penetrate " Eudaimon Arabia." In the third century B. C., the Greek Theophrastus collected the reports of botanical experts who had been sent by Alexander to study Arabian aromatic herbs. Greek sea captains (as witnessed by the *Periplus maris Erithraei*) surveyed the shores of Arabia. In the first century A. D., Hippalus discovered the regular incidence of the opposing monsoons in the Red Sea and Indian Ocean, thereby making navigation a less hazardous adventure than it had been in the past.

The Greeks had not succeeded in gaining possession of Arabia's wealth in aromatics and gold, but they did divert the bulk of the trade from her desert routes to the sea. The merchandise of India and Africa was laden more and more often onto the ships of the Graeco-Egyptian Ptolemies, whose fleets plied their way cautiously through the coral reefs of the Red Sea. The oases which lay along the old caravan-tracks, Mecca and Yathrib among them, saw their most lucrative means of livelihood disappearing.

The Romans made greater inroads into the heart of Arabia than did the Greeks. In 24 B. C., Aelius Gallus attempted to launch an attack on the south of the Peninsula. In 106 A. D., Trajan occupied Petra and created around the rock-hewn city the Roman " Provincia Arabia." Great Roman cities were built at Bosra, Jerash and Palmyra.

In the Arab world, however, as elsewhere in countries with vigorous cultures of their own, the local artists' interpretation of the Graeco-Roman style was to prevail, bringing about the flowering of a new eclectic art. In territories that were

17. A South Arabian limestone idol, undated. Height 20 cm.

occupied by the Parthians, Hellenism encountered not only the native artist's own temperament, but also the vivid strength of the nomadic conquerors from Central Asia, their gods, their costume and their animal emblems. It was in regions ruled by the Parthians, in Dura-Europos and Palmyra, that the naturalistic Graeco-Roman style was adapted to the portrayal of the Orient. The results were so attractive that the Jews were led to abandon a strongly-held tenet of their religion, and had the walls of a synagogue decorated with pictures representing, among other things, Moses and the Ark. In fact, the style of plastic art evolved at Dura-Europos, that cross-roads of civilisation, was typical of a specifically Oriental naturalism that was adopted throughout the Near East, from Byzantium to South Arabia, and probably also in Macoraba ("holy site" in Ethiopian), as Mecca was now called by Ptolemy. Meccan chronicles mention that in the sixth century A. D. there were mural paintings within the Ka'bah; it may well be that these works bore lingering traces of the Dura-Europos influence.

There are no objects of Hijazi art of this period available to us, so we must again seek information from the two regions lying directly to the north and south of Mecca: Arabia Petraea and Arabia Felix. Here too artists became imbued with

Reconstruction of the Ka'bah as it must have been rebuilt in Muhammad's lifetime.

the spirit of the Graeco-Romans, but they adapted it to their own inclinations. The beautiful façades of Petra, though designed and carved in the Graeco-Roman era, bearing all the elements of classical architecture, represent nonetheless the fantastic compositions of the unfettered, unconventional desert-dweller. In Southern Arabia, however, Graeco-Roman architecture remained almost unknown, and historical records indicate that it did not reach the Hijaz either.

GRAECO-ROMAN INFLUENCES

In sculpture, though, the realistic approach of Graeco-Roman art was a major inspiration for the Arabs. The monoliths and static figures began to take on more developed human characteristics, often wearing garments of Graeco-Roman style. Statues of al-Lat, for example, in the garb of Pallas Athene, are typical of this period. Manaf, the principal Meccan idol, took on the aspect of a Hellenised solar deity. Stele portraits were now made to resemble the dead person's features more closely. A second century alabaster carving in the British Museum, showing a large-eyed young woman with covered hair, is an example of this new trend (*ill.* 42). Some Arabian sculptures, such as the pair of bronze Amors of Timna', riding on lions, were mere copies of Alexandrian originals.[30]

The representation of movement was a new concept for Arabian artists, and they revelled in it. An Arabian bas-relief in the Istanbul Museum, made of basalt and believed to date from the first century B. C., shows a man wearing a knee-length cloth secured at the waist by a belt, who is seated on what appears to be a galloping horse. This figure has sometimes been described as a centaur. He holds the reins of his mount in one hand, and a flaming torch in the other. The rider's hair, the horse's tail and the flame of the torch all seem to be blown backwards, giving the impression of headlong speed, as in the pre-Islamic Meccan poem describing a warrior " running to portentous deeds, like a flame burning in the torch-bearer's hands." [31]

Even in the archaic period, in fact, some Arabian artists had portrayed animals with a certain degree of robust realism, though usually in static poses. Now, with the growing taste for naturalism, animals were shown as living beings, caught in mid-movement. On the drum of a red sandstone column from al-Hijr there is a carving which shows a procession of antelopes, all in motion. Another relief shows a huge bird of prey carrying off an ibex in its claws; in yet another, a composite creature, half bull, half tree, moves against a veritably surrealistic background of foliage.

In the Graeco-Roman period, then, the Hijaz must undoubtedly have been affected by the spirit of the age, and realistic representation of the human shape probably began to replace the stiff, monolithic idols. Yet the gradual transformation of the formless masses into recognisable shapes could not fail to arouse anxious uncertainty in the Arab mind, preparing the way for further evolution.

JUDAISM AND CHRISTIANITY IN THE HIJAZ

THE STAR of Bethlehem rose as the Near East was in a state of religious turmoil. New faiths were springing up everywhere, and there is evidence that the Chaldean-Sabean star cult, the celestial hierarchy of Zoroastrianism, and many other beliefs flourished in the Hijaz at this time. Arabia had colonies of Magians and possibly even Manicheans.[32]

Stronger than any others, though, were the influences of Judaic monotheism and Monophysite and Nestorian Christianity. Jewish tribes, called by the Arabs " the authentic sons of Aaron and Isaac," had long been living in the Hijaz; no doubt they had made a number of converts among the Arabs, though the extent to which they did this is a matter for conjecture. They had become integrated in Arabian society to a considerable extent themselves, for they spoke in Arabic and bore Arabic names.

The historian Ibn Hisham tells of a mass conversion to Judaism that apparently happened some time in the first four centuries of the Christian era,[33] under the leadership of As'ad Abu Karib, a king of Southern Arabia, and a member of the Himyar branch of the old monarchs of Saba. The name Himyar means red; the dynasty was so called because the princes draped themselves in purple mantles, in imitation of the Egyptian Pharaohs. Leading his armour-clad troops, Abu Karib crossed the Hijaz on an expedition into the northern part of the country. When he arrived in Yathrib, he found there two Jewish tribes, called " the priestly ones," and the Southern tribes of 'Aws and Khazraj—some of those who had fled from their homes on hearing the prophecy of the rupture of the Marib dam and later helped in the overthrow of the Jurhum. Abu Karib left his son in Yathrib, and continued his journey northwards. During his absence, the young man had a quarrel with a native of Yathrib and was stabbed to death in the date-palm groves. When the king heard of this, he immediately brought the Sabean army back and stationed them in a field outside Yathrib. He then ordered his soldiers to enter the city, and to inflict on it the old oriental penalty of deporting the inhabitants and cutting down the fruitful palm trees.

On learning of the fate that was to befall the town, two rabbis from the Jewish community came to the king's camp to plead with him to spare Yathrib. One day, they said, it would be the refuge of the founder of a monotheist religion. The king asked what they meant by this, and they explained to him the faith of the One God. Deeply impressed by the strength of their belief, Abu Karib became a convert to Judaism.

18. The head of a colossal statue in red sandstone, c. 700 B. C., from Madain Salih in the north of the Hijaz. Height of head 52 cm.

19. An onyx stele, dating from about the beginning of the Christian era, with a relief showing a camel-rider and bearing an inscription in archaic South Arabian characters. Height 19 cm.

20. Alabaster slab, carved in a design of bull-heads and grapevines, and bearing an archaic South Arabian inscription, dating from about the first century B. C. 43×60 cm.

18 19

20

چوكدي عبد المطلب ول فيلك قولاغنه سويلدي ايتدي يا
مبارك بن محمد بن عبد الله جذيم ددي چون فيل رسول آدني
يشتدي درحال يوزيني يره اوردي عبد المطلبك اوكنه
باش قودي يوزن يره سوردي و ديزن چوكش ايكن ديخي

21 22

23 24

شول قدر اوردیلر کیرو یورومدی اسود بن مقصود ایلر

He then prepared to depart. He had not intended to go through Mecca, but some Ishmaelites of Yathrib told him of the treasure contained in the Ka'bah. " O King," they said to him, " shall we lead thee to an ancient hoard of riches, unrevealed to the kings who have preceded thee? It contains pearls, topazes, rubies, gold and silver."

Again the two rabbis intervened, this time to warn him that the Ishmaelites were trying to bring about his downfall. The valley of the Ka'bah, they said, was known as " the breaker of tyrants' necks." Abu Karib thereupon ordered that the hands and feet of the Ishmaelites should be cut off as a punishment for their treachery, and then he set off again, to pay homage in Mecca. The rabbis did not go with him, as they were afraid that they would be polluted by the blood of the victims that were being sacrificed to the pagan idols of the Ka'bah.

Abu Karib followed the time-honoured ritual at the sanctuary, shaving his head and walking barefoot round the temple. He distributed to the poor gifts of meat from the animals he sacrificed, honey, and a beverage made from barley, and ordered that a gate which could be locked should be made for the monument. In a succession of dreams, the king was directed to lay upon the Ka'bah a cover made of palm leaves, and then to replace this by striped Yemenite fabric. So began the tradition of draping the holy edifice with a covering of fine cloth, as is still done to this very day.

When Abu Karib returned from Mecca, he tried to persuade his subjects to embrace his new-found faith. They showed considerable reluctance, however, and in order to convince them the king organised a trial by fire. The rabbis emerged from it alive and the idolatrous Arabian augurs were burned to death. The Sabeans thereupon decided that their king had proved his point, and became converts to the faith of Moses.

The heterogeneous races and religions which invaded Arabia during this period are reflected in her art. Southern Arabia, in particular, extending on the east towards India and on the west towards Africa, was a meeting-place of many cultures. When ships from India and China called at her ports, they brought new ideas as well as merchandise. First the Abyssinians, then in 570 the Persians, invaded and occupied the land of spices; all left their mark on the native cultural image. A bronze statue of a woman found in the temple of Sumhuram at Zafar, for instance, shows the characteristic anatomy, the large breasts and swelling hips, of an Indian Gupta figure. On a Himyarite flat relief, now in the Louvre, the camel-riders and other figures no longer wear the Arabian knee-length draped cloth, but the tight-fitting tunics of their Sassanid conquerors (*ill.* 29).

Monophysite Christianity seems to have penetrated quite early into Southern Arabia. An Indian missionary, Theophilos, apparently played a considerable part in spreading it in the fourth century, building churches in Aden and Zafar. An inscription dated 542, after the second Abyssinian invasion, reads: " By the power and grace and mercy of the Merciful and his Messiah and of the Holy Spirit, this memorial stone was inscribed by Abrahah, the governor of the Geezite (Axumite) King Ramhis Zubaiman, the King of Saba and Dhu-Raidan and Hadramawt and Yamanat and the Arabs of the high and low lands."

Christianity also came to the Hijaz from the north. The Arabs were in any case closely connected with Rome; Marcus Julius, who was Emperor between 244 and 249, was a man of Arabian stock. After the Eastern Roman Empire had embraced Christianity as its official faith, monasteries were built along the southern perimeter of the orthodox Empire, and monks began to mingle with the crowds at Arabian fairs.

Some of the princes of Arabia and their courtiers entered the fold of the Christian church. The most famous of these were the Ghassanids, whose ancestors had

21.* The Yemenite army, led by Abrahah, invading Mecca and being destroyed by pebbles thrown by a flock of birds.
37×27 cm.

22.* 'Abd al-Muttalib, in Abrahah's camp, whispering the name of his grandson Muhammad, as yet unborn, into the ear of an elephant, as it kneels in token of respect.
37×27 cm.

23.* The Qorashi merchant Muttalib and his nephew, the young archer 'Abd al-Muttalib, arriving in Mecca.
37×27 cm.

24.* Abrahah's elephants, charging upon the Ka'bah.
37×27 cm.

invaded Mecca along with other Sabean tribes but subsequently migrated again to Syria. The Byzantines did not altogether approve of the Ghassanids' Monophysite concept of Christianity, but they found the Arab dynasty useful allies. In 529, therefore, Justinian granted to a Ghassanid the title of phylarch, the highest Byzantine rank under that of the Emperor himself. This did not mean, however, that the Arabian phylarchs gave up their pagan customs; indeed, they continued to sacrifice camels to the spirits of their ancestors, even though they addressed the spirits as " the sons of Mary ".

In the sixth century, a celebrated Arabian prince of the royal house of Kinda, Imr al-Qais, sought the protection of Byzantium. His ancestors, who were scions of the Himyarite dynasty, had come to Central Arabia in the fourth century. An Arabic inscription dated 328 states that one of these ancestors regarded himself as " king of all the Arabs who wear headbands." As his name indicates, Imr al-Qais had been dedicated at birth to Qais, consort of Manat, the Arabian goddess of fate. The prince led a dissipated life, devoted to drinking and to the composition of poetic tributes to his mistress. He is, however, regarded as one of the greatest Arab poets and is said to have invented the *qasidah* literary form. His father died in circumstances that made it imperative for his son, as next of kin, to avenge him, but the prince was drinking when the news was brought to him and said: " Today for wine, tomorrow for business." His attempt at vengeance was unsuccessful. For a time he lived with another poet, Samaw'al, a Jewish noble who had a fort near the Taima oasis. Then in 530 he went to Constantinople, where he was made a phylarch. According to Arabian romance, he courted a Byzantine princess, but never married her as he died in Ancyra from the effects of a poisoned robe sent him by Justinian.

At this time Byzantium was engaged in a perpetual struggle with Persia for political control in the Near East, a struggle in which the Abyssinians and the Turks also played an important part. The Turks allied themselves with Byzantium, as did their cousins the Khazars—a valuable asset for Byzantium, as the Turks were greatly feared, even by the Sassanids, although related by marriage to their kings. In ancient Arabic poems there are frequent references to the " gates of the Turk," which were supposedly at Kabul and through which the Turks and the Khazars would one day menacingly stream.

In order to counter Byzantium's warlike ambitions in Arabia, the Persians lent their support to the Lakhmid dynasty, inveterate rivals of the Ghassanids, and the Lakhmid princes built a citadel for themselves in Hira, the city where Nebuchadnezzar II had once massacred the Arabs.

There were many poets at the court of Hira. They would recite Arabian epics, such as the lament of Zenobia, Queen of Palmyra, who died in 270, chained in a Roman prison, and the romance of 'Antarah the negro poet, as well as love stories, fables, riddles and drinking songs. One of the most famous, Nabighah, was the boon-companion of a Lakhmid prince. Chancing one day to catch sight of the king's consort as she stood without her veil in the privacy of her room, he could not restrain himself from describing her statuesque beauty in verse. The poet would have paid for this indiscretion with his life had it not been for the king's attachment to him, which overcame his outraged sense of honour.

Eventually Christian influences, both religious and political, did penetrate as far as Mecca. In the sixth century A. D., the inhabitants were one day surprised to see their fellow-citizen 'Othman ibn al-Huwairith returning home from Constantinople, riding on a mule with a gilt saddle, to proclaim himself the first King of Mecca, appointed by the Eastern Roman Emperor. 'Othman's self-assurance so impressed the Meccans that they were on the point of crowning him when they remembered just in time that there had never been a king in the holy city—no

25.* The newly-born Muhammad, in his mother's arms, is shown to his grandfather 'Abd al-Muttalib and to the wondering Meccans. The infant Apostle and his mother are shown veiled, as is usual in Islamic orthodox painting, as a sign of reverence. The holy figures are often represented with flaming haloes. 37×27 cm.

26. An alabaster head of a youth or girl, from Southern Arabia, dating from about the beginning of the Christian era. Height 13 cm.

27. A bronze horse, bearing an archaic South Arabian inscription: « Gabhai, mistress of Ba'dan, an offering of... Lihathat ". Length 11 cm.

28. Stone bas-relief of two heads, with a South Arabian inscription. Height 28 cm.

25

26 27

28

doubt out of deference to the God of the Ka'bah—and they sent 'Othman back to Constantinople.

JUDAISM AND CHRISTIANITY IN THE HIJAZ

An ascetic Christian hermit, Faymiyun, was brought by slave-dealers from the Syrian desert, where his miracles had healed many sick people, to a large and prosperous settlement and caravan station in the province of Najran on the southern border of the Hijaz, east of the Yemen. Here, although he was now in servitude, he succeeded in converting his master's native city to Christianity. In the sixth century, the Yemenite King Dhu Nuwas, who was himself of Jewish faith, persecuted the inhabitants of Najran for their beliefs. Their sufferings are related in the Qoran, in Ibn Hisham's history and in the martyrology of St. Arethas.

The Ka'bah murals at this period contained a picture of Mary and her Child, probably painted in the later Dura-Europos style, and the early Christian Arabs were still not forbidden to participate in the traditional pilgrimages to the Temple of Allah, the One God of Mecca.[34]

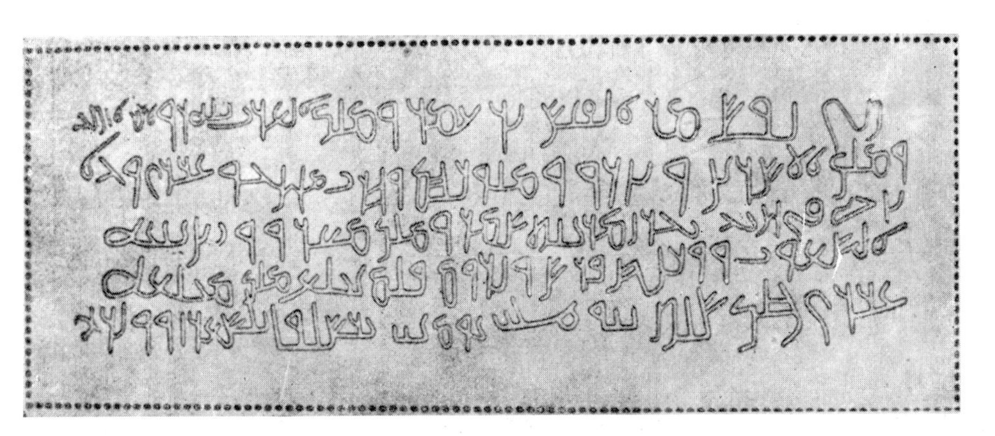

Transcription of the oldest known inscription in historical Arabic, dated 328 A. D., found on a tombstone near Damascus.

THE QORAISH

THERE WAS a large group of Ishmaelites in the Meccan region whose generic name was Qoraish. The earliest member of the tribe to make his mark in the annals of history was Zayd, the fifth forefather of Muhammad, born about the year 400 A.D. His father Kilab died soon after, and Zayd and his elder brother Zuhrah (to whom Muhammad could also trace his ancestry, on his mother's side) were left in the care of their mother Fatimah. She married again quite soon, a man from 'Aqabah who had come to Mecca on pilgrimage. Fatimah left Zuhrah behind with his father's family and took the baby with her to her new home.

There, near the river Yarmuk, in the old country of the Nabateans, Zayd grew up with his mother's second family, and was called " Qusayy," " the little stranger." In spite of this, it was not until he was of adult years that he learned of his foreign origin. He resolved to pay a visit to his father's family, and so joined a group of pilgrims travelling south along the desert route.

Once in Mecca, the handsome young Ishmaelite met a girl from the Khuza'ah tribe and sought her hand. This young woman, whose name was Hubba, was the daughter of the Gatekeeper of the Ka'bah, a man who belonged to the holy family of his tribe and was thus a descendant of the 'Amr ibn Luhayy who had first brought idols into Mecca. When in course of time he became too old to carry out his ritual duties, he passed them on to his daughter, who in turn transferred them to her husband. The Khuza'ah tribe were incensed that a sacred dignity should be thus arbitrarily handed on to an outsider, and Zayd was forced to send to his relatives, both Ishmaelites and Nabateans, for help. They came in force, riding swiftly and silently by night along the flat beaches of the Tihamah, and a pitched battle ensued at the Mina gorge, at the entrance to the Meccan vale. Zayd and his kinsmen won the day, and, following Arabian custom, the opposing sides sought the advice of an arbitrator to decide upon the fate of the defeated faction. The judge ruled that as the Khuza'ah were related to Qusayy by marriage, they should not be expelled from Mecca; but Zayd became to all intents and purposes the city's priest-king.

So, after two thousand years of exile, the Ishmaelites were free again to settle in Mecca. While his kinsmen celebrated their success and the Khuza'ah stood waiting to be released from their chains, Qusayy, following Arabian custom, spoke an *epos* beginning with this couplet:

I am the son of the virtuous Lu'ayy (Ishmaelite)
Mecca is my home, where I became a lord.

29. Stone stele from South Arabia, showing several human figures and camels, and dating from about the beginning of the Christian era. Height 55 cm.

29

30

It is believed that during his reign Qusayy rebuilt, or at least repaired, the Ka'bah. Adam's gem throne was still there, in spite of many attempts to steal it, but the generations of impure hands which had touched it had darkened its milky whiteness, and it was now called the Black Stone, though it still shone with dark splendour.

Qusayy was the first man to construct a town in the sacred valley itself. No houses had ever stood there; the nearest habitations to the Ka'bah had always been on the lower slopes of the Red Mountain and Abu Qubais, overlooking the valley. Now the shrubs were cleared away from the plain and, as the site of the Zamzam had long since been forgotten, new wells were dug.

The new houses were arranged in concentric circles round the Ka'bah, according to strict rules of caste and tribal precedence. The houses of Qusayy and his children, each of whom had been dedicated to and named after one of the gods worshipped in Mecca, enclosed the square, sandy courtyard which had been left round the temple; his own house faced the northern side of the Ka'bah. The rows behind were occupied by people in descending degrees of importance; accommodation was also provided for people of allied tribes whom the Qoraish regarded as their equals, such as the Ghassanid phylarchs. The outskirts of Mecca were left to undistinguished foreigners, outcasts, slaves, and mercenary soldiers.

Judging from later accounts, dating from the seventh to ninth centuries A. D., the Meccan houses were cubic in shape, with a single entrance. They were generally built of rough or shaped stones, or of bricks, either baked or unbaked. Occasionally they were decorated with marble, coloured stones, or with the curiously-shaped shells found along the Arabian Gulf. The wealthier citizens had lofty ceilings in their houses, supported on pillars. There were few gardens, but here and there a solitary palm tree grew in a courtyard. Along the narrow streets, merchants sold spices and perfumes, local and imported cloths, garments and sandals, water-skins, stone vessels, honey and dates, the juice of Taif grapes and the millet that was their common food. There were wells with cisterns (*siqayahs*) in the town squares, and caravan camels would be brought there to kneel, deposit their burdens and to drink.

In theory, Mecca was a republic, administered by an oligarchy of men over the age of forty. Qusayy's house also did duty as a kind of city hall where the men would meet to discuss public affairs. But in fact Qusayy himself was in overall charge of both temporal and spiritual matters. He was " lifter of the veil " in the Ka'bah and in this capacity led the ceremonies there; it was he who consulted the oracles, and organised the distribution of food and water to the pilgrims. If a member of the Qoraish wished to marry outside the tribe, he had first to seek the permission of Qusayy. In time of war, Qusayy unfurled his banner and took command of the troops.

When Qusayy died, and was buried in a house near the Ka'bah, the duties he had performed were divided among his family. Quarrels soon arose between his sons, and a civil war broke out. Members of the two factions swore allegiance by rubbing their hands, dipped in scent or blood, against the walls of the Ka'bah. When the hostilities abated, Qusayy's twin grandsons 'Abd al-Shams (" the Servant of the Sun "), forefather of the 'Omayyad dynasty, and Hashim (" the Bread-breaker"—so-called because he distributed bread to pilgrims), the great-grandfather of Muhammad, shared their grandfather's administrative responsibilities between them. They were both imbued with the courtesy and moderation for which the Qoraish aristocracy was famous, and did their best to alleviate the worsening conditions of the Meccan people. Times were so hard that the inhabitants of the Hijaz were even known to bury new-born female babies alive, for the starving mothers could not nurse them and girls were regarded by the Arabs

30.* Muhammad's marriage to Khadijah, who is seen sitting in a recess, while her proxy speaks her consent.
37×27 cm.

generally as a liability. Mecca's prosperity depended on the trade brought by her caravans, and although these were protected by trade agreements and still journeyed towards Abyssinia every winter and to Syria-Palestine every summer, the sea routes now took much of their business from them.

On a visit to Yathrib, Hashim met a widow of noble birth called Salma; he married her, and she bore him a strange silvery-haired child. Not long afterwards Hashim died, and the boy grew up in Yathrib with his mother. Some years later his uncle Muttalib of the Qoraish tribe came to fetch him back to his people. The boy had taken up archery, and as they rode into Mecca—Muttalib in the saffron robes and purple sash of the high-born Qoraish, the boy in the sober garb of an archer—the citizens thought the old man must have acquired a new slave, and therefore called the newcomer 'Abd al-Muttalib, " Muttalib's servant " (*ill.* 23).

The boy now settled in Mecca and in due course assumed the functions of his father and uncle as the dispenser of food and water to the pilgrims. He longed to have a large number of sons, and vowed that if he were blessed with ten children he would sacrifice one of them at the Ka'bah. In time his wish was granted and he had no choice but to fulfil his promise. The children drew lots with marked arrows and the choice fell upon the youngest son, 'Abd Allah (" Servant of God "). Of all his sons 'Abd al-Muttalib loved his youngest child best of all and was horrified that fate should have chosen him. The distraught father sought the help of a sibyl, who advised him to redeem his vow with expiatory sacrifices, and in this way the boy who was to be the father of Muhammad was saved from an untimely death.

About the year 570, Mecca was threatened by calamity. A series of events was set in train in Southern Arabia, then under Abyssinian rule. The Ethiopian

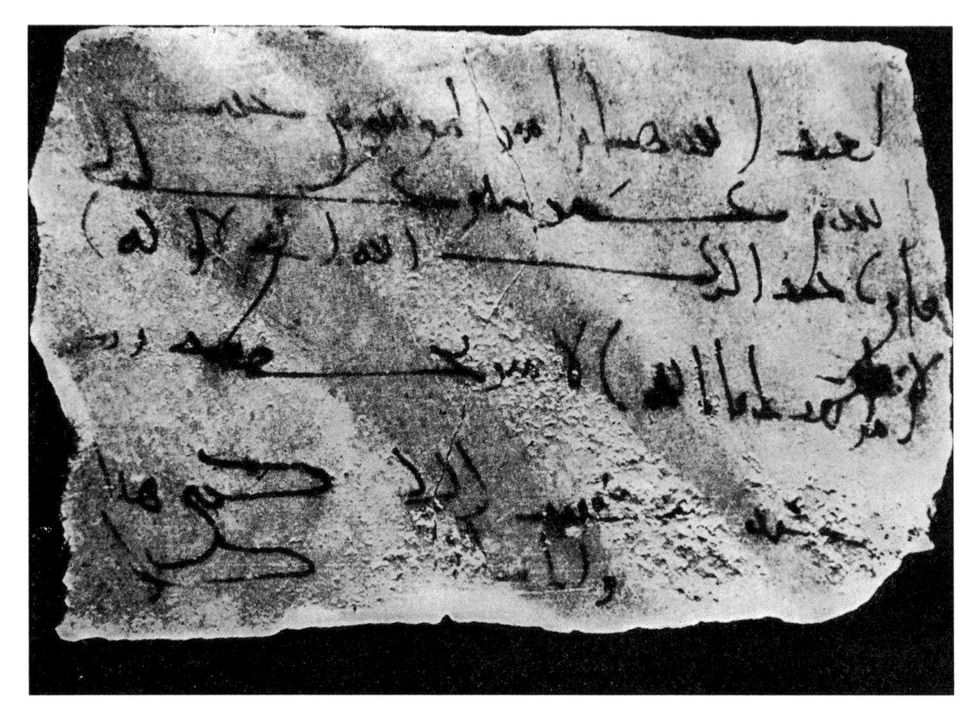

Graffito inscription in Arabic from the palace of Khirbat-al-Mafjar, giving the name of the Caliph Hisham (724-743 A.D.).

governor there, Abrahah, who was a Christian, decided to initiate a proselytising campaign. With the intention of diverting Arab pilgrimage from the Meccan Temple and its Black Stone, he built a magnificent church at San'a, decorated with polychrome marbles, gold and silver inlay, and studded with gems. At the gate of the church he set an enormous ruby, perfumed and blackened with musk, and hung a curtain across it. Then he suggested that the Arabs should come to worship in the church adorned with this Jewel instead of at the Ka'bah, and indeed some tribes did break away from their old beliefs to worship there. A young votary of the Meccan temple, angered by this defection, went to Abrahah's church and defiled it. This offence so enraged the governor, that he swore to take his revenge upon the Ka'bah Temple itself.

Flying his flag of battle, on which was represented the Cross of his faith, Abrahah set out for the Hijaz at the head of a tremendous army. He wore a crown on his head, a ruby pendant hung across his forehead; he rode upon a giant elephant. His face had been badly gashed in an earlier combat, and altogether his appearance struck such terror into the people he met along the way that they gladly showed him the route to Mecca so that he would leave them in peace.

When Abrahah arrived at the edge of the sacred valley, he drew up his cavalry on the plain and sent his infantry into the mountains overlooking the Ka'bah. The Meccans were terrified to find themselves surrounded but made no attempt at defence, relying on the sacredness of the sanctuary to protect them. Abrahah sent them a message, asking to see their king. As their only king was the invisible Lord of the Ka'bah, the venerable 'Abd al-Muttalib was deputed to go to the Abyssinian camp (*ill.* 22). He came back bearing the decree that the Meccans were to retreat to the mountains and allow Abrahah and his army to destroy the Ka'bah.

Quickly the inhabitants of the valley departed, and again the Ka'bah stood alone, as in earlier years, in the bowl-like valley. 'Abd al-Muttalib was the last to leave and, grasping the metal knocker on the door of the Ka'bah, he offered up this prayer before he abandoned the temple to its fate:

> *O God, in truth* (even) *the servant defends*
> *his camel, defend thou Thy city.*

At dawn next day, the Abyssinian troops were drawn up in battle order to enter Mecca (*ill.* 24). As they advanced upon the Ka'bah, the governor's elephant suddenly kneeled down and refused to get up, even though it was severely beaten on the head with iron bars. The sky grew dark and a huge flock of birds appeared, each one carrying a pebble in its beak (*ill.* 21). As they flew over the plain, the birds dropped the stones on the invaders. At the same moment, the soldiers were struck by a terrible plague: their faces were pocked and their limbs fell away. Those few who survived fled in terror towards the Yemen, leaving bloody, putrefying corpses along the way. The valley of Bakkah, " the breaker of the necks of tyrants," had punished the invaders.[35]

THE BIRTH OF MUHAMMAD

In the second half of the sixth century A. D., religious unrest still prevailed in Arabia and the surrounding countries. The religions of the scriptures had large followings, but they had not yet succeeded in conquering paganism entirely. Many were still awaiting the coming of divinely inspired teachers: the Jews expected their Messiah; some of the multitudinous Christian sects hoped for the arrival of the Comforter who had been promised to them in St. John's Gospel. Members of dualist religions also, such as the Zoroastrians, sought a human manifestation of their principle of light. In Arabia itself, the last heathen strongholds were gradually falling. The idols' doom was being foretold at their own altars. Minstrels who had chanted praises to the pagan gods now sang a different song; and when the illustrious poet Labid said: "Lo, all things but God are vain," the idols trembled upon their pedestals and their crowds of adherents wondered what lay in store for them.

The truth sought by the monotheist hermits of the Hijaz was to be neither Judaism nor Christianity. Already there was a House of the One God, in Mecca: now it began to figure more and more often in the poets' verses. At a ceremony in Mecca itself, four men were shocked to see a great congregation gathered together to worship a stone, and they agreed secretly to revive their ancestor Abraham's forgotten religion. Three of them, in fact, adopted Christianity, but the fourth, Zayd ibn 'Amr, felt that neither of the prevailing monotheistic creeds could satisfy him. When he became an old man, he would lean upon the wall of the Ka'bah and say:—" O God, if I knew which is the rite Thou deemest best, I would worship Thee thus. But I know not." Prostrating himself, he would praise his God:—

31.* The young Muhammad, on a caravan expedition to Syria, being served a meal by Christian monks. 37 × 27 cm.

32.* Muhammad meeting a monotheist shepherd. 38 × 26 cm.

33.* Muhammad pacifying a giant reptile. 38 × 26 cm.

34.* Muhammad hearing from hunters the complaint of a doe: " O Apostle of God, I have two dearly-loved little ones that I suckle... " 38 × 26 cm.

> I renounce entirely al-Lat and al-'Uzza
> I will have no faith in al-'Uzza, nor in her two daughters
> Nor in Hubal, although he was our Master.
>
> . . . .
>
> I looked with wonder, for there are many marvels in the nights
> And in the days, that are clear to those endowed with vision.

One who was thus endowed was 'Abd al-Muttalib. He was standing one day in meditation before Hagar's tomb, when a voice told him to dig into the earth and find the spring of water that had belonged to his people for all eternity, the water that was as much part of them as their own blood and entrails. This was

31

33

32

34

35
36

the long-lost Zamzam, once struck from the barren ground by an angel to succour Hagar, the Egyptian woman who had borne their ancestor Ishmael. 'Abd al-Muttalib dug at random; at the bottom of the hole shone the waters of the ancient well, and he blessed the name of the God of Mecca.

His youngest son, 'Abd Allah, had now reached the age of twenty-five—which was to be the last year of his life. His father had consecrated him to the service of the One God, and a mysterious light seemed always to shine about him. A Meccan woman who was well versed in the Scriptures believed that this light indicated that 'Abd Allah was to be the father of the promised Comforter, and she tried to ensnare him. But 'Abd Allah preferred the girl chosen for him by his father: Aminah, a descendant of Qusayy's brother Zuhrah. Like other nubile maidens of the Qoraish, Aminah had been kept a virtual prisoner in her father's house, near the corn market. Very soon after he had married her and she had

Late eighteenth century Turkish oil painting of Mecca.

conceived a child, 'Abd Allah died. This was the year in which Abrahah and his army set out to attack the Ka'bah, and one of the fugitives who fled to the mountains must have been the young widow, sheltering in her body the future Prophet Muhammad and his ever-present aureole.

Like her father-in-law, Aminah now heard a commanding voice:—" Thou bearest the Lord of this people. When he comes to Earth, confide him to the care of the Unique One, away from the danger of all malign influences. Then name him Muhammad (" He for whom thanks should be offered ")."

In the inky darkness of the Arabian skies, desert dwellers saw multitudes of falling stars, presaging the end and the beginning of an era.[36] A silent promise wafted among the stony wastes:

> He cometh, he cometh, Muhammad cometh!
> The soul who will animate the lifeless world cometh! [37]

Outside Arabia, the world was unaware that revolutionary changes were soon to take place. An Arab girl was about to give birth to the founder of the last great

35. A desert plant, near Mount Hira and in the vicinity where Muhammad heard the bushes and stones speaking to him.

36. Boulders half-way up Mount Hira, near the place where Muhammad, fearing insanity, thought of throwing himself down to his death.

37. The desert round Mecca, seen from Mount Hira; the mountain's flat peak appears in the foreground.

38. View from within a cave on Mount Hira – possibly the same one where Muhammad had his first vision.

monotheistic religion. The new faith of Islam was to attempt a fusion of the preceding monotheistic faiths which it should succeed, declaring:

"... *we believe in God and in what is revealed to us and what was revealed to Abraham and Ismail and Isaac and Jacob and to the tribes and in what was given to Moses and to Jesus and to the prophets from their Lord. We make no distinction between them. And to Him we submit.*" (*Qoran*: III, 83).

It was to be the task of the gentle and unassuming Muhammad to destroy age-old conventions and fetishes, to raze the social and religious hierarchies of ancient Asia, and to open a direct dialogue between God and Man.

Muhammad (*ill.* 25) was born on a Monday, on the twelfth night of the Arabian lunar month Rabi al-Awwal, in the year 569 or 570 A. D., fifty-five days after Abrahah's onslaught on Mecca. Aminah was living in a house not far from the Ka'bah, on the eastern side of the valley under the towering shadow of Mount Abu Qubais, Adam's supposed burial place. From accounts of Aminah's poverty, it can be assumed that the house must have been extremely modest, perhaps consisting only of a single room with an earthen floor. On the night of the birth, the young mother was probably alone and in darkness:

" And I felt not the pains of delivery. And when he was cut away from me, the light he shed illumined both the east and the west. Then he fell upon the ground, confidently, on his two hands. He took up a piece of earth, held it firmly and raised his head toward heaven."

Across infinite expanses of time and space echoed the immense voice of the millions of Moslems who in centuries to come would rise on the Night of Nativity to salute the new-born Muhammad:

Hail to Thee, O Soul of souls most tender, hail!
Hail to Thee, Cupbearer of God's mysteries, hail!
Hail to Thee, O Pleader for the fallen, hail!
Hail to Thee, O Refuge of all sinners, hail!
Hail to Thee, O Mine of lore, all hail to Thee!
Hail to Thee, O secret of the Scriptures, hail!
Hail to Thee, O Epiphany of Mercy, hail! [38]

37
38

صلى الله عليه وسلم حرى طاغنه چقمغا عزم ايلدى چون
طاغ وستونه چقدى كير ورسول حضرتنه كوكدن آشغه
براون كلديكم يا خيرة الله من خلقه ديو رسول عليه السلام بواوا
اشديجك بو نوبت يوركني بركتدى كندوزني جمع ايلدى ايتدى

MUHAMMAD THE TRUSTWORTHY

THE WOMEN of the Banu Bakr tribe rode on their asses to Mecca, to look for suckling babies that the mothers of the city might wish to have nursed in the healthier climate of the hills. Among them was Halimah, who was to be the foster-mother of Muhammad.

> She had left her region with her husband and her own infant son, along with the other women of the tribe, to offer her services as a wet nurse. She said: "And that was a year of drought. We had nothing more left. I rode on a she-ass the colour of the moon. We also had with us a she-camel, but she yielded not a drop of milk. And none of us could sleep at night because of the hungry baby's crying. My breast was dry and the she-camel gave no milk for our breakfast... Thus I rode along on my weak and emaciated donkey, its slow pace keeping back the others, until we came to Mecca...
>
> "And there was no woman among us who did not refuse the Apostle of God as he was offered to us, because it was said that he was an orphan... We expected to receive a handsome present from the child's father. And we said: 'An orphan! And what can his mother and his grandfather provide?' And we spurned him.
>
> "And there remained no woman without a suckling except I. When we gathered to leave, I said to my husband: 'By God, I hate to go home amongst my friends without a suckling. I really think that I should take that orphan.' As soon as I took him to my bosom, there came milk for him from my breasts. He drank till he was satisfied, and his foster-brother also. And they both slept... My husband went to our she-camel and lo! she had milk... We spent a happy night. Then I went and mounted my she-ass, carrying him (Muhammad) with me. And it went at such a pace that none of the other donkeys could overtake it, until my friends called to me: 'Confound thee! Wait for us. Is that she-ass the one thou hadst as we came?' And I said to them: 'Aye, by God, the very same!' So they said: 'By God, it has surely become a proud beast'."

Muhammad grew up in his foster-father's tent, in the highland region near Taif. Halimah's husband was a shepherd, and they found that their flocks prospered as never before. This they attributed to the luck brought by the Qorashi child, but they were nonetheless a little afraid of the supernatural atmosphere that surrounded him. There seemed to be a cloud constantly over his head, as if to shade

39.* Muhammad hearing a voice and seeing a vision on the horizon, as he thinks of suicide while on Mount Hira. 37×27 cm.

him from the sun. When the family went to the local fair at 'Okaz, Arabian seers, Jewish rabbis, Christian monks and others all showed extraordinary interest in Muhammad, and even asked to examine the egg-shaped white birthmark between his shoulder-blades. This later became known as the " Seal of Prophecy".

When Muhammad was four years old, he was out one day tending lambs when his foster-brother saw two angels, dressed in white, appear before them. They seized the little Muhammad, cut his chest open and washed his heart with snow. When Halimah was told of this, she rushed to the spot and found Muhammad standing there, apparently unhurt but very pale. She decided there and then that she would return the child to his mother in Mecca. Aminah said, when she heard about the incident: " There is something extraordinary about my little boy."[39]

For the next two years Muhammad lived with Aminah. Many years later the Prophet was to make the only reference to this part of his life: " Paradise is under the feet of mothers." When he was six years old, his mother and her maid took him with them on a journey to Yathrib, to stay with some members of a related tribe. The young Muhammad played with his cousins, swimming in a large well, and counting the birds that perched on the crenellations of the fortress-like enclosure where the tribe lived. As they were returning home through the desert, at a place called Abwa', Aminah suddenly died; she could not have been more than twenty-five years old, as her husband had been when he had died. Later when the grown Muhammad visited her dilapidated tomb, he said: " I remembered her mercy and I wept."

His mother's maid brought Muhammad home and gave him into the care of his grandfather. 'Abd al-Muttalib was now a blind old man, who spent his days sitting at the Ka'bah, while his multitude of sons stood respectfully round him. After two years, he too died, nodding in approval as his daughters composed elegies for him, evoking the " princely hero" and his tall elegant figure as a youth. Muhammad was adopted by his uncle Abu Talib, who brought him up with his own large family.

Contemporary witnesses of Muhammad's growth towards manhood say: " The Apostle of God became a young man. God protected him from the loose behaviour of the pagans. He was the most generous of his people... kind to his neighbours, courteous, faithful... and trustworthy, so that his people called him by no other name than ' the Trustworthy ' (al-Amin). He was the bravest of men... the most sensitive." He smiled readily and often, yet he was of a serious disposition. He would sometimes fall into deep thought, becoming oblivious of his surroundings. " I have never seen, either before or since, anyone like him," said those who knew him.

His cousin 'Ali and others have described Muhammad's appearance:—" He was neither tall nor short, but of the medium height common to his people." His shoulders were broad, his chest well-developed, and his waist slender. " His skin was white, tinged with red "; there was a glow about it that caused his contemporaries to compare it to the pearly light of the moon or the shimmer of silver. " He was not fat, not round-faced "; his forehead was high, his nose aquiline, his neck long. His eyes were large, black and long-lashed. His hands and feet were finely shaped. He walked rapidly, and " lightly, with long strides." His clothing generally consisted of two pieces of cloth about four ells long, one of which he draped round him, while the other, called a *ridâ*, was thrown across his shoulder like a toga.

Like most of the men who lived in this barren region, Muhammad earned his living by going on the caravans which departed from Mecca twice a year; in this way he probably made several visits to the lands bordering on the Hijaz. On one occasion, he went as the agent of a wealthy woman, his distant cousin Khadijah.

40.* Muhammad's vision of ascension. Here the Apostle is represented in the house of 'Ali's sister Umm u-Hani. According to one tradition, he sat there, surrounded by his disciples, as the vision was vouchsafed to him. 65×42 cm.

عاد قومن هلاك قلدوم سنك دوشمنلروكی داخی شویله هلاك
قلایم ددی اندن رسول علیه السلام اول برسنی دخی ایلرو
اوقدی ایتدی سن نیه موکل سن ددی اول فرشته دخی ایتدی
بن دکزلو صولرا وستنه موکلم حق تعالی بلوتدن انز یغمورلری

41

42

This brought about a closer acquaintance between Muhammad, now twenty-five years old, and this twice-widowed woman of forty who already had several grown-up children. She wrote to him: " My cousin, indeed I esteem thee ... because thou deservest consideration in the midst of thy people for thy trustworthiness, friendliness and veracity." Her high regard was reciprocated, and Muhammad and Khadijah were married (*ill.* 30). Their union lasted twenty-five years and was most happy. Four daughters were born to them—Zaynab, Roqqiyah, Um Kulthum and Fatimah—and three sons who all died in infancy. They lived in a house with a peristyle, on the eastern side of the Ka'bah, in Upper Mecca.

In 605 A. D., when Muhammad was thirty-five, an accident befell the Ka'bah. A woman was carrying round it a tray of glowing charcoal and frankincense, to perfume it, when a spark fell on the red-striped cloth covering the shrine, and the resulting blaze scorched the stone quite badly. After this, there was a flood, which caused the weakened masonry to crumble, and it became necessary to demolish the whole structure and rebuild it. Providentially, the wood needed for the task was easily available, from an Egyptian ship that had been wrecked on the Red Sea coast. Among the shipwrecked crew there was a Copt, a carpenter by trade, who agreed to undertake a task that would have been beyond the capabilities of the Meccans, living as they did in a treeless valley—the fashioning of a wooden roof for the Ka'bah. This was virtually a necessity now, as there had been so many attempts to steal from the roofless building, some of which had even been successful.

Before the work began, a snake that had lived for years in the treasury of the Ka'bah came out of his hiding-place, and caused some alarm among the by-standers (*ill.* 33). But a crane swooped down from the sky and carried the snake off; this was regarded as a good omen for the task which lay ahead. Even so, the Qoraish hesitated to begin the work of demolishing the old temple, for fear of committing a sacrilege. At last an elderly man summoned the courage to tear down the first stone, and after that the work could proceed. When the walls had been removed, some green Cyclopean stones appeared; these were the substructure of Abraham's original edifice. When the Qorashi tried to break them, the first splinter sprang back to its place with a blinding flash, and the sanctified ground trembled.

The Qorashi therefore left Abraham's foundations where they were and began to rebuild the shrine on top of them. They went—Muhammad among them—into the mountains to look for suitable stones and carried them back on their shoulders. Four groups of workers were formed, each to build one wall. This, however, gave rise to considerable argument, as each group claimed the privilege of placing Adam's gem-throne at the eastern corner of the new sanctuary, where Abraham had first put it. In no time sides were taken and oaths of allegiance were sworn by dipping hands in blood, pledging loyalty unto death between one group and another. As a last-minute effort to avert violence, it was suggested that the next man to enter the Ka'bah's enclosure should act as arbitrator. The person thus designated by fate was Muhammad, " the Trustworthy." He asked one delegate to come from each faction, to hold the stone between them in a cloth. Then he took it from them and placed it in position himself.

In order to safeguard the treasure, the Ka'bah was now raised to a height of eighteen ells. Fifteen layers of stone, fastened together with metal dowels, and thirteen rows of wooden planks, formed the body of the edifice, and the Coptic carpenter set a flat roof on top. The area occupied by the new Ka'bah was smaller than that of the old; this was mainly due to a shortage of building materials. Whereas in the past the whole of Ishmael's bower-dwelling had been included in the temple, now a part of it had to be left outside. However, its perimeter was marked on the north-eastern side by a low semicircular wall.

41. The ruins of Nabatu (Petra), the rock-hewn city of the Nabateans in Arabia Petraea.

42. A calcite gravestone of about the second century A. D., probably from Qataban in Southern Arabia, showing a young woman holding cornstalks, together with an inscription of the name " Aban ". Height 32.5 cm.

The Ka'bah was now ready to be decorated. According to tradition, it had been profusely ornamented both inside and out during the 'Amalik period, but nothing was known of the nature of these embellishments.

The Qoraish built six pillars, in two rows, within the sanctuary, and covered them, as well as the walls, with paintings of trees and figures of prophets and angels. There was, for instance, a representation of Abraham consulting the pagan oracular arrows, and one of Mary with the Infant Jesus in her arms. These paintings may have been in a provincial Byzantine style, perhaps containing some traces of Abyssinian influence. Historians refer to the existence of painters of the human figure and image-makers in Arabian territories adjacent to Mecca, if not in Mecca itself.[40] The golden gazelles and other precious objects once buried by the chief of the Jurhum in the dry Zamzam well and found there centuries later by 'Abd al-Muttalib, were now replaced in the Ka'bah.

These alterations set the door of the temple well above the ground, so that it could only be reached by a stairway. Visitors were allowed to enter on Mondays and Thursdays; before going in they would remove their shoes as a sign of respect. Also they were expected to give a suitable present to the official in charge of the door—a source of constant regret to Muhammad, who thought that the Ka'bah ought to be freely and easily accessible to all.

MOUNT HIRA

THE SOCIAL order of the Meccan community was being threatened by such dangers as extreme poverty and inter-tribal dissension. Periodic years of famine were a common occurrence in the barren Hijaz, and the Meccans said that, shut in by their mountains as they were, no people on earth had a harder life than they.

Since the income from caravan trading had been so greatly reduced by rival maritime transport, and the foreign pagan temples—hitherto Arabia's best customers for aromatic herbs—had fallen into neglect, the Meccans were forced to seek other sources of revenue. In spite of their poor economic situation, they were addicted to gambling, drinking and festivities. The sound of flutes and singing often echoed along the streets of Mecca at night. Money must be found for these pleasures, if not for food. So the pilgrimages to Mecca were turned to account, and some of the members of the priestly aristocracy proceeded to exploit this potentially rich source of revenue. Among those who indulged in this practice were the Homs, who considered themselves to be an " elect " caste by virtue of their long residence in Mecca and their religious strictness. It was they who granted permission to enter the city and were in charge of the worship at the idols' altars, and their methods of exacting payment for such permission were summary, to say the least. If, for instance, a pilgrim did not offer a large enough bribe to the gatekeeper of the Ka'bah, he might be pushed off the top of the high stairway; a number of deaths resulted from this procedure. Pilgrims were told that their garments were impure and must be removed; the " guardians " of the Temple then sold them new ones. Quite often the women who came to worship at the sanctuary were kidnapped by the Meccans, and this would lead to reprisals from the men of their tribes. A few citizens disapproved of these excesses, but they were forced to hide their resentment or face being driven into exile by the young braves of the Qoraish.

When Muhammad was twenty years old, however, a number of such public-spirited citizens revived a traditional association which had fallen into obsolescence. Its aim was to protect the weak and oppressed against the tyranny that threatened them, and Muhammad became a wholehearted member of this group. Their pledge to " fight against the usurpation of rights " was later to inspire the semi-religious artisans' guilds that were to play such a prominent part during the Islamic Middle Ages.

One of the meanings of the word " Islam " is " salvation," and Muhammad was already doing his best to bring salvation to his corrupt and poverty-stricken people. During his travels and in conversations with strangers, he was also discovering the thoughts and aims of humanity in the world beyond the Hijaz. But the man who was to say: " Consult the law of thine own heart, even if law-givers decree for thee a law," and for whom religion represented nothing but " sincerity, sincerity and again sincerity," had not yet heard the call of the Spirit.

As Muhammad approached forty, he began to seek solitude, and for a month each year he would go into retreat on Mount Hira, which is seen from Mecca as a steep, conical peak on the north-eastern horizon. From his house he would follow the deep ravine paths until he came to the black sands of the desert, where he would be in sight of the two mountains of Hira and Thabir. Mount Thabir, where Abraham was said to have attempted the sacrifice of Ishmael, rose sharply like a pyramid, while Hira now looked like a crouching sphinx, with its head raised in the direction of Mecca. In the shady plain between the two mountains grew the Meccan opobalsam, petrified-looking thorny bushes, and a few tropical trees with thick juicy leaves and white blooms. It is said that as Muhammad walked among them, the plants and stones would greet him in human speech; hearing them, he would turn but see no one (*ill.* 35). Then he would climb the curving, rocky backbone of Mount Hira, where the boulders grew gradually larger as he neared the top, until they were as huge as cliffs and hid the summit from sight (*ill.* 36). Then the peak again came into view, capped with its golden sand. Rock-doves flew about him, calling, so says Meccan lore, the name " Khadijah." Blue lizards flashed across the sun-warmed boulders. At the windy top of the mountain, Muhammad found himself on a small, flat expanse. It seemed to be an island in the sky, floating towards the blue haze of the Meccan vale. Along the horizon lay the barren Hijaz desert and the chains of rocky peaks (*ill.* 37). The blazing sun flung the giant shadow of Hira across the plain.

On the southern flank of the mountain, about five hundred feet from the top, is the cave where Muhammad was wont to meditate. Inside it is high and deep enough for a man to stand or lie down; the walls and ceiling are of clean-cut rock (*ill.* 38), and the floor of the cave is covered with fine golden sand. Here, in the Arabian month of Ramadan, during the hours of darkness, Muhammad had his first vision. He described it like this:

" One came to me with a written scroll, while I was asleep, and said ' Read! ' I said ' I cannot read '... He pressed me with it, until I thought death must be nigh... And he said

> ' *Read in the name of thy Lord who created;*
> *He created man from a sensitive drop of blood.*'
> (*Qoran:* XCVI, 1-2)

And he departed ... And I awoke ... And it was as if the scripture were written on my heart."

Muhammad got up, " *as the star set,*" afraid that he must be losing his mind. He thought: " I will throw myself down that I may gain rest." " I went until I was midway on the mountain and I heard a sound from the sky saying: ' O Muhammad, thou art the Apostle of God and I am Gabriel ' (*ill.* 39). I raised my head to heaven and saw him standing, in the shape of a man, with his feet upon the horizon. And I stood staring at him, and could move neither forward nor backward. Then I turned my gaze away from him, along the horizon, but wherever I looked I saw him."

Muhammad rushed home in terror. He clung to Khadijah, trembling and saying: " Hide me! Hide me! " She covered him with a cloth until his fears subsided, but still he could see the vision everywhere, even when his eyes were closed. He said to his wife: " I have heard a sound and seen a light, and verily

43. Two plaster heads from the 'Omayyad palace at Khirbat al-Mafjar, near Jericho, built for the Caliph Hisham between 106 and 125 A. H. (724-743 A. D.). Height 25 cm.

44. A stone head from the 'Omayyad palace at Khirbat al-Mafjar. Height 30 cm.

45.* Muhammad, leading the Moslems' prayer at the Ka'bah, is attacked by the pagan Qorashi Abu Jahl, who attempts to crush him under a rock. 37×27 cm.

46.* Muhammad prays alone in the Ka'bah. 37×27 cm.

43
44

45

46

I fear that I will become insane." But she comforted him: "Oh no, God will never grieve thee, for thou art merciful to thy kin and takest upon thee their burden and through thee the fallen rise again ... These are glad tidings, O my cousin. I hope that thou wilt indeed be the apostle of this people."

MOUNT HIRA

But for months, years even, nothing more happened. Muhammad still carried in his memory a persistent and dazzling image of the angelic figure in which the Divine Spirit had appeared to him at Hira, and doubt and fear of insanity still gnawed at him. He was so obsessed by this anxiety that he wished the awful experience would recur and give final proof that it had indeed been a revelation. He climbed both Hira and Thabir over and over again, hoping to find his lost vision in one of these hallowed places; the Meccans now called him "he who goes up and down Hira." The towering precipices and slippery rocks constantly tempted him to return to his original intention and to fall to oblivion.

Then one day as he was walking yet again towards the mountains, deeply immersed in thought so that he did not notice the thorns that caught at his garment or the stones on which he stumbled, he suddenly heard a sound that made him fall down in awe. "He then looked up and saw Gabriel, sitting cross-legged on a throne between heaven and earth, who said to him: 'O Muhammad, thou really art the Apostle of God'."

Now Muhammad left his house and spent all his time in the Ka'bah, praying and awaiting God's will (*ill.* 46). Sometimes he would be convinced that God had forsaken him, but the Archangel spoke to him thus: "*Thy Lord hath not forsaken thee nor doth He hate thee.*" (*Qoran:* XCIII, 3).

At last the divine commands came, ringing like bells in the ears of the ashen-faced man as he lay prostrate and trembling under the folds of his mantle:

> "*O thou who enwrappest thyself!*
> *Arise and warn*
> *And magnify thy Lord.*"
> (*Qoran:* LXXIV, 1-3)

Muhammad's soul heard the message and accepted the heavy burden of apostolate.[41]

MUHAMMAD THE SERVANT AND THE APOSTLE OF GOD

Verily this is a revelation from the Lord of the worlds
The Spirit of Truth has descended with it
Upon thy heart that thou mayst be one of the warners.
(*Qoran:* XXVI, 192-4)

During the remaining twenty years of Muhammad's life, he was to receive a continual stream of revelations, in the course of which, according to the Moslem faith, the divine injunctions were vouchsafed. The text of the revelations is called the Qoran, a word the significance of which lies somewhere between " lecture " and " sermon," and consists of prose versicles, varying in length. The Divine Spirit which imparted the verses to Muhammad was generally made manifest to the Apostle in a form perceptible to human senses. At the beginning of Muhammad's apostolate, he had vivid dreams that were exactly realised. Later, the revelations came during his waking hours; " the Spirit whispered to his soul," or the commands sounded in his ears like bells. The Spirit appeared to him also in the guise of the Archangel Gabriel, sometimes in human shape, or, as on Hira, in superhuman aspect. Only once, in his ascensional visions, did Muhammad contemplate the mysteries of God in the abstract, without the medium of a definable human experience.

In his moments of inspiration, Muhammad's body would sag, as if under the burden of an intolerable weight. His face would become pale and his eyelids would close. Vainly he would try to stop his lips from trembling; in one revelation he had been told not to move his lips in repetition of the divine words, because they could never vanish from his memory. When the vision was over, the Apostle would recite the verses to his disciples, who would learn them by heart. They were also written down, on palm-leaves, the shoulder-blades of animals, or any other material that was readily available.

The Qoran describes the vast and harmonious creation of the universe as a " Book " of which Man can see the writing but cannot understand its meaning. Therefore it has to be presented to him in the form of " parables." Man is assured that, although it may not seem so to him, the universe is governed by an immutable justice. " The Book " beginning " In the Name of the Merciful and Compassionate God " may be described as a long monologue in which the Creator addresses Man, in the persons of Adam, Abraham, Moses, Judaic prophets, Christ and Muhammad. The perennial story is told of Man's struggle against Evil, which is nothing but a temporary illusion, and of his ultimate return to Absolute Truth.

Although it contains many rulings on aspects of personal and social life, the Qoran lays stress primarily on the monotheistic creed. The only essential condition of Islam, which is an Arabic word meaning conjointly submission to " God," " peace " and " salvation," is to believe in the oneness of God. All monotheists who lived before Muhammad are also referred to in the Qoran as Moslems, meaning " those who have attained salvation through belief in God," so that Islam appears to be synonymous with monotheism.[42]

There is another part of Muhammad's teaching which is not regarded as divine revelation. This consists of the Prophet's interpretation of Qoranic text, or his personal opinion on matters about which he was consulted, or his course of action in various circumstances, as reported by his contemporaries. The teaching thus imparted, by instruction or example, forms the " Islamic tradition " (*hadith*) on which Moslems model their conduct in any matter not specifically mentioned in the Qoran.

For some years, the new religion hardly extended beyond the Apostle's own family circle. Muhammad's first, and for a time only, disciple was his wife Khadijah, and then their three unmarried daughters (the youngest, Fatimah, was at the time a child of five) also embraced the faith. The Divine Spirit, in the shape of the archangel, appeared to Muhammad as he walked in the hills above Mecca, and taught him the ritual ablutions and forms of prayer, which included standing, bowing, kneeling and prostrating oneself before God. Prayer itself was to be regarded as a temporary retreat from earthly life, a " farewell to the world " which allowed the spirit to enter into direct communion with God.

Muhammad and his family prayed together in this fashion, and one day 'Ali, Muhammad's cousin, who was then a child of ten, came upon them as they prayed and enquired what they were doing. Next day, he asked if he might join them in their worship, and took to accompanying Muhammad on his wanderings around Mecca. To Muhammad, the whole earth was a temple to God, and he would pray with his young companion in the open air, under the wide dome of heaven.

The next converts were Zayd, Khadijah's slave whom Muhammad had freed and adopted as his son, Abu Bakr, a cloth merchant and Muhammad's greatest friend, and his future son-in-law 'Othman ibn 'Affan. The Moslems were afraid that if their new faith was discovered they might be persecuted, and at first they spread it surreptitiously, by word of mouth. Even after three years, the total number of adherents could not have been more than sixty. Their services were held in the cellar of a private house, where the Prophet or one of his disciples would recite verses from the Qoran and teach the Islamic ritual. From the very first there was, as Muhammad said " no priesthood in Islam."

About the year 612, the Apostle was inspired to attempt public conversion to Islam. He embarked on this venture with some misgivings, for it amounted to a head-on clash with Arab tradition. His first attempts met with little success. To begin with, he gathered together his nearest relatives, the tribe of 'Abd al-Muttalib. He said to them: " God has ordered me to call you to Him. Which of you will help me in this mission? " An uneasy silence was the only answer. Impulsively, young 'Ali, now a boy of thirteen, got up and stood beside Muhammad. The Apostle placed his hand on the youth's head and said: " This is my brother, my executor and my successor among you. Hearken ye to him and obey him." Loud laughter greeted this injunction and the tribe dispersed.

On another occasion Muhammad addressed the Qoraish tribe from the top of the Safa Hill. They replied with taunts and jeers, calling him " the Sleepwalker," and challenging him to perform miracles, to bring his God down to earth, to prevail upon Him to remove from Muhammad the slur of having no male heir, or to raise to life their long-dead ancestor Qusayy.

As was to be expected, when Muhammad persisted in his campaign against Meccan polytheism and idolatry the attitude of his fellow tribesmen began to change from derision to threats, for by proclaiming that the Qorashi ancestors were purging their idolatry and their evil deeds in fire, Muhammad was attacking not only the tribesmen's pride in their ancestry but also the interests of the priestly aristocracy. The Apostle and his followers began to encounter physical violence. During this Meccan period of Islam, which lasted for ten years, they endured persecution and physical violence without resistance, and offered forgiveness to their oppressors, perhaps out of respect for the holy city of Mecca.

The slave converts suffered the most severely, for they were at the mercy of their masters. Even so, it was a slave woman's son, 'Abd Allah ibn Mas'ud, who first had the courage to recite the Qoran publicly in the Ka'bah. The Moslem slaves were beaten and dragged through the streets with ropes round their necks, as well as being subjected to a form of torture which was peculiar to Mecca—they were placed in the blazing sun with stones on their chests and left there to die. The first martyr of Islam was Sumayyah, an old slave woman. As she lay under the stone, side by side with her husband and son, a Qorashi aristocrat drove his lance into her chest. An African slave called Bilal continued to proclaim the One God, repeating aloud: " One, one, one..." even while his polytheist master tortured him.

Moslems began to migrate to other lands. The largest group, consisting of eighty families, went to Christian Abyssinia, where the members of this new monotheistic cult were welcomed with kindness. Muhammad stayed in Mecca. His influence had become so potentially dangerous that the Qoraish were forced to resort to coercion; they even offered him a position of high honour in the community if he would agree to proclaim the divinity of their idols along with that of his own God. When this proved unsuccessful they determined to ostracise Muhammad, and all his relatives along with him if they persisted in supporting him.

The most prominent member of the family was Abu Talib, the uncle who had brought up Muhammad. Hitherto his attitude had been benevolent towards his nephew's new religion, though he remained somewhat sceptical. Now, under the threat of ostracism, he advised his nephew to be more discreet in the dissemination of his ideas. Muhammad answered: " If they place the sun on my right and the moon on my left, to induce me to abandon my course, I will not do so until God makes his purpose manifest, or I perish thereby." He turned away from his uncle in tears, but Abu Talib, moved by this strength of purpose, called him back and promised that he would continue to protect him.

The Qoraish enforced their ban; Muhammad and Khadijah were confined with the rest of his family in their part of the city, which was then virtually sealed off. All trade relations and ties of friendship with other groups of Qoraish were cut. Food supplies could only be taken to them secretly; they were grateful to find a piece of animal hide in the street which they could boil for stew. Muhammad's second and third daughters had both recently become betrothed; their suitors abandoned them. If Muhammad ventured out of the house where he was living, he was liable to be seized and assaulted by ruffians who were lying in wait for him. Nevertheless, he continued to go with Khadijah and the rest of his disciples to the Ka'bah, where they prayed under the very eyes of the pagans. They would stand at the south-eastern side of the temple, so that they faced Jerusalem, the stronghold of monotheism. As they prayed, the crowds of onlookers would jeer and throw stones and filth (*ill.* 45); Khadijah's son by her former marriage was killed in this way.

47. The oratory at 'Aqabah, near Mecca, on the site where Muhammad received the pledge of the Madinese, so that the persecuted Moslems could find refuge in Madinah.

Muhammad's most potent weapons were his recitations of Qoranic verses. He

48
49

would speak slowly and distinctly in his slightly husky voice, only just loud enough to be heard at close quarters. As the Arabs heard him reciting the rhythmic cadences, extolling the wonders of creation and the mysteries of the Ineffable God, they could not help but be impressed. They would sidle closer to him when darkness fell, sometimes hiding under the cloth cover of the Ka'bah. They would follow him through the dark narrow streets when he went home at night, and there they would secretly affirm their new belief in Islam. The redoubtable Qorashi warrior 'Omar ibn-al-Khattab was so moved when he heard his sister reading the Qoran that he became converted to the Islamic faith.

The soft-hearted Abu Bakr had transformed his cloth-shop into an oratory; there he would stand and recite the Qoran, weeping with emotion. The Qorashi men laughed at him, but their womenfolk, children and slaves listened to him clandestinely.

The year 619 was the " year of sorrow " for Muhammad. Worn out by her struggles, the Apostle's unfailing prop and stay Khadijah died, at the age of sixty-five. She was buried in a graveyard in Upper Mecca. Muhammad took her body in his arms and descended into the tomb, where he laid her down. He was stunned by grief so that years afterwards if anything reminded him of Khadijah, when for instance he heard a voice that sounded something like hers, he was overcome with emotion.

Abu Talib, Muhammad's uncle and protector, died at about the same time, still refusing to acknowledge monotheism even though his nephew pleaded with him as he lay dying.

In 620 or 621, Muhammad had the visions that became known to posterity as the " nocturnal journey." In many literary works, Islamic authors have interpreted Muhammad's visions of ascension as a symbol for the mystic soul's gradual elevation towards higher spheres; they were also a direct inspiration for Dante's *Divine Comedy*.

The exact spot in Mecca where the Apostle's body rested as " his eyes were closed and his soul awake " is a matter for conjecture, and there are various conflicting versions of the visions he saw (*ill.* 40). The essence of all the versions, however, is much the same: Gabriel led Muhammad, by night, to a heaven peopled with allegorical and symbolical figures. The Apostle saw the sinners, with " *the wind-blown ashes of their deeds*," burning in the fire of regret that " *rises upon their hearts*." Then the " *Lord of the Way of Ascent* " showed him the gardens of Eternity, where the flowers and trees represented good deeds and prayer.

Glory be to Him who transported His servant by night
from the Sacred Mosque to the Further Mosque.
(*Qoran:* XVII, 1)

Muhammad prayed with Jesus and the prophets of the Scriptures in the " Further Mosque," the symbol of the human soul in worship, of which the Ka'bah, the Temple of Jerusalem and all other temples are earthly reflections.

After gazing upon the created universe, the Apostle came to the threshold of the Uncreated. Here the figure of Gabriel and all other forms receded, and Muhammad's soul contemplated the Infinite Unknown.[43]

48. A plaster statue of the 'Omayyad period, representing a man wearing a loin-cloth, in ancient Arabian fashion. Height about 125 cm.

49. A polychrome plaster statue of the 'Omayyad period, representing a dancer holding a posy. Height about 125 cm.

THE HEGIRA

And thou wilt be liberated from the responsibility of this city.
(*Qoran:* XC, 2)

In 622, the year which is accepted as the beginning of the Islamic era, idolatry was more firmly entrenched in Mecca than ever before. When Abu Talib died, his brother 'Abd al-'Uzza (" the servant of 'Uzza ") had become head of the family. He was openly hostile to his nephew's faith, and withdrew the family's protection from Muhammad. This meant that the Apostle and his followers could only continue to live in Mecca through the goodwill of such sympathisers as were willing to take the risk of guaranteeing their protection. It was clear to Muhammad that he and his disciples would have to find a permanent home in exile; in dreams he saw the ideal place, but in reality no solution seemed to present itself.

Muhammad's task was complicated by the fact that the large group of Moslems who had emigrated to Abyssinia were now coming back because they had heard a false rumour that an agreement had been reached between the Qoraish and the Moslems in Mecca. When they arrived back, of course, they found nothing but hostility and persecution awaiting them, and their presence only added further weight to Muhammad's already heavy burden of responsibility.

He took advantage of the annual pilgrimage season to enter into relations with people from other Arab regions, thinking that in this way he might hear of a suitable refuge for the Moslems. The Qoraish realised what he was doing and posted agents on the roads leading into Mecca, to warn pilgrims against the " mad poet " who might accost them in the city. Most of the foreigners therefore either avoided Muhammad altogether or stopped their ears, naively thinking to protect themselves against his " magic incantations." Some, though, did listen to him and took his ideas with them when they went home. A group of Christians from Abyssinia embraced the Islamic faith. It probably did not seem to them that they were making any alteration in their beliefs; like Muhammad, they saw Christ as an Apostle, as one of the prophets of the scriptures.

In spite of these minor successes, Muhammad was still unable to find a home for Islam in another part of Arabia. Tribe after tribe refused pointblank to allow any Moslem immigrants into their territories. Muhammad thought of Taif, where he had some friends who would surely give his proposal a warmer welcome. He walked for several days until he reached the mountain city, with its famous temple to al-Lat, where he told his acquaintances of the straits in which the Moslems found themselves and of his hope that Taif might afford them a refuge. The citizens of Taif were angry at his suggestion, accused him of encouraging the slave class to rebellion, and drove him out of the town with stones, one of which wounded him. A Christian slave gave him soccour and received his blessing, in the famous orchards outside Taif.

Help was to come, however, from the city of Yathrib. In the year 620 Muhammad had gone to 'Aqabah, in the Mina gorge, to look for possible converts. There he had entered an enclave in the rock at the base of Mount Thabir, and found six men sitting in a natural amphitheatre, partly concealed by fallen boulders (*ill.* 47). He asked them who they were and, on learning that they came from the tribe of Khazraj in Yathrib, Muhammad introduced himself as their cousin, through his great-grandmother Salma, the wife of Hashim. He then took the opportunity to explain his faith to them. The men from Yathrib, remembering that their Jewish fellow-citizens often spoke of a Messiah whom they were awaiting, believed that this might be the new religious leader and accepted his creed. A year later, the Apostle met twelve men from Yathrib at the same place, and they also embraced Islam. These eighteen converts then began to propagate the new religion in their native city.

In 622, Muhammad went to meet the people of Yathrib for the third time. His life was at a turning-point, for a fundamental change had taken place in his attitude towards the enemies of Islam. He was fifty-three years old, and his health was failing. He had already been an apostle for over ten years, yet his followers were only a handful of long-suffering people who might well succumb under the pressure of their hostile environment. There seemed to be no hope that in the span of years left to him Muhammad could find general acceptance for the faith of Islam as he had felt it was his destiny to do. But a momentous event had occurred; whereas formerly patient endurance had been enjoined upon the persecuted Moslems, now a Qoranic verse allowing active resistance in defence of faith had been revealed:

> *Permission is given (to resist) to those on whom war is made, because they are the oppressed... those who have been driven out of their homes without justification only because they have said God is our Lord. Had not God repelled some of mankind through others, cloisters and churches and synagogues and mosques wherein God's name is praised would have fallen.*
>
> (*Qoran:* XXII, 39-40)

So the seventy-one men and two women of Yathrib who left their pilgrims' encampment secretly one night in 622 to meet Muhammad in the ravine near 'Aqabah vowed themselves not only to the monotheistic faith, but also to its active defence.

Solemnly Muhammad renounced his birthright as a Qorashi and accepted the protection of the Arab tribes of Yathrib. It is said that the Spirit of Evil shouted to the assembly: " O pilgrims, what is this rebel and his apostates to you? They are conspiring to fight against you." Muhammad replied: " O Enemy of God, I vow that I will expose thy falsity."

The people of Yathrib said to Muhammad: " We accept thee at the risk of losing our earthly possessions and the lives of our leaders. If we prove faithful, what shall be our reward? "

" Paradise," replied Muhammad.

So the citizens of Yathrib, who were to go down in history as " the Succourers of Islam," said to the Apostle: " Give us thy hand," and one by one they pledged themselves to the " covenant of God."

THE HEGIRA

The exodus of Moslems to Yathrib began as soon as this pledge had been made. Although the emigrants were careful to leave Mecca only in small groups and as surreptitiously as possible, their going could not altogether escape the attention of their fellow-citizens. Men were sent to overtake and arrest the fugitives, and a few Moslems lost their lives in the ensuing skirmishes. Others were wounded and imprisoned, some were persuaded, or forced, to return to idolatry, but the majority succeeded in escaping their pursuers. The Meccans thereupon appropriated the property they had left behind, and installed themselves in the empty houses.

Two months after the pledge at 'Aqabah, it had already become clear to the Meccans that they could not afford to allow the formation of a new Moslem community at Yathrib, as it presented a potential danger to their caravan trade.

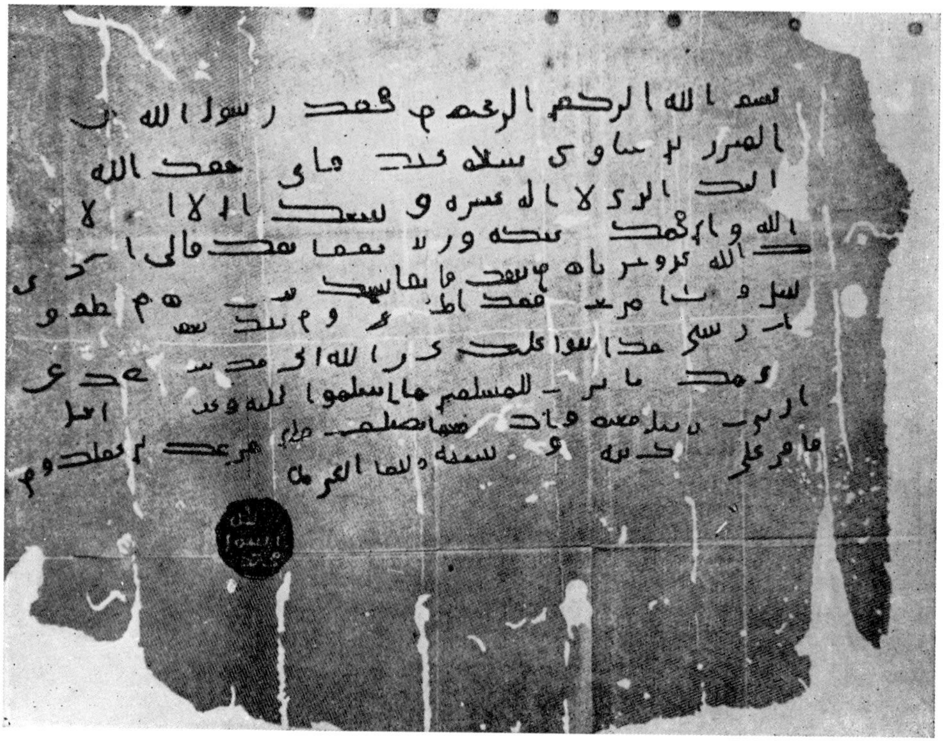

Letter attributed to Muhammad and bearing his seal.

Muhammad was still in Mecca, with his friend Abu Bakr, and the Qoraish decided that if he were prevented from joining his disciples in Yathrib the group would disintegrate from lack of leadership. They met in the city hall to discuss ways and means of achieving this, and came to the conclusion that Muhammad must be assassinated. No one clan, however, was prepared to take sole responsibility for his death, so it was arranged that the deed would be done by a group consisting of ten young men, one from each tribe, who would all strike with their swords at the same moment. This conspiracy was hatched in the morning; by midday Muhammad had been made aware of it, and went straight to Abu Bakr's house to arrange for their departure that same night.

When darkness fell, the ten would-be assassins surrounded the Apostle's house and settled down to wait for the dawn, when they could make their attack without fear of killing the wrong man. They peered into the house, and could make out the form of a man whom they took to be Muhammad, lying under a blanket.

50. Head of a plaster statue of the 'Omayyad period. Height 25 cm.

51
52

In fact it was 'Ali, now a stalwart young man of twenty, who had taken his cousin's place. Muhammad himself left the house during the night and passed unnoticed between the waiting men, reciting a passage from the Qoran, including this verse: —"*And we have placed before them an obstruction, and behind them an obstruction, and we have screened them and they do not see*" (*Qoran:* XXXVI, 9). He went to Abu Bakr's house, and together they made off for the desert south-west of Mecca.

They had decided to take refuge on Mount Thawr, and near the summit they found a cave which would hide them both satisfactorily. The entrance to the cave was low and narrow; once they were inside a spider wove a web across it, and a pair of doves began to build a nest above.

Meanwhile the Qoraish had found out that their prey had escaped them and they were following close on his trail, guided by a Beduin who was an expert tracker of footprints. Muhammad and his companion heard the men as they came up the mountainside, beating the bushes with their swords. They came right up to the mouth of the cave, but seeing the intact spider's web they did not trouble to look inside.

The two exhausted men were then free to relax for a while. They spent three days in the cave, where Abu Bakr's daughter Asma' and his son visited them and took them food. When the hue and cry over the escape had died down, the cloth merchant's freedman brought a guide and two camels to the cave, and the two friends set off for Yathrib, Asma' bidding them an anxious farewell.

It was the 13th September 622, in the Arabian month of Safar. The Islamic era begins on the first day of Muharram in that year.

Muhammad and Abu Bakr followed little-used tracks, parallel to the sea coast. Only a few people, mostly desert Beduin, saw them as they passed, but it seems they must have realised that the two travellers were making a momentous journey for they observed them keenly and left descriptions of them for posterity. One desert warrior heard that the Qoraish were offering a reward of one hundred camels for the capture of Muhammad, so when he observed two distant figures, not far from Yanbu', he put on his armour, took his lance and galloped his horse towards them. As he came close, he saw that one walked on, moving his lips in silent prayer. The other, who was Abu Bakr, turned to look at him. Suddenly his horse began to stumble; the warrior decided that this was a bad omen and forthwith abandoned his attempt to capture Muhammad for the Qoraish.

Elsewhere a man came upon the two friends riding on the same camel and asked what they were doing. Abu Bakr replied metaphorically: " I am one who has lost his way and the man before me is my guide." [44]

51.* Madinah in Ottoman times: a book-painting by Osman Yumni, 20 × 11 cm.

52* The early Moslems building the Apostle's original mosque in Madinah. 38 × 26 cm.

THE PROPHET'S CITY

For more than ten days, Muhammad and Abu Bakr toiled across monotonous wasteland. At last they came to a vast plain of reddish, damp earth, dotted with palm groves, wild cypresses, and tamarisks. To the west lay the dark blue chain of the Sarat mountains; white clouds floated upon their jagged peaks from the direction of the nearby sea. Muhammad knew that he was approaching the promised land of Islam as it had been revealed to him in dreams during the years of hardship in Mecca: " the alkaline earth where date-palms grow, set between two plains strewn with lava."

On the outskirts of Yathrib, the Moslem population were watching the horizon. They had come out from the city each day since Muhammad's imminent arrival had been announced. Now, on the twelfth of Rabiʿ al-Awwal, which happened to be Muhammad's birthday, they came once more. At midday the burning sun drove them back to their houses, but a Jew who chanced to be on the roof of his fortress-like house and knew that the Moslems were awaiting their Prophet, called to them that he could see a small group of travellers in the distance. The Moslems rushed eagerly out to look.

From the mirage caused by the sun's reflection on the plain, there did indeed emerge a group of white-clad men. The Moslems began to beat their tambourines and chant songs of welcome. As the riders alighted from their camels, some of the citizens of Yathrib recognised Abu Bakr and hurried to greet him. Not so many of them knew the apparently younger man who sat down in the shade of a tree and seemed immediately lost in thought.

Muhammad had many reasons to be thoughtful. Now that he had arrived in Islam's promised land, he was responsible for seeing that his small community were able to live there in security. Furthermore, it would be necessary to create an enduring framework for his monotheist society, so that " the Prophet's city " (Madinat al-Nabi), as Yathrib was a little later to be called, would be a radiant torch showing the way to all future generations of Islam.

At last Muhammad rose from his meditations. He invited the Moslems to build, in all humility and awe of God, a house of worship there in the spot where they stood. So this, the first mosque, was constructed at Quba, a league south of Yathrib. It was a simple, square enclosure, of a kind traditional in the Yathrib region as well as in other Hijazi oasis towns. Muhammad traced its outline in the sand with the lance which he had inherited from his father. Each side was 66 ells long, and the walls were built with stones brought from the mountains nearby. The Apostle himself carried a rock which he placed inside the enclosure to indicate the direction towards which the believers had to turn in prayer—at this time it was still towards Jerusalem. Part of the court, an area of 50 × 26 ells, was covered, probably with thatching of palm branches and earth in the usual Hijazi manner. The building was completed in a few days, and on the following Friday Muhammad led his Moslem congregation in prayer, in the first mosque built especially for the Islamic faith (*ill.* 60).

Then the Prophet remounted his camel (it was called Qaswa—" she of the clipped ear ") and rode towards the centre of the city. About a hundred of his followers, both Madinese and emigrants from Mecca, accompanied him, arrayed in their armour for this solemn occasion. In the centre of Yathrib, Muhammad noticed the old fort where his father's tomb lay, and thought of his childhood and the visit to his cousins. Now some of these cousins, as well as many other citizens, were anxious to receive him as their guest. But Muhammad dropped Qaswa's reins and asked to be allowed to descend wherever the camel chose to stop. Eventually it knelt down in an empty field. Nonetheless, Muhammad said: " God willing, this is our alighting place and our final station." It was here that the great Mosque of Madinah was built (*ill.* 51), and later Muhammad's own tomb.

The field turned out to belong to some orphaned children, from whom it was purchased. It contained part of an old graveyard, and the remaining tombs were transferred elsewhere. A palm tree and some *Garqad* bushes (small thorny trees with red berries) were cleared away. The Meccan emigrants, the Madinese converts, and Muhammad himself set to work, chanting poems as they cleared the ground (*ill.* 52). The new mosque, like the one at Quba, was a square enclosure. The sides were about a hundred ells long; the central courtyard was covered with black sand, and the walls were of bricks and clay. Some of the brickwork was arranged on a pattern of alternating verticals and horizontals. Again there was a covered area inside the mosque, to shelter worshippers from the sun. It was supported on eight palm trunks and the roof was of intertwined palm branches—" like Moses' cradle," said Muhammad, probably thinking that the Madinese mosque seemed as insecure in hostile Arabia as the cradle of the infant Moses had been in the Nile.

The mosque had three entrances, on the east, west and south respectively. There was no doorway in the northern side, for this was the direction in which the Moslems turned to pray. It was not until the second year after Muhammad's arrival in Madinah that, while leading prayers one day in a mosque on the outskirts of the city, he suddenly changed his direction and turned towards Mecca. The congregation naturally followed his example, interpreting his movement as a formal renunciation of the union with Judaism and Christianity which he had tried to bring about during the earlier years of his apostolate. By turning towards the Ka'bah, Islam was associating itself with the older form of monotheism represented by Abraham. The southern doors of all the mosques in and around Madinah—by this time there were many of them—were walled up, and the Moslems have ever since turned towards Mecca when they pray.

When the Apostle himself was not present, the service would be led by the member of the congregation who was most conversant with the Qoran. For instance, during this somewhat informal initial period of Islam, a tribalistic community saw nothing extraordinary in assembling for religious service under the guidance of a child of seven, who was the only one among them to have learned some verses of the Qoran by heart. He was therefore their *imam*—their " leader in prayer "—and the Beduin collected money to buy a length of cloth to make a garment for the naked child.

Considerable discussion took place among the Moslems about the manner in which they should be summoned to prayer; some suggested that the Jewish trumpet might be used, others thought a clapper as used by the Christians would be suitable. Then one of them dreamed that he heard a voice calling the faithful to prayer, in these words: " God is the Most High. I witness that there is none to worship except God. I witness that Muhammad is the Apostle of God. Arise to prayer. Arise to divine service." This method was accordingly adopted, and the first man appointed to chant these words from the mosque was Bilal, the African slave who had been tortured by his Meccan master and had afterwards been ransomed by the Moslems. Five times a day, at dawn, at noon, in the afternoon, at sunset and again at night, the Madinese would hear Bilal's beautiful voice and foreign accent calling them to prayer.

When they first came to Madinah, the Moslems probably observed certain Jewish fasts, but later a Qoranic revelation enjoined them to follow rites of their own. Each year during the month of Ramadan—the month in which Muhammad had had his first vision on Mount Hira—his followers abstained from all forms of indulgence. Between sunrise and sunset they would neither eat nor drink, and even the scent of a beautiful flower was considered a breach of the rule of self-denial.

Within the Madinah mosque there was a dais which was reserved for the poor and infirm. These people, who had no other shelter and were often poverty-stricken to the point of starvation, were given the dates from the palm-trees in the mosque, and lived on alms from the worshippers — particularly from Muhammad himself. Some of them learned the Qoran by heart and in time they became Islam's first teachers and mystics.

When Muhammad was preaching in the mosque, he formed the habit of leaning against one of its palm-tree columns. It tired him, however, to stand for long periods of time, and a craftsman who noticed this constructed a bench for him out of tamarisk wood (*ill.* 53). At the moment when Muhammad sat on this bench for the first time, the palm tree against which he had been accustomed to stand, broke, with a sound that was like a human cry. This phenomenon was the subject of much comment and speculation among mediaeval Islamic mystics.

The Mosque with the palm-tree columns was considered one of the " Gardens of Eternity," the site where flowed the Kawthar, " a paradisiac river that was to quench the thirst of souls as numerous as heaven's stars " (*ill.* 54).

Islamic writers have said that the Ka'bah in Mecca is a symbol of the monotheistic faith, but the mosque in Madinah represents Muhammad's heart. There he preached that every child of Adam, no matter what his earthly lot, had the privilege of direct communication with God. Thus, each must make his own distinction between good and evil, for no action was good or bad in itself, but depended in the intention behind it. " People will be resurrected according to their intentions," said Muhammad. He also advocated a balanced life, adding: " No extremism, even in religion."

Seen against the prevailing pagan cults, with their human sacrifices and their priests' pretensions to supernatural powers, this new humanist religion seemed revolutionary indeed. It flouted the ancient traditions of aristocratic privilege and tribal affiliation, and discounted differences of race and tongue. The Moslem, whether he was of Arabian or foreign origin, whether high-born or lowly, was the equal before God of all the other members of his religious community.

Equality of status was thus a social as well as a religious concept. The rights and responsibilities of Moslem citizenship were strictly laid down. Even women, children, and slaves, who had counted for little in ancient Arabian society, now acquired legal rights that could not be contravened without serious consequences. A slave could free himself, if he wished, by doing additional work for his master, and this was encouraged by the Moslems. In fact, however, slavery

53.* Muhammad preaching on his bench in the Madinah mosque, surrounded by the first four caliphs and the wise men of the dais. 17×9.5 cm.

54.* The archangel Gabriel inspires Muhammad in the Madinah mosque. 38×26 cm.

55.* The Apostle praying for rain to relieve the Moslems' thirst (*Qoran* VIII, 11), before the battle of Badr. 38×26 cm.

56.* Muhammad pledging his daughter Fatimah to her cousin 'Ali in marriage. 38×26 cm.

53

54

55

56

57 58

lost much of its stigma, and marriages even took place between slaves and people of aristocratic birth. Muhammad prevailed upon his own first cousin, Zaynab, daughter of Jahsh, who was proud of her blood relationship with the high-born Qoraish, to marry a man who had formerly been a slave, Zayd ibn Harithah.

A few women in the first Islamic community might be termed ardent feminists, such as the elderly warrior Nusaybah. She asked Muhammad why it was that in the Qoran God always addressed mankind, never womankind. It is said that God acknowledged the validity of her question, because afterwards both " the believing men and the believing women " were mentioned in revelation. Even so, although women now had some freedom of decision in certain spheres, even including marriage, most of them were still considered to have dependent status. Muhammad believed that the majority of women were " as fragile as glass," needing help and protection.

In the Prophet's city, women apparently exercised the traditional Arab right of granting protection to a stranger; indeed, Muhammad's own daughter once took advantage of this (*ill.* 61). Zaynab, who was the eldest of his family, had been married before the emergence of the Islamic faith. In time she embraced her father's religion but her husband, Abu al-'As, remained a polytheist. When strife broke out between the Meccans and the Moslems, Zaynab and her husband were forced to part. They remained attached to each other, however, and in the year 7 A. H. Abu al-'As was taken prisoner in Madinah, where he had come in the hope of seeing his ex-wife. In the mosque, the Moslems discussed what was to be done with him. Then Zaynab rose, and declared that she granted her protection to the captive. After a moment's thought, Muhammad asked the congregation if they had heard the declaration and what they thought of it. As a result, Abu al-'As was freed and returned to Mecca, but later came back and accepted his wife's faith.

The territory of the Madinese Moslem theocracy was bounded by the two lava plains on the east and west, and the mountains of Thawr and 'Air on the north and south. A number of non-Moslem communities lived within this domain—in particular, three Jewish tribes—and they were allowed to remain there as self-governing groups in accordance with the Qoranic concept of non-compulsion in religion. By agreement with the Prophet and the Arab tribes, their only duty was to contribute towards the defence of the land they shared with the Moslems.

As Muhammad had hoped, his community at Madinah eventually served as a model, at least theoretically, in all the countries where Islam became the accepted faith. Tradition relates that the Prophet wrote to the rulers of the Yemen, Abyssinia, Egypt, Byzantium and Persia, to invite them also to embrace Islam. He frequently expressed the hope that his faith would spread throughout the world and across the centuries.[45]

57. A pulpit in carved wood inlaid with ivory, bearing an inscription from Qoran XXXIII, 56, which was presented to a Cairo mosque by the Mameluk Sultan Qayit Bay (1468-1490 A. D.), who rebuilt the Madinah mosque.

58. Persian *mihrab* in blue ceramic of the Selçuk period, *c.* 700 A. H. (1300 A. D.). 60 × 30 cm.

THE APOSTLE OF THE PORTIONLESS

MUHAMMAD, WHO LED to monotheism the descendents of Hagar, the servant-girl abandoned in the desert, is called in Islamic liturgy the "Apostle of the Portionless" (Nabi al-Ummi). The Arabs of the Hijaz were indeed ill-endowed with worldly possessions; not only were they steeped in the evil consequences of superstitious beliefs, but their desert land with its merciless climate afflicted them with famine and disease.

During the ten short years that he lived in Madinah, the Apostle tried to organise every aspect of life for the benefit of his community. In the preceding chapter it has been described how he formulated the institutions of the ideal Islamic city and defined the status of its citizens. But in their private life the Arabs were still bound by pagan custom. Untrammelled polygamy was considered a normal state of life, and transitory unions were quite common, so that many children were deprived of paternal protection and left in the care of their destitute mothers. As previously mentioned, girls were often buried alive in infancy. The lot of these unhappy women and children is described in the Qoran:

And when the one buried alive is asked
For what sin she was killed

. . . .

Every soul shall know what it has prepared.
(*Qoran:* LXXXI, 8-9, 14)

In order to provide some measure of security for a man's dependents, Muhammad instituted the practice of contractual marriage, with a dowry given by the husband to safeguard the wife's future. Polygamy was still accepted; the custom was so deeply rooted in Arabia and in ancient Semitic tradition that a man was almost certain to have children by more than one woman, and possibly Muhammad did not wish the father's protection to be withdrawn from all except the offspring of one wife.

It was then the Apostle's task to demonstrate the responsibilities of a head of the family, and impress these upon an Arab community accustomed to the boundless liberty of pagan social life. Gradually Muhammad gathered round him an increasing number of dependents. For twenty-five years he had remained happily married to one wife, Khadijah; after her death he contracted about eleven other unions, mostly, apparently, for reasons totally unconnected with personal inclination. The Apostle's later wives were either needy widows of men who had died in the cause of Islam, or they belonged to families or tribes whom the Prophet wished to rally to, or at least be friendly towards, Islam. In Arabian custom, intermarriage between families, tribes, or even different ethnic groups, established rights of kinship that, theoretically, brought about inviolable peace between the parties. One consequence of this was that captives previously taken from each other by the two sides in time of war were automatically released from the condition of slavery to which they were otherwise condemned.

Some years after Khadijah's death, just before he left Mecca, Muhammad married " Sawdah the tall," the elderly and indigent widow of a Moslem who had died in exile in Abyssinia. Already the Apostle's friend Abu Bakr had offered him in marriage his daughter 'Aishah, who at that time was still a child. Muhammad delayed the marriage so long that at last Abu Bakr asked him whether he wished to break the engagement, but in fact he hesitated only because he had not the means to buy a wedding present for the young bride, and the marriage did at length take place, in Madinah. 'Aishah was the only woman Muhammad ever wed who had not been married previously. He saw in this vivacious young girl the symbol of Arab womanhood, whose lowly condition he sought to raise, and insisted that she should learn to read, a rare accomplishment at the time. " You treat us as if we were camels or cattle," said 'Aishah in later years to the Arab men; " the Apostle respected us as human beings." Her lively and impulsive nature made her the target of gossip, but Muhammad, who loved her both for her own sake and her father's, said to those who complained about her: " But she is Abu Bakr's daughter." Once, following a particularly slanderous rumour, 'Ali implied that he should divorce 'Aishah. She heard of this and never forgave 'Ali for it. The poet Hasan ibn Thabit also attacked her, but Muhammad supported her unfailingly.

Hafsah, the daughter of 'Omar ibn al-Khattab, lost her husband in the battle of Badr. 'Omar, seeking protection for his homeless daughter, offered her in marriage to several people, who either did not answer or refused outright. Muhammad, however, agreed to shelter the widow. Like her father, Hafsah was of an energetic disposition, and was known to scold the Apostle.

After the battle of Ohod, Muhammad married another widow, who had been bereaved of her husband. Known as " the mother of Salamah," this woman had four children. When Muhammad proposed marriage to her, she observed that she was too old to marry; he replied that he was even older.

In the fifth year after the Hegira, he married a widow from a tribe against whom the Moslems had been fighting and who had therefore been taken into captivity. He called her Juwairiyah, " the Unhappy One," by which name she has been known ever since. All the prisoners from her tribe held by the Moslems were thereupon released. In this same year, Muhammad also wed his first cousin Zaynab, the daughter of Jahsh, who had managed to get a divorce from the former slave she had previously married. As she had contracted this union on the Prophet's advice, when it failed Zaynab made it clear that she felt some compensation was due to her for her hurt pride and ruined life.

The Apostle also married another Zaynab, a twice-widowed lady, known because of her charitable disposition as the " Mother of the Poor." She died shortly afterwards.

A daughter of Abu Sufyan, the Qorashi notable who fought so bitterly against Islam, had herself become a Moslem. With her husband and children she had emigrated to Abyssinia, where the husband had embraced Christianity while she remained faithful to Islam. When she was widowed and alone in an alien country, Muhammad sent word to the Negus that he wished to marry this woman, the " Mother of Habibah," by proxy.

After the battle of Khaybar, Muhammad met Safiyah, a Jewess who had been taken prisoner. He liberated and married this woman, who had been wed twice before. From caustic remarks made about her by 'Aishah, it is clear that Safiyah must have been unattractive. Muhammad and this " daughter of Aaron," as he called her, were on terms of close friendship.

Maria the Copt, a Christian, was sent to Muhammad as a slave by the Ruler of Egypt. This must have reminded Muhammad of Abraham's Egyptian servant-girl Hagar, because he called the much-desired son that Maria bore him after the Patriarch. Abraham was Muhammad's only child by any of his later wives. Like Khadijah's sons, Abraham died in infancy.

Finally, in the seventh year after the Hegira, Muhammad married, no doubt for political reasons, a widow called Maimunah who belonged to a tribe hostile to the Moslems.

These unions brought Muhammad no particular happiness. Indeed, when his wives complained of the poverty in which he made them live, he readily suggested that any of them who wished to contract a more prosperous marriage could obtain a divorce. None of them, however, took advantage of this, choosing to remain with him and accept his self-imposed hardship.

It was evident to the Moslems that Muhammad's personal feelings did not incline him towards polygamy. Indeed, he more than once expounded the advantages of monogamy, saying: " When a man looks only at his wife and she at him, God looks at both of them," probably remembering his tender relationship with Khadijah. When the Apostle's polytheist son-in-law fell a prisoner to the Moslems, his wife Zaynab sent as a ransom a necklace she had inherited from her mother. The Moslems who saw the look Muhammad gave the ornament realised that he would always miss Khadijah. " You will never forget that toothless old woman of Qoraish! " 'Aishah angrily said once.

Besides his wives, Muhammad's other daily companions were his daughter Fatimah, her husband 'Ali (*ill.* 56) and their two infant sons, Hasan and Husain. The men who lived in the mosque, on the dais reserved for the poor, were also continually with him. Five times a day he would pray with them and listen as they recited the verses of the Qoran that he taught them.

Muhammad's circle was also enlarged by the families and tribal connections of his wives and friends. Many of his closest disciples came from among such people, as well as some of the scribes to whom he dictated the Qoranic text.

Such a crowded mode of existence must have held few attractions for Muhammad. According to his contemporaries, he had a pronounced taste for solitude, but he tried to curb it as a manifestation of egocentric self-indulgence. Nevertheless he made a revealing observation:—" I envy the man who lives in a solitary house and prays in the joy of meditation... no one knows him, he is not pointed at with the finger... He dies without cares, leaving no succession and none to cry over him." [46]

The troubles and occasional quarrels of his companions weighed on the Apostle. At times he found it difficult to reconcile the members of his entourage, when these were pushed by their tribal connections into the position of faction-leaders. He had to be careful not to show particular favour to any of the groups, for fear of sowing enmities that would grow into serious weaknesses in the Islamic community after the Apostle's own death. This constant arbitration tired him, to such an extent that he even expressed his relief at having reached the end of his life. Someone childishly suggested that the Apostle should be given a golden throne, to restore his inclination to live; at this Muhammad made one of his rarely impatient remarks:—"As I have lived amongst them, they have never ceased to quarrel, pulling at my garment, covering me with their dust, until I wished that God would give me rest."

59. An undated monument erected at a site in Quba where Fatimah, Muhammad's daughter, is said to have stayed overnight on her journey from Mecca to Madinah.

60. The mosque at Quba, near Madinah, where Muhammad built the first Islamic house of worship. The present building dates from the reign of the Turkish Caliph Mahmud II – 1199-1255 A. H. (1784-1839 A. D.).

59
60

61 62
63

It was clear to his contemporaries that although Muhammad was devoted to Madinah "the Mild," the promised land of Islam, and to the "Succourers" of the exiled Meccan Moslems, he nevertheless felt, in this the evening of his life, a nostalgia for his native town and the obscurity of his youthful life. In the religious strife, Muhammad had been exiled from his country and separated from his friends. Warring against his own tribe and family, he had seen the death of many close relatives, bearing arms against his disciples. Some of his faithful companions had lost their lives; Zayd his freedman and adopted son, Hamzah his uncle, and many others, lay in battlefields, shrouded in their inadequate armour, their corpses mutilated by the vengeful enemy. Near Madinah was a plot of land named Baqiʿ al-garqad, after the crimson-berried bushes that grew there. Many hundreds of years earlier, Abu Karib, the South Arabian invader, had camped there and discovered Judaism. Now it was the Moslem cemetery, where Muhammad often came to conduct funeral rites. Here were the graves of many of the Apostle's "companions" and family, where lay the beautiful Roqqayah and Umm Kalthum, his second and third daughters, who had successively married ʿOthman ibn ʿAffan. Here too lay Zaynab, Muhammad's eldest daughter, who through her constancy had brought about her husband's conversion to Islam. At her father's request, Zaynab had been buried with her hair divided into two tresses, a coiffure that had been becoming to her. The infant son of Maria the Copt, Abraham, was also buried here.

THE APOSTLE OF THE PORTIONLESS

Muhammad's own health began to fail. When he attended public meetings that involved long hours of standing, he felt the need to lean on a crutch. His appearance had not greatly changed with the passing years. He still had the spare figure, the rapid walk which had been remarked in him when he was young. His face still had a luminous quality. He had only a few white hairs. But with age his pensiveness had increased. He hardly noticed his surroundings. His companions said:—"There was in his glance nothing but meditation." His profound earnestness intimidated those who met him for the first time, but on better acquaintance his kindness invariably inspired a lasting affection.

"Plunged in multiple sorrows," Muhammad took comfort when he heard Bilal calling the worshippers to the mosque. As God's call to man rang out across the city, the Apostle found the courage to hope that he had satisfactorily accomplished the mission entrusted to him.

In dealings with his fellow-men, the Apostle's principle was to serve them with selfless devotion. He seemed to be disengaged from his own person, "as if already dead." Although he was relentless in his attacks against anything he regarded as sacrilegious behaviour, nevertheless he forgave all offences committed against him, even various attempts on his life. He never made a harsh comment on any person, whether in their presence or their absence. His severest reproach was silence.

To the underprivileged, the "fragile ones," as he called the aged, the infirm, the slaves, the women and children, who were sometimes mercilessly ill-treated in the ancient world, the "Apostle of the Portionless" devoted especial care. When he encountered one of these vulnerable people, Muhammad tried to give the impression that he was the humbler of the two. He always came to an appointment first, and gave to the visitor his only sand-filled pillow, while he sat on the ground. Determined to help as best he could, his attention would never waver from the problem being presented to him. Clasping hands in farewell, Muhammad was always careful not to draw his away before the other person did so.

The Apostle liked animals and condemned their useless killing, maintaining that even predatory beasts have rights that are worthy of respect. He tried never to tread on grass, to avoid crushing a blessing given by the Creator to the desert land.

Muhammad's thoughts were dominated, in all aspects of his daily life, by the

61.* Zaynab, Muhammad's elder daughter, escaping from Mecca to Madinah.
38×26 cm.

62.* Hind, the wife of Abu Sufyan, and other pagan Meccan women prepare to mutilate the corpses of the fallen Moslems at the battle of Ohod and to devour the liver of Hamzah, Muhammad's uncle, who is seen lying on the ground.
38×26 cm.

63.* Muhammad tries to persuade the Moslems to await the attack of the pagan Meccans within Madinah, instead of meeting them at Ohod.
38×26 cm.

omnipresence of God. When he sat, it was always in the uncomfortable position of a slave, ready to rise at his master's sign. As well as the ritual five services, the Apostle prayed far into the night, though, so as not to impose an example of supererogatory worship on his companions, he would retire to his own quarters or to a tent made of straw.

The poverty of his people was a constant source of anxiety for Muhammad. He promised them consolation in the next life, and tried to see that in this world he lived in conditions as lowly as the poorest in his community. The smallest luxury seemed to him a theft from " the fragile ones." He had no house of his own, but lived in turn in the modest huts that belonged to his wives, on the eastern side of the Madinah mosque. He helped the members of his family in their work about the house, and looked after their children. Sometimes he would sit at prayer with a child asleep on his lap. He did not even permit himself the expense of an oil lamp; " if we had oil, we ate it," said the outspoken 'Aishah.

Muhammad had no bed; he slept upon his mantle, which was folded twice and laid on the earthen floor. A scrupulously clean person, he washed and mended his own garments and sandals. As in his youth, he draped himself in two lengths of cloth, but now he also wore a sleeved shirt underneath. The *izar*, as the cloth draped below the waist was called, was arranged in such a way that instead of dragging behind, in the aristocratic manner, it was gathered to the front, in token of humility. Muhammad's coat was of Yemenite or Persian cut, fashioned from wool so rough that it left marks on his skin. The touch of silk seemed to him a brand of fire, burning the self-indulgent wearer while others went in rags.

Muhammad would starve for days at a time, so that the mendicants who surrounded him might have enough to eat. He would tie a stone on his stomach, to allay the pangs of hunger, as poor Arabs so often did. " The Apostle left this world," said his companions, " without once eating adequately."

To those who would have liked to see their leader adopt the pomp of Caesar or Khosroes, the "Apostle of the Portionless" replied:—" My poverty is my pride." [46]

THE RELIGIOUS WARS

As mentioned in Chapter XII, Muhammad's attitude to the enemies of Islam changed shortly before he found a new home for his followers. No longer did he impress on them the need for patient submission, for the Qoranic verse permitting active resistance against religious persecution had been revealed. This change in outlook inaugurated a long period of strife, which began soon after the Moslems had fled to Madinah, and more than once their small community was threatened with extinction. Their situation became even more precarious when the Qoraish managed to form alliances with other Arabian tribes in the Hijaz, and even intrigued with some of the Jewish tribes in Madinah itself. Among the rest of Arabian society, however, there was growing approval for the social reforms which were an integral part of the Islamic code, and in spite of the crucified bodies of Moslem neophytes that were sometimes seen hanging on the pagans' gallows, many conversions to Islam were still made, both in secret and in public.

Muhammad himself led some twenty of the battles and skirmishes in which the Moslems engaged during their first ten years in Madinah, and there were at least fifty others during that time in which he did not take part. They brought fearful hardship to the struggling community, but the Moslems were inspired by their Apostle's convictions and strengthened by their desire to keep the security they had at last obtained.

The first great battle took place in 623 A. D., the second year of the Hegira, at Badr, a rocky pass about twenty leagues south of Madinah. An army from Mecca, approximately a thousand strong, was there defeated by three hundred and thirteen Moslems. This victory of an amateur militia, inadequately armed and ill-disposed to fight, against superior odds, seemed nothing short of a miracle. Indeed, before they fought Muhammad had prayed: " O God Almighty, help them, for if they are annihilated Thou shalt be worshipped no longer," and the Moslems saw a vision of angels, who came to shield and lead them (*ill.* 64). For the Qoraish, this defeat at the hands of a paltry handful of renegades was a severe blow to their prestige. Furthermore, it meant that one of their valuable caravan-routes was still in danger—the problem that had troubled them when they had plotted to kill Muhammad.

Thirteen months after the battle at Badr, therefore, an army of three thousand Meccan soldiers marched on Madinah, intending to end this threat once and for all. They were commanded by Abu Sufyan, who belonged to the 'Omayyad branch of the Qoraish. A skilled politician, he first of all tried to split his opponents by sending word to Madinah that the Qoraish were only waging war on Muhammad and his Meccan disciples; if, he said, the Madinese would withdraw their protection from these rebellious members of the Qoraish, they would be left in peace and their city would be spared the devastation of war. This approach, however, met with no response from the " Succourers of Islam ".

The Qorashi force, which also contained soldiers from allied Arab tribes, and some African mercenaries, therefore took up their positions near Mount Ohod, about a league north of Madinah. A horde of women had accompanied them on their journey from Mecca, and they now chanted warlike songs to encourage their menfolk. Abu Sufyan's wife Hind had come with him, and she moved haughtily among the others, her ankle-bracelets jingling.

In Madinah the women and children, the sick and the aged, were taken to the relative safety of the fortified enclosures, and the male population, along with one or two women soldiers, prepared to fight. Muhammad thought they should wait until the enemy attacked the city, but he was prevailed upon to lead his disciples out to engage the Qoraish in the plain (*ill.* 63).

The elderly and weakened Muhammad, who had some difficulty in putting on his armour and helmet, rode out at the head of about a thousand men. Some of them, seeing the vast array of force set against them, withdrew before the battle had even been joined. The rest went on to the foot of Mount Ohod, under the banner of Islam which bore the words: " There is none to worship but God," and challenged the army of Abu Sufyan to combat.

During the *mêlée* that ensued, as clouds of arrows and thrusting spears felled many men on both sides, the Qorashi women beat their cymbals and tambourines, and sang:

If you advance, we embrace you
And we spread soft carpets.
If you retreat, we part from you
A parting without love.

In spite of this encouragement, the first successes went to the Moslems and the Qoraish began to fall back. But one of their women soldiers found their banner lying on the ground, picked it up and rallied the retreating army round her. The Moslems had been thrown off their guard by their unexpected success, and the Qoraish now managed to attack them in the rear. The Moslems lost ground. A rumour ran through the ranks that Muhammad had been killed; in fact he had been cut in the face by a stone. As the enemy pressed their advantage, the Prophet encouraged his followers to resist. Arrows were falling thickly in every direction, and the Moslems tried to shelter their leader with their bodies. He was losing blood from his wound and some of his disciples carried him to a cave near the top of Mount Ohod where he lay till the battle was over. It was not long before the Moslems were forced to concede defeat.

Abu Sufyan and his wife both climbed to the top of the mountain and improvised poems in honour of the victory and of their god Hubal. Then Abu Sufyan asked the Moslems whether it was true that Muhammad was dead; hearing that he was still alive, the Meccan leader challenged them to battle again a year later.

The Qorashi troops, as exultant as their commander, proceeded to mutilate the bodies of their dead opponents, cutting off the ears and noses to thread into necklaces for their women. Muhammad's elderly but stalwart uncle, Hamzah, had been killed with a shrewd javelin thrust delivered by an Ethiopian soldier, who now ripped open the corpse's belly and tore out the liver as a trophy for Hind. To express her loathing for Hamzah, who had killed one of her relatives in battle,

64.* Qoran III, 199 is revealed to Muhammad during a battle. 38×26 cm.

وفی اصحابك اوزرینه كم یا ایها الذین امنوا اصبروا وصابروا ورابطوا
واتقوا الله لعلكم تفلحون حضرت رسالت صلی الله علیه وسلم
اصحابنك وستنه الله تعالینك قولین اوقودی کادکن قریشك
جرسن صف باغلیوب یقین کلدیلر رسول حضرتی اصحابنه

65

66

she tried to eat the liver, but only managed to chew a tiny piece and threw the rest away (*ill.* 62).

To the surprise of the Moslems, the victorious Meccans did not attack the city of Madinah, which was now virtually defenceless and might have been captured without difficulty. Instead they mounted their camels and rode home, leading their horses beside them. The Madinese were left to pick up their wounded, with the help of the women who now came out of the forts. The dead were buried where they had fallen (*ill.* 66). The anguish of the bereaved families was accentuated by the terrible mutilations that had been perpetrated upon the bodies, and Muhammad thereupon forbade the Moslems ever to indulge in the ancient Arabian custom of disfiguring both human and animal bodies. Then he tried to comfort his distressed followers, reminding them that martyrdom was an exalted state. Mount Ohod had been that day, he said, one of the gateways to Paradise.

In the sixth year of the Hegira, the Meccan army and its allies again attempted to besiege Madinah. This time the Moslems dug a trench round the city, and the battle is accordingly known as the Battle of the Ditch.

If the Qoraish and their allies had achieved their aim on this occasion too, the name of Islam might never have become a part of history. But the fortune of war had begun to favour the Moslems, and now they started to mount raids on their enemies' strongholds, destroying pagan temples in various parts of the Hijaz. Deputations began to come to them from other Arabian tribes, seeking treaties of alliance or non-aggression.

In 630 A. D., after a two-year period of truce between Muhammad and the Qoraish, this wave of success culminated in the occupation of Mecca itself. A large army, led by Muhammad, rode out of Madinah. It was the month of Ramadan and the soldiers were observing the ritual fast. On the road to Mecca, they were joined by contingents from the various tribes who had become their allies until at last it was an army of ten thousand men that pitched camp outside the holy city. The inhabitants of Mecca watched thousands of fires lighting up the night sky, and knew that this was the end of their supremacy in the Hijaz.

Next day the Moslem forces poured into the valley from every direction. Muhammad, coming from the southern gorge, planted the banner of Islam at the entrance to the city. Then he rode on his camel into Mecca, reciting a Qoranic verse: "*Verily we have expanded before thee a true expansion*" (*Qoran:* XLVIII, 1) (*ill.* 67).

Muhammad had promised that all Meccans who remained in their houses or went to the Ka'bah would be safe, and the streets were empty. The Apostle rode to the temple and circumambulated the Ka'bah, touching the Black Stone with his long hooked camel-stick at the end of each circuit. Then he turned towards the idols that stood in the courtyard of the Ka'bah. With his stick he knocked down each one of the three hundred and sixty images, repeating every time: "*Truth has come and falsehood has vanished.*" (*Qoran:* XVII, 81). Figurative art has ever since been prohibited in Islamic houses of worship.

The Apostle dismounted and asked for the keys of the Ka'bah. They were brought, after some show of reluctance, by the guardian who held the hereditary right to keep the entrance to the temple. Muhammad entered the building, and immediately ordered his followers to wash away all the paintings from the walls. But he put a protective hand over the picture of Mary with the Infant Jesus; he had once said that none could love Jesus more than himself. The effigies of Abraham and Ishmael were destroyed, however, because they were shown holding the pagan soothsayer's arrows. Muhammad then purified the interior of the Ka'bah by uttering the monotheistic creed at each of its corners. He prayed there behind a pillar, on a slab of red marble.

65. Plaster bust of the 'Omayyad period, representing a warrior. Height about 95 cm.

66. Undated tombstone on the battlefield of Badr.

When he came to the doorway of the Ka'bah, Muhammad stopped on the threshold as he saw the Qoraish gathered in the courtyard to await judgment. He said to them: " There is none to be worshipped but God. He is the Unique One and has no equals. He has fulfilled his promise... and he alone has vanquished the confederates... O people of Qoraish, verily God has removed from you the vanity of the ignorant and the veneration of lineage. All men are descended from Adam, and Adam was nought but earth. Henceforth let there be no difference of caste between you; the best among you is he who is most deeply in awe of God. O assembly of Qoraish, what do you think I will do to you? "

The members of the tribe answered: " We expect kindness from thee, good brother, good nephew," and Muhammad replied: " In truth, I will repeat what Joseph said to his brethren: *let there be no reproach today* (*Qoran:* XII, 92). Disperse, you are free."

Bilal went up to the roof of the Ka'bah to call the Moslems to prayer for the first time in the holy city. After leading the congregation at prayer, Muhammad climbed the neighbouring hill of Safa, where he had first spoken publicly of monotheism. There a stream of converts came to make their promises that they would abstain from major sins and accept Islam. The men shook Muhammad by the hand, and the women followed the ancient Arabian custom of dipping their fingers in a bowl of liquid—only this time the liquid was water, instead of blood as it would formerly have been.

Now that the idols had gone, the Meccan valley was reconsecrated. No blood was to be shed there, no animals were to be hunted, and no trees could be cut down. Stones were set at the entrances to the sacred area, so that no confusion could arise.

Muhammad had owned two houses when he lived in Mecca; when he left they had been confiscated, and he made no claim to them now. He asked all the other emigrants from Mecca to follow his example, promising them eternal homes in Paradise as a reward for their self-denial on earth. The Madinese, noting Muhammad's forbearance towards the Qoraish, wondered whether he intended to stay and settle down again in his native city. But Muhammad reassured them that his dwelling in life and in death would always be Madinah.

Before returning home, he sent out parties of Moslems to destroy the pagan temples in the vicinity of Mecca. The Arabs who watched the ancient monolithic images being thrown from their pedestals saw that no retribution appeared to descend on the Moslems. They began to be convinced that Muhammad's faith must therefore be the true one, and tribe after tribe sent deputations to Mecca to accept Islam.[47]

At this, the culmination of his career, Muhammad received a revelation that included in its purport the announcement of his approaching death:

When God's succour and the expansion comes
And thou seest mankind entering in multitudes into God's faith
Celebrate thy Lord and entreat His pardon.

(*Qoran:* CX, 1-3)

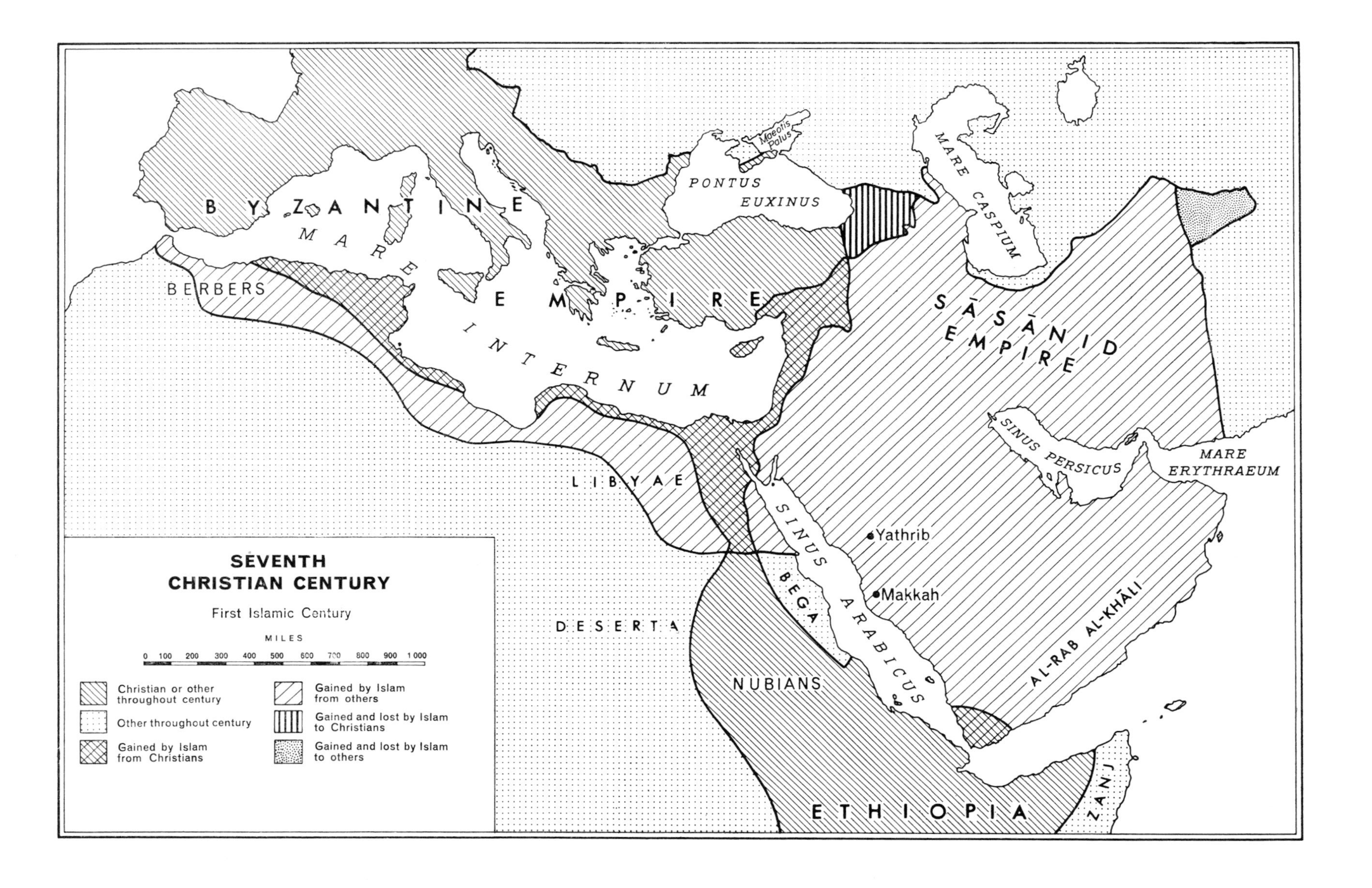
SEVENTH
CHRISTIAN CENTURY
First Islamic Century
MILES
0 100 200 300 400 500 600 700 800 900 1 000
Christian or other throughout century
Other throughout century
Gained by Islam from Christians
Gained by Islam from others
Gained and lost by Islam to Christians
Gained and lost by Islam to others
BYZANTINE EMPIRE
MARE INTERNUM
PONTUS EUXINUS
Maeotis Palus
MARE CASPIUM
SĀSĀNID EMPIRE
SINUS PERSICUS
MARE ERYTHRAEUM
BERBERS
LIBYAE
DESERTA
SINUS ARABICUS
Yathrib
Makkah
BEGA
NUBIANS
AL-RAB AL-KHĀLI
ETHIOPIA
ZANJ

MUHAMMAD'S FAREWELL

One of God's commands to the members of the Moslem faith was that each one of them who was able should make a pilgrimage to the Ka'bah at least once in his life-time. In order to establish a proper ritual for Islamic pilgrimage, Muhammad decided to undertake one himself. In the tenth year after the Hegira, therefore, he rode out of Madinah about a fortnight before the tenth of Dhu al-Hijjah, the date on which Abraham's sacrifice was thereafter celebrated by the Moslems. A young disciple rode with him on the same camel. It was intended that this boy should observe the Apostle's movements and describe them to others throughout a presumably long span of years, so that the rites should be accurately perpetuated.

The route began in the valley of the 'Aqiq (Cornelian valley), which was so named because of its red sand. At each resting-place along the way, the people of the neighbourhood would assemble. Muhammad would place his lance on the ground, indicating the direction of the Ka'bah, and invite the congregation to join in prayer, which he had said was Man's greatest combat, waged against his own self.

At Baida Muhammad took the vows of pilgrimage—abstinence from sin, avoidance of evil thoughts, and of harming any living thing, either morally or materially—and put on the traditional garment, which consisted of two pieces of unseamed cloth. Then he walked towards the symbol of monotheism, repeating the words that embody mankind's obedience to Abraham's call to pilgrimage: "At Thy command, O God."

Muhammad entered the Meccan valley from the north, crossing Mount Kada on the way, where he prayed that the Ka'bah might for ever be a goal for pilgrims. When he arrived at the temple, he entered the courtyard through the gateway generally used by the members of his own tribe, and then walked round the Ka'bah and saluted it in the customary way. He prayed beside the stone that was said to have served as Abraham's ladder. Then, to symbolise Hagar's search for water, Muhammad ran backwards and forwards seven times between the hills of Safa and Marwah. He felt unwell after such a strain, for he was no longer a young man. He had to return to his lodgings and rest there for some days.

On the ninth of the month of Dhu al-Hijjah, Muhammad had recovered sufficiently to resume the pilgrimage rites. He rode out of Mecca to the 'Arafat plain; in years gone by the common people had gathered there, while the high-born Qoraish stayed within the Meccan precincts. This gesture was therefore interpreted by those who were watching as a final blow to the Ishmaelites' conviction

67. The oratory built on the site near Madinah where the expansion of Islam was prophesied to Muhammad, in Qoran XLVIII, 1.

68. The site in the plain of 'Arafat where Muhammad prayed on his farewell pilgrimage.

67
68

حضرتی علیه السلام منبرینه آغدی خطبه اوقودی عبدالله

بن ابی مسجده کلدی کندو قاعده سنجه اوروطوردی

کیم رسول علیه السلامی اوکه مسلمانلر دورت

یکادن اتکنی چکدیلر ابتدیلر اشغه اوتورسن اول

that they were the chosen of God. As the sun began to go down, a vast crowd of people gathered in the plain to listen to Muhammad as he preached. His voice, always inclined to be low, did not carry as far as the outskirts of this huge concourse, so criers were posted at various points to repeat his words to the people near them.

After his sermon, Muhammad rode towards the heap of boulders where Adam was said to have asked God for mercy, and stayed there for a while in meditation, on his faithful camel Qaswa' (*ill.* 68). Towards sunset, the silent crowd saw the Apostle's face turn pale and his body fall forward in prostration. This meant, as always, that he was receiving a divine revelation, one of the last that were to come to him:

> *Today I have completed your religion and perfected*
> *My grace upon you and consented to Islam as your faith.*
> (*Qoran:* V, 3)

At sunset, Muhammad rode on to the next station, at Muzdalifah. A fire had been lit there to guide the multitude who had joined the Prophet on his journey. Muhammad spent the night meditating beside the fire.

The following day was set aside for the celebration of Abraham's sacrifice. After the morning prayer, Muhammad rode to the Mina gorge, where the patriarch was believed to have killed the ram. There he threw stones at the monolith of the Evil Spirit that had tempted Abraham and mankind, symbolising with this gesture his refusal of temptation. After that, he too sacrificed a ram, thereby indicating man's relinquishment of his wordly possession, in order to approach God purified by sacrifice.

Turning towards Mecca, Muhammad invited the congregation to join him: the emigrants from Mecca stood on his right and the Madinese on the left, with the rest of the assemblage in between. As he spoke to them, there was a vibrant note in his voice that made criers unnecessary this time. He said:

" O mankind, listen well. I may not be with you after this year. Just as these days, these months, this city, are sacred, so your lives, your property and your honour are sacred to one another. The weak, the weak among you—feed them on what you eat, clothe them as you are clothed. You will meet your Lord, and He will call you to account for your actions... Do not fall back into error... Let those here present warn those who are not with us. May those to whom these words are repeated understand them better than some who now hear them. Have I delivered (God's) message? " The congregation assented, and Muhammad added: " Witness, O God."

Muhammad returned to Mecca, to drink for the last time from Hagar's well, and then began on the journey back to Madinah. He had only eighty more days to live, and was never to visit Mecca again.

Towards the end of the month of Safar, 11 A. H. (632 A. D.), Muhammad felt the first symptoms of his fatal illness. He became troubled about the fate of Islam after his death. One night he went with a friend to the burial ground in Madinah and prayed: " O people of the graves! Soon dawn will arise over you, a more favourable dawn than upon the living, for here dissensions will follow one upon another as the hours of a sombre night."

For some days the Apostle did his best to continue his normal life and still conducted prayers in the mosque. When it became evident that he must lie down, he asked his other wives to allow him to stay in the hut next to the mosque that was reserved for 'Aishah. This was Muhammad's first indication that he would prefer Abu Bakr to succeed him as leader of the Moslem community. Later he

69.* Muhammad delivering his last sermon, in the Madinah mosque.
38×25 cm.

gave more precise signs, asking his old friend to lead the prayers in his stead, ordering all the doors of the mosque to be closed except the one which faced Abu Bakr's house, and making frequent allusions to the great qualities of the former cloth merchant. He did not, however, seek to impose his choice of successor by any direct announcement.

Muhammad's illness lasted for thirteen days. During that time he appeared repeatedly at the door of 'Aishah's house, leaning on the arm of one of his cousins, and wearing a black bandage round his aching head. " One of God's servants," he once said to the congregation, " given the choice between here below and His vicinity, has preferred God's vicinity." He asked for the forgiveness of any he might have offended, so that he would appear before his Judge untainted by anyone's ill-will. One man asked for the return of three dirhams he had lent Muhammad to give to a beggar. Others asked for his blessing (*ill.* 69).

The illness worsened and Muhammad tossed and turned feverishly, lying on his mantle, which had been folded and placed on the earth. He did not complain, but said: " O soul, what has happened to thee that thou now seekest every possible hiding-place? " 'Aishah began to pray for his recovery. Quickly the Apostle interrupted her with his own prayer: " Let me meet the Most Exalted Friend! ", and begged to be made to bear the dark hour of death.

Gradually he lapsed into unconsciousness. His friends poured an Abyssinian medicine into the corner of his mouth, threw buckets of water over him to reduce his fever, and attempted other treatments some of which, in his moments of lucidity, the sick man resented. In these moments too, Muhammad invariably remembered something that must be done. He asked that his money, which only amounted to seven dinars, should be distributed among the poor. To his grief-stricken younger daughter Fatimah he whispered that she would soon join him in death. To Safiyah, his Jewish wife, the dying man found a kind word to say. Usamah, the son of Muhammad's freedman Zayd, came to see him, but the Prophet was by then past speaking: he blessed his adoptive grandson by moving his hand up and down, with the forefinger raised.

As he lay there dying, his thoughts turned again and again to the dreadful possibility that a new form of paganism might come into being, in which he would figure as an idol. Repeatedly he warned the Moslems not to worship tombs; once he asked for writing implements so that he could make a permanent record of his last admonition, but he did not pursue the attempt. He asked those around him whether they thought he had conscientiously fulfilled his mission, and they reassured him.

On the anniversary of his birth, Monday the twelfth of Rabi' al-Awwal in the eleventh year of Islam (the seventh of June, A. D. 632), Muhammad made an effort to rise from his bed and perform his ablutions before dawn. The curtain covering the doorway of 'Aishah's house was lifted, so that the Prophet could see his followers praying in the mosque. He smiled at them, silently. He was as white as a sheet, but those who looked at him thought they had never seen such a noble expression on his face. When they had finished their prayers, Muhammad came into the mosque, with the signs of approaching death already unmistakably on his features. In a ringing voice he cried: " O mankind, the fire is kindled. Dissensions have come as the hours of a sombre night. Indeed, God is my witness that you cannot reproach me. Verily, I have allowed what the Qoran allowed and forbidden what the Qoran forbade."

He returned to 'Aishah's hut. Those who stayed with him seem to have been 'Aishah, Fatimah and 'Ali. As the sun rose towards noon, they began to see a vision. The humble room was filled with thousands of angels, led by Gabriel, the Spirit of Truth who had inspired Muhammad throughout the twenty years of his apostolate. Gabriel asked the Prophet how he was. " O Gabriel, I am sad and melancholy," he replied. "Apostle of God," said the Archangel, " Death asks for permission to enter." The Angel of Death came in and asked: "Apostle of God, shall I strike at thy life? " and Muhammad answered: " Fulfil, O Death, the command " (*ill.* 70).

The watchers by the bedside came out of their trance. One of them, who was supporting Muhammad's head, felt that his body had become heavy. His head turned upwards and his eyes became glassy. His last words were: " To the Most Exalted Friend."

Muhammad's companions washed his body, without removing the shirt in which he had died, perfumed him with musk, and wrapped him in three lengths of Yemenite cloth. Then they laid the body back in the spot where he had died, and his followers came in groups to pray beside him. His nearest relatives came first, then the Meccan emigrants, then the Madinese Moslems, and then the rest of the men, women and children. ʻAli said to them: " No one shall lead the prayers beside him. He stands before us always, in life and in death." One by one his disciples filed past the dead Prophet, reassuring his spirit on the question that had weighed so heavily on his living heart: " Peace be upon thee, O Apostle. We witness that thou hast truly delivered the message, that thou hast endeavoured in God's way until God glorified His religion and perfected it." For thirteen centuries, all Moslems have saluted the Apostle's grave in the same words.

Three nights after his death, towards dawn, the sound of mattocks was heard as Muhammad's grave was dug, in the place where he had died. His body was laid in wet sand, on a piece of of spongy red cloth, and was facing towards the Kaʻbah. His friends looked for the last time upon the face of Muhammad the Trustworthy, then covered him with earth and little red pebbles. They knew that, as he had promised, he would lie there always, untouched by the earth's corruption, and when one of the living saluted his grave, Muhammad's spirit would return the greeting.[48]

THE APOSTLE'S COMPANIONS

Has any day when mortal was mourned
Equalled the mourning on the day Muhammad died?

THE POET HASSAN ibn Thabit thus expressed in his elegy the sorrow felt by Muhammad's companions at his death. Many of them, in fact, were incredulous; to them it seemed inconceivable that such a man, the most extraordinary man who had ever appeared among them, could die like anyone else. There was a tumultuous meeting in the mosque at Madinah when 'Omar stood up to harangue the crowd, uttering threats against anyone who dared to confirm the rumour that Muhammad was dead. If the Prophet had indeed left them, he said, it could only be for a very short time; he would return again, like Moses from Sinai or the Risen Christ. The congregation took some comfort from this, panic-stricken as they were at the thought of losing their Prophet.

But while 'Omar was still speaking, Abu Bakr entered the mosque from the hut where Muhammad's body was lying. His mild features were blurred with tears. He pleaded with 'Omar to sit down, and then spoke himself to the assembly: " If it was Muhammad whom you worshipped, he is dead. But if you are servants of God, indeed He is the Ever Living One, the Eternal." At this, the frightened crowd fell silent. The man who was soon to be elected Muhammad's successor at the head of the Moslem community continued with his words of comfort, reminding his audience that the proof of the miracle of prophecy, the Qoran, would remain with them for all time.

" O father, father! " mourned Fatimah; to her weeping eyes, the blazing dome of the Madinese sky had been plunged into the " gloom of the nights," as she said in her elegy for him. She stayed shut within her " house of sorrows," thinking of nothing but the beloved father who had taught her the joys of poverty and humility. For ten years she had lived next to him in Madinah, ministering to her family and trying to model her life according to his wishes. She had worked sometimes till " her breast ached," drawing water from the well, grinding corn, and tending her tiny garden. As in life her father had wakened her before dawn for prayer, so she now waited alone for him to call her; only six months after his death she too was laid to rest.

70.* The angel of death asking permission to take Muhammad's life. Fatimah is standing beside her father. 37×27 cm.

Muhammad had been buried in 'Aishah's house, and for a time she continued to live there in the room with the tomb. Then she dreamed that Muhammad asked her to withdraw, so she placed a partition down the middle of the room;

السلام عليك يا رسول الله

even so, her bed was not more than a yard from the grave that lay on the other side of the wall. The Prophet had been afraid that the ill-feeling between 'Aishah and 'Ali might flare up after his death, endangering the political stability of the Moslem community. He had therefore warned 'Aishah against meddling in public affairs. She was to ignore his advice, however, and later she did as Muhammad had feared she might—she joined a faction which opposed 'Ali, thereby sowing some of the first seeds of dissension in the Moslem world. The " mother of the believers," as she was called, bitterly regretted this rash action, feeling that she had forsworn Muhammad. She died at the age of fifty-seven, moaning: " Would that I were a tree, a stone, a nameless object, anything condemned to oblivion."

Bilal the African could no longer bear to call the faithful to the mosque, now that Muhammad was not there to lead the services, nor even to stay in the city where every corner brought back a memory of the Prophet. He went to Syria and to Tarsus, in Anatolia. Only once did he ever again chant the invocation to prayer: when the second caliph, 'Omar, visited Syria.

One of the " people of the dais " who had become a teacher of the Moslem faith was Abu Hurairah, " the father of the little cat," who had once seen Muhammad perform a miracle. The Prophet had noticed the signs of starvation on Abu Hurairah's face and had given him a pitcher of milk, telling him to share it with some of the other people who were living in the mosque. Understandably, Abu Hurairah doubted whether so many starving people could obtain much benefit from one jug of milk. Yet in fact all of them were able to drink their fill from it.

Another of Muhammad's companions, Salman, was a Persian. He was born near Isfahan, the son of a Zoroastrian priest. As a boy he guarded the fire altar in the temple, until one day he heard a Christian service being conducted and was so impressed by it that he became a convert. He fled to Syria, and was a devoted follower of some Christian ecclesiastics there; he is even said to have seen Jesus himself, when he appeared in the desert to cure the ailing and infirm. Salman was inspired to direct his steps towards Arabia; on the way, he was captured by slave dealers, and sold to a Jewish landowner in Madinah. There he worked in the gardens, drawing water and picking fruit, and was actually up a fruit-tree one day when he overheard his master telling a friend about Muhammad's arrival in Yathrib. Salman felt that this must be the living teacher for whom he had been searching, and became so excited that he fell out of the tree. Next day he went to see Muhammad. The two men recognised each other and embraced. Salman was bought from his master and later, became the first man to translate part of the Qoran into Persian. After Muhammad's death, he left Madinah and wandered back to his native land, teaching the Islamic faith as he went.

It seems that, before he died, the Prophet had sent a message to a solitary hermit living among the sand dunes of the Yemen. Uwais al-Qarani had never been to Madinah or met the Apostle as he did not wish to leave his blind mother alone, but Muhammad's greeting was perhaps a sign that he regarded the hermit as one of his spiritual successors. This possibility is strengthened by later versions of the episode, in which a gift is added to the greeting. The Apostle is said to have asked 'Omar and 'Ali, as a last request, to give Uwais the mantle in which he was about to die. They did not know Uwais and had to enquire his whereabouts. Those who knew him told them:—" He is an extravagant madman who does not dwell amongst his people. He shepherds his camels in a plain. At night he comes to an encampment to buy bread, but does not stay there overnight and returns to the desert. He speaks to no one. He knows neither sorrow nor joy. When others laugh he weeps, and as they cry, he is merry." When at last 'Omar and 'Ali found Uwais, he was at prayer and an angel was guarding his herd. The hermit finished his devotions, and the two companions went closer to him, to make certain that

71. The inner gate of one of of the pavilions at the Topkapu Palace in Istanbul, dating from the time of Mehmed II. The first Turkish caliph, Selim I, dedicated this pavilion to the relics of the Apostle and of his companions, and it was subsequently known as the " Pavilion of the Holy Mantle ".
The flower-patterned tiles are amongst the best examples of sixteenth century Turkish ceramics. The inscription over the gate, in Jali Thuluth characters, reads: " Salutations to thee, O Apostle of God ".

he was the man indicated by Muhammad. 'Omar said to him: " The Apostle has sent to thee his salutation and begged of thee to pray to God for his congregation and to intercede for them."

" 'Omar," said Uwais, " thou shouldst endeavour for this purpose."

" But I repeat to thee the Apostle's message," insisted 'Omar.

" Take care, 'Omar," responded Uwais. " Perhaps it is a mistake and another man was intended."

Uwais was at last persuaded and took the mantle. He died in 37 A. H., during the battle when 'Ali, the last elected caliph, was defeated by the temporal princes who, in the view of the Prophet's companions, usurped the supreme seat of Islam. It is said that the fragment of the Prophet's mantle, a piece of white handwoven woollen cloth, which is now kept in an Istanbul mosque, is the remains of his gift to Uwais.

One of the companions of the Prophet was a mere child when he died, but he had received the blessing of Muhammad. This was 'Abd-Allah ibn 'Abbas, who retired to Mount Thawr, to the entrance of the cave where Muhammad and Abu Bakr had hidden from the Qoraish, where he is said to have written the first commentary on the Qoran.

The " people of the dais," who had made it their task to memorise and recite passages from the divine revelations while the Apostle was still alive, now set themselves, with the help of the first caliphs, to establish a text of the Qoran. These humble beggars also passed on their knowledge of Muhammad's precepts to posterity and were instrumental in beginning Islamic exegesis, theology, jurisprudence, mysticism and historical documentation.

The disciples of Muhammad travelled far and wide, propounding the ideal of the Islamic community. They went to Syria, Palestine, Byzantium, Persia and North Africa, in the wake of the Arab armies to Khorassan, Turkestan, and wandered across the Eurasian steppes, from China to the Volga. Slowly their work and their inspiration had their effect. Moslem communities started to grow up alongside Magian, Christian or Buddhist groups. Some of the neophytes even began to think with longing of the birthplace of Islam, and left their native lands to live in the Hijaz.

Muhammad's official successors as head of the Moslem community were the caliphs. The first four caliphs, who were elected by the congregation, resided in Madinah, and their seat of office was the lower steps of Muhammad's bench. Each year, at the time of pilgrimage, they would send a caravan to Mecca, or lead it themselves. The rule of the first caliph, Abu Bakr, lasted only three years, but during that time he was greatly troubled by unmistakable signs that paganism was resurgent throughout Arabia, and even in Mecca. He died in the thirteenth year of the Islamic era and was buried at the feet of Muhammad, shrouded in the vestments of a pauper so that he should appear before God in humility.

The second caliph, 'Omar ibn al-Khattab, now took his place on the steps of the Apostle's bench. " 'Omar was so tall," it is said, " that when he stood amid a crowd, one thought he was on horseback." His personal seal bore the inscription: " Death is the best preacher, O 'Omar!" He has been compared to St. Paul, because like the Christian Apostle, his loyalties had undergone a dramatic change of direction. 'Omar had been a Qorashi warrior, a vehement enemy of Muhammad, when suddenly the Qoran seemed to open the way to the only possible truth, and 'Omar became an ardent supporter of Islam. His greatest claim to fame is the establishment of the Islamic system of justice. His own son transgressed the laws of the community, and 'Omar sentenced him severely. The penalty for the offence was flogging, which resulted in the young man's death. 'Omar practised conscientiously the humility enjoined upon his disciples by Muhammad; when the

" Commander of the Faithful," as he was known, entered Jerusalem after its conquest by the Moslems, he was leading a camel on which his freedman was mounted. It had fallen to the servant's turn to ride as they neared Jerusalem, so 'Omar entered the city on foot.

From 17 to 35 A. H., under 'Omar and his successor 'Othman ibn 'Affan, extensive alterations were made to both the Meccan and Madinese temples. The Ka'bah had to be repaired in 17 A. H. Some of the houses which Qusayy had built overlooking the Ka'bah were pulled down, so that the courtyard of the temple could be enlarged. A wall was built round it, in the manner of the Madinese mosque, and lanterns were hung up to illuminate it at night. Improvements to the Madinese mosque were complicated by the fact that it had been built during the Apostle's life-time and under his direction, so that to alter it might be considered impious. After considerable theological discussion, it was decided that Muhammad himself would have agreed that the needs of the Moslem congregation must come first. The people who owned houses adjoining the mosque were persuaded to donate them, so that the Madinese mosque could also be enlarged. By 35 A. H., its area had been extended towards the north, south and west (Muhammad's family had lived on the eastward side) until it measured 150 × 170 ells. The supporting columns were correspondingly increased in number, and stone or stuccoed pillars were substituted for the palm trunks originally used. Mosaics of coloured stones decorated the lower parts of the walls and pillars. The covered part of the mosque was enlarged to the size of Muhammad's original building, and given a ceiling of teak.

As caliph, 'Omar held himself personally responsible for the mosque. He chased away the minstrels who had followed the example of their patron, Muhammad's poet Hasan ibn Thabit, and formed the habit of chanting loud improvised verses in the mosque courtyard. When in Madinah, 'Omar always stayed in the mosque until the last worshipper had left, then put out the lights and closed the doors himself.

During the time of the first four caliphs, the Apostle's mausoleum was left as a building separate from the mosque. A canopy made of layers of waxed cloth was placed over 'Aishah's hut, and a low fence was built round it. The partition she had made in the hut was still there, and her room was now an antechamber for visitors. They would enter through one doorway, offer their salutations to the Prophet and leave by another door. A casket of aromatic herbs was set facing the place where his head lay in the tomb. The dead as well as the living came here, brought by their relatives to receive a blessing from the Apostle's spirit.

Muhammad had once described 'Omar as Islam's strongest barrier against the counter-attack of old idolatries. As the victor over the Sassanid Empire, he was extremely unpopular with the Persians, and he was eventually murdered at the age of sixty-three, in 23 A. H., by a young ironmonger of the Magian faith. 'Omar too was buried beside Muhammad, the second and last of the companions to be so honoured.

The third caliph was 'Othman ibn 'Affan, a modest and retiring man, who was already sixty-eight when he took office. His contemporaries described him as a man of pleasant aspect, with a blond beard and golden teeth. He had rendered great services in the codification of the Qoran. As mentioned above, he carried on the work of enlarging the mosque, extending it towards the south and placing against the new wall a slab to indicate the direction of Mecca. He also built an enclosure within the mosque as an oratory for his own private use, although Muhammad had wished that in the temples of Islam everybody should worship together. 'Othman founded the city of Jiddah, as a port for Mecca. His predecessor 'Omar had built a monument there, in the place believed to be Eve's grave; while in the neighbourhood, 'Othman visited this memorial, and also discovered the pleasures of sea-bathing.

After the death of Muhammad, his seal had been passed on to the first caliph, and subsequently to those who followed. Accidentally, 'Othman dropped it in a well, not far from the Quba mosque. His administration was consistently mishandled, and nepotism was rife. At last, in 35 A. H., he too was murdered, by a dissident group. " They murdered a white-haired old man, whose brow bore the signs of prostration and who spent the night in vigil and Qoranic recitation," said the contemporaries. 'Othman was in fact killed on the day when Abraham's sacrifice was celebrated. Muhammad's " night of dissensions " had come. The Qoran 'Othman was reading was stained with the blood which gushed over it as he was stabbed to death. It is said that this same Qoran was taken to Turkestan, in the late Middle Ages, and kept in a dervish convent in Samarkand, until the city was occupied by the Russians.

Difficulties beset the caliphate on every side. It was proving almost impossible to govern the whole of Islam from Madinah. In the countries where Moslem communities had come into being, in the former empires of the Pharoahs, of the Sassanids, of the Kushans and the " Celestial Turks," pre-Islamic religions and local cultures still held sway, threatening to engulf early Islam's republican institutions and fundamental monotheism. In Mecca itself, the remaining members of the old sacerdotal aristocracy were dissatisfied with their loss of power; their position might, they thought, be improved if the caliphate could be transformed into a hereditary monarchy.

It was in such circumstances that the fourth and last orthodox caliph, 'Ali, Muhammad's cousin and son-in-law, took office. It appears that some of his followers had begun to regard him and his sons as holders of a divine right over the caliphate—a conviction which was to lead to perpetual conflict within the Moslem world.

'Ali had a complex personality. The " Knight of Islam," as he was called, had made countless sacrifices in the cause of his faith ever since he had so enthusiastically embraced it at the age of ten. He was heroic and generous in spirit, with a tendency to bluntness; Muhammad had once smilingly called him " the earthy one." In many ways, no two natures could have been more at variance than the impulsive 'Ali and his quiet, withdrawn wife Fatimah, who had shut herself away from human society to mourn her father and await her own death. Yet 'Ali was a mystic. He knew the Qoran by heart and, characteristically, spoke his prayers aloud. (Many Moslems still follow his example in this, while others adopt Abu Bakr's method of silent concentration.) Ali was also artistically inclined; in the Middle Ages he was considered the patron of Islamic painters, and there is a volume of mystic poetry which has been attributed to him.

When he acceded to the caliphate, 'Ali was fifty-five—dark, corpulent, almost bald, with large lustrous eyes. He always wore black, perhaps as a sign of mourning for Muhammad. As soon as he took office, 'Ali determined to go and challenge his opponents. In 36 A. H., he set out from Madinah. He never returned there again.

With the departure of the last of Muhammad's " companions " to become caliph, came the fulfilment of his prophecy that the " mild city " of Madinah would be abandoned for places where Muhammad and his republic were not remembered.[49]

72. A golden casket in which the Apostle's mantle was kept during the reign of the Turkish caliph Murad III – 953-1004 A. H. (1546-1595 A. D.). 53 × 53 × 12.5 cm.

73. The southern side of the iron and brass-work railing which surrounds Muhammad's mausoleum within the Madinah mosque. The brass disc indicates the level of the Apostle's head. The inscription, repeated in several rows, reads: " There is none to worship but God, the Rightful and True Lord. Muhammad is God's Apostle and the faithful attester of the certain promise."

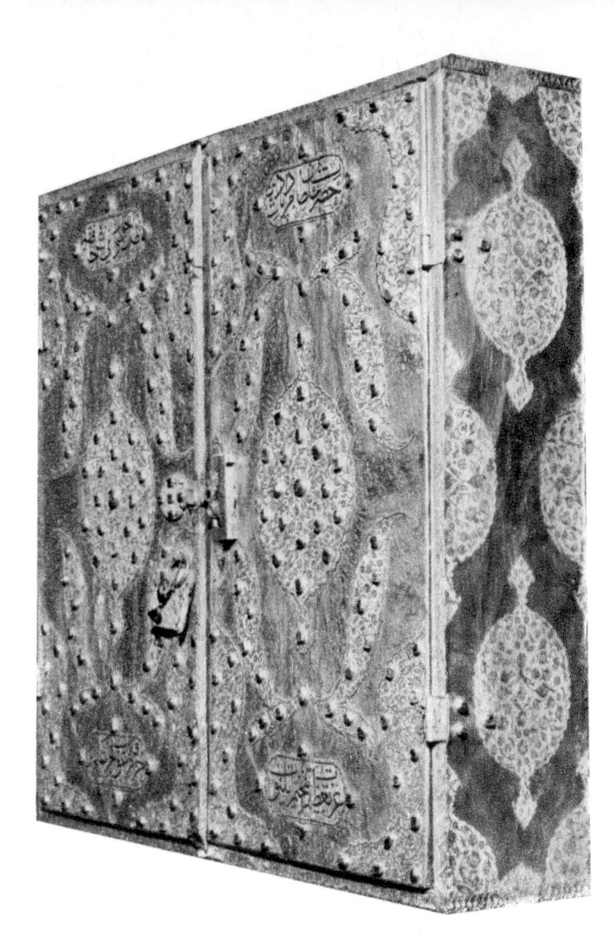

72
73

'OMAYYAD DOMINATION

'ALI'S ARMY met with its first opposition near Basrah, where it was challenged by a force led by Moslem pietists. Among them was 'Aishah, mounted on a camel. Their complaint against 'Ali was that he had not taken sufficiently stringent measures to avenge 'Othman's murder. The caliph won this battle, however, and sent the remorseful 'Aishah safely back to Madinah under escort.

At Siffin, on the right bank of the Euphrates, 'Ali fought against the Syrian army of the 'Omayyad. On the point of triumph, he fell victim to a trick which the defeated 'Omayyad managed to play on him and during a conciliatory meeting was manoeuvred into a semblance of abdication. At this meeting the Khariji, a " Protestant " group of pietists, walked out to express their contempt for both parties. 'Ali continued his opposition to the 'Omayyad until in 661 A. D. one of the Khariji struck him a fatal blow with a poisoned sabre.

Already, only thirty years after Muhammad's death, the bitter dissension he had prophesied had split the Moslem world into violently opposing factions, forcibly removing the leadership of Islam both from Muhammad's " companions " and from the birthplace of the Moslem religion. In 40 A.H. (660 A.D.) the 'Omayyad installed their first caliph: Mu'awiyah, the son of Abu Sufyan and Hind. The ceremony took place in Jerusalem. Mu'awiyah's only claim to this dignity was that, having embraced Islam when Mecca was conquered, he had then lived in Madinah with his elderly sister, one of Muhammad's wives, and had acted for a short time as secretary to the Apostle. The pietists were shocked to see the son of Hind upon the caliph's throne. " He was a tall and corpulent man, with white skin, fat thighs, a tiny head, protruding eyes, a dyed beard and a grim expression. Of a subtle turn of mind, he was crafty, perspicacious and yet firm. He knew how to make use of opportunities. In difficult matters he would feel his way with circumspection, and if he seemed to be losing ground in an argument, he would interrupt his adversary with a jocular remark."

Meanwhile, in countries which were accustomed to dynastic monarchy, and even, as in Persia and Turkestan, to attributing supernatural powers to their leaders, the Moslems still regarded the Prophet's descendants as the natural successors to the throne of Islam. In Madinah, therefore, Hasan, the elder son of Fatimah and 'Ali, was proclaimed caliph. Although his father had nominated him as his heir, Hasan felt compelled to forego the honour thus accorded him, for it is said that when he was a child the Prophet had told him that if in later life he found himself in a position where two sides warred on his account, he should withdraw.

74. The " Green Dome " above Muhammad's mausoleum, built in 1277 A. H. (1860 A. D.), under the Turkish caliph 'Abd al-Mejid. The " Head Minaret ", on the south-eastern corner of the Madinah mosque, near the mausoleum, was rebuilt in neo-Mameluk style during the repairs made by the Saudi government in 1948-55.

He therefore abdicated, in favour of his younger brother Husain. In spite of this, he met with an untimely death at the age of forty-five, probably by means of poison.

Husain set out with an army to try to establish his claim to the caliphate by defeating the 'Omayyad. In 61 A. H., however, the 'Omayyad forced him into the desert near Kerbela, west of the Euphrates, where he and some of his family and adherents were first left to suffer the pangs of thirst and then finally killed. The 'Omayyad cut off Husain's head, carried it away in triumph, and threw it at the feet of their own new caliph, Mu'awiyah's son Yazid. Pietist Moslem literature has left a striking portrait of this man:—" He was dark and his face was pock-marked." " He wore silk robes worth tens of thousands of dinars, for which human beings had been flogged and the veils of their honour torn to shreds." " He did not hide his inclination for pleasure, indeed he made a public parade of his shameful manners and gloried in his sins." " Yazid the wine-drinker, Yazid the lover of monkeys, Yazid the master of tigers! " " Besotted with vice, he died at the age of thirty-three."

The martyrdom of Husain and his family divided Moslem opinion for all time. The Shiites, as the adherents of the 'Alids (the descendants of 'Ali and Fatimah), were known, continued to maintain that the only rightful caliphs must come from this family. In Madinah, therefore, unofficial homage continued to be offered to twelve generations of 'Alid anti-caliphs. Some extreme Shiites accorded the 'Alids a devotion so intense that it amounted almost to worship; the puritans considered this heretical, and the 'Alids themselves apparently did not approve of such exaggerated veneration. Throughout the centuries, however, they continued to challenge the legitimacy of their rivals' position. Some of them managed to achieve secular power in the Hijaz, but they never permanently regained the caliphate.

Nevertheless 'Alid followers continually harassed the official caliphs in many ways. As a sign of allegiance, for instance, Arab ladies of the 'Omayyad period took to wearing a coiffure brought into fashion by the poetess Sakinah, a charming and talented daughter of Husain. To discredit the 'Alids and the pietists who lived in Madinah, the 'Omayyad encouraged rumours that pleasure parties were being held on the red sands of the 'Aqiq valley where Muhammad had walked in fervent prayer.

A small pietist faction, considered by the others to be fighting a lost cause, remained faithful to the ideal of Muhammad's republic and disapproved of the dynastic tendencies of both the 'Alids and the 'Omayyad. Its members wore black, as a sign either of mourning for Muhammad, or of protest at Islam's deviation from its initial democratic and austere ideology. The pietists fought stubbornly against the 'Omayyad, organising rebellions or in guerilla warfare. Though at the time their aims were considered impractical, tendencies akin to theirs have constantly been in evidence throughout the centuries and still survive in Islam today.

The majority of Moslems, while disliking the excesses of the 'Omayyad, nonetheless did their best to avoid stirring up additional dissension that might further weaken the Islamic state in an already troubled world. To be fair, it should be mentioned that the information which has come down to us concerning the misdeeds of the 'Omayyad dynasty was recorded either by historians who served their successors and enemies, the 'Abbassid caliphs, or else by the pietist Moslems, whom they persecuted. Some of the criticisms they levelled against the 'Omayyad might therefore be exaggerated.

Opposition from the 'Alids, and their own addiction to luxury and pageantry, which was so remote from Muhammad's ascetic ideals, made it impossible for the 'Omayyad ever to reign from the Hijaz. The Caliphs of their dynasty, which lasted from 40 to 132 A. H., held office in Damascus, Mu'awiyah's former seat of

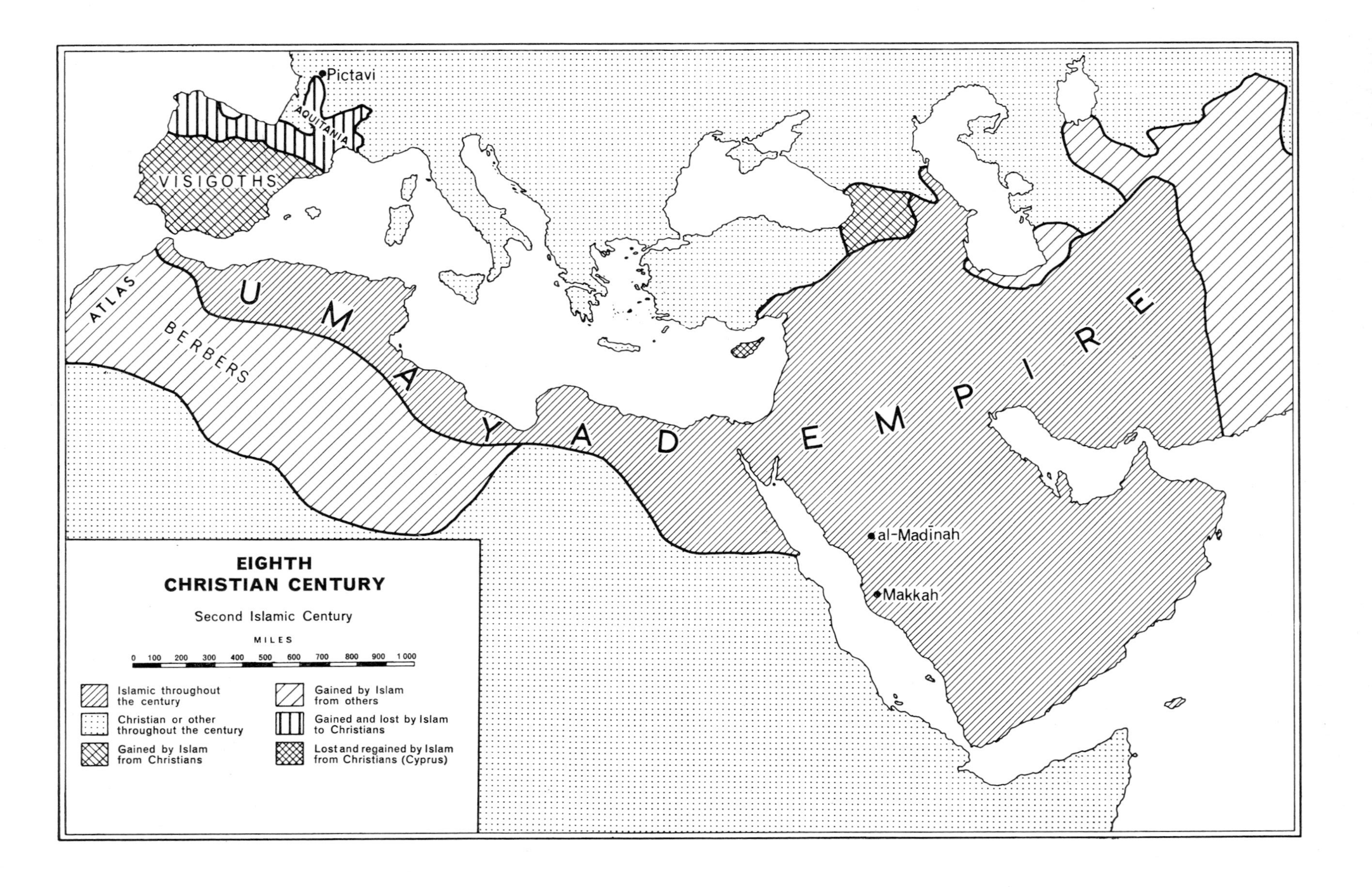
EIGHTH
CHRISTIAN CENTURY
Second Islamic Century
MILES
0 100 200 300 400 500 600 700 800 900 1 000
Islamic throughout the century
Christian or other throughout the century
Gained by Islam from Christians
Gained by Islam from others
Gained and lost by Islam to Christians
Lost and regained by Islam from Christians (Cyprus)
Pictavi
AQUITANIA
VISIGOTHS
ATLAS
BERBERS
UMAYAD EMPIRE
al-Madinah
Makkah

governorship. Here, in a setting of Byzantine splendour, near the magnificent residences of the old Ghassanid phylarchs, the 'Omayyad built their great monuments. Their mosques in Damascus and Jerusalem were intended to rival the sanctuaries of Mecca and Madinah, and sacred associations were invoked for the two cities—the relic of John the Baptist in Damascus, and for Jerusalem its connections with Solomon, Christ and with Muhammad's ascensional vision.

The 'Omayyad also built palaces and hunting pavilions, and adorned them with figurative sculpture and painting.[50] Here was the fourth stage of Arabian art, after the archaic, the Hellenistic, and the style influenced by the Parthians and Sassanians. New influxes, principally Mediterranean Christian art, and Buddhist art from those areas of Central Asia recently converted to Islam, continued to give Arabian art an eclectic character. In early Arabic texts, the Central Asian contribution to 'Omayyad culture is represented by means of a picturesque image. It is said that a king from the region of China, who lived in a palace of gold bricks with stabling for a thousand elephants, and was waited on by a thousand kings' daughters, sent an unusual gift to Mu'awiyah, who passed it on to his successors. The present was a book, in which were written the secrets of arts and crafts.[51]

In Qusair 'Amrah in Transjordania, at Khirbat al-Mafjar near Jericho, at Qasr al-Hair in Syria, and elsewhere, wall-paintings, earthen sculpture and Byzantine mosaics have survived the centuries, showing us the life of the 'Omayyad. At Qusair 'Amrah the caliph is shown as Pantocrator, among sovereigns contemporary with him: the Emperor of Byzantium, Roderick the Visigoth, the Sassanid monarch, Yazdgird III and three others believed to be Kultekin the ruler of the Celestial Turks, the Negus of Abyssinia, and the ruler of Egypt. Round the figures are set Heaven, in the form of the zodiac, and Earth, symbolised by palm-trees and clusters of fruit. In this and other 'Omayyad mansions, there are paintings and statues showing scenes of hunting in the desert, of water-parties and of many other festivities where the real and fantastic personages of a gay court are seen at play (*ill.* 48, 50). There are guards (*ill.* 65), archers on horseback, negroes, nude bathing girls, dancers holding posies (*ill.* 49), galloping centaurs, and the monkeys so dear to Yazid, performing upon musical instruments.

To quote the pietist writers again, in the privacy of his apartments, the caliph sat " between the (singer girls) Habbabah on his right and Sallamah on his left, as they chant for him. And when wine has intoxicated him, he tears his vestments and turns to one of the maids and asks: 'Shall I soar up to heaven?' The puritans add their own answer to this query: 'Aye,' they say, 'soar thou to hell!'.

This lavish mode of life, adornment and architecture, so reminiscent of the extravagances of the pagan Arab world and so abhorrent to the pietists, was eventually to be imposed on the Hijaz itself. In 63 A. H. (682 A. D.) the pietists of Madinah, exasperated by reports of the 'Omayyads' unrestrained behaviour, rose in rebellion. The revolt was led by 'Abd-Allah, the son of Hanzalah, a saintly man who all his life had fasted between dawn and sunset and always kept his head bowed in humility. A battle took place near the north-eastern lava belt of Madinah in which the pietists suffered a crushing defeat, barely escaping wholesale massacre at the hands of the 'Omayyad soldiers. 'Abd-Allah removed his armour, in order to receive the dignity of a martyr's death. For three days the invading 'Omayyad troops sacked Madinah, perpetrating atrocities upon the inhabitants.

The caliph, Walid son of 'Abd al-Malik, decided to obliterate the memory of the early Moslems in Madinah by building a new and opulent mosque in the style of the temples in Damascus and Jerusalem. At his request, the Byzantine Basileus Philippus, an Armenian precariously supported by the Khazar Turks, sent to Madinah a hundred Byzantine and Coptic artisans, and quantities of gold slabs and mosaic stones.

75. The southern porticoes of the Madinah mosque, built in 1277 A. H. over the site of Muhammad's original mosque.

It will be remembered that the Apostle's mosque had already been extended by 'Omar and 'Othman, on all sides except the eastern where there were the huts that had belonged to Muhammad's family. Now, in spite of the tears and entreaties of the Madinese, the Prophet's dwellings were ruthlessly destroyed. Fatimah's little house was torn down while one of her descendants, a young man, continued to sit there in meditation. The palm-trees in her garden were felled.

Amid this wholesale destruction, an outer wall of Muhammad's mausoleum collapsed. The sweet fragrance from the holy graves, borne upon the air, warned the Madinese of what had happened. The space where the Apostle, Abu Bakr and 'Omar were buried lay open to view. The mound covering 'Omar's body had crumbled slightly, and his feet became visible, causing the 'Omayyad prince who governed Madinah and the architect, Ibn Wardan, who saw them, to faint with fright. When they regained their senses, they were able to observe that the enclosure also contained a set of camel trappings and a jug for ablution. It was impossible to know which of the three men had owned these objects, so piously left beside his body.

The funeral chamber was curtained off, and as it would have been improper for the 'Omayyad to do it, the 'Alids were summoned to rebuild their ancestor's mausoleum. Double walls were now constructed round the burial place. The mausoleum had been square, like the Ka'bah; in order to avoid the possibility of people making ritual circuits round it in the same way, the shape of the exterior wall was altered by means of a triangular projection towards the north. The walls were built up to a height of two ells above the vaulted roof, as an additional protection. The funeral chamber could now only be entered through the hole left in the roof above it. The casket of aromatic herbs and a lighted lamp were placed outside the walls, facing the Apostle's head.

The area of the mosque now extended as far as the mausoleum and the site of Muhammad's dwellings, and covered some 300 × 200 ells of surface. As before, it consisted of an open, sandy courtyard surrounded by a wall; this wall was now not only crenellated but also ornamented with turrets. Inside, the walls were inlaid with marble and decorated with gold slabs or mosaic. There were colonnaded porticoes on each side of the courtyard. The columns, which may have been cylindrical, or four-sided as in ancient Yemenite temples, were in marble or faced with stucco; their capitals and bases were gilded. There may have been arcades above the colonnades. If so, the arches might have been pointed or in horse-shoe shape, in the characteristic style of Buddhist architecture that the 'Omayyad had borrowed from the conquered territories of Khorassan and Turkestan.

For the first time, minarets were erected on the four corners of the outer wall. Perhaps fashioned to resemble the first minaret of Islam, built in Cairo in 58 A.H., these were four-sided, each side being 8 ells wide, and about 50 ells high. They must have looked like towers, and were in fact an organic development from the pre-Islamic Madinese fortified enclosures.

Some relics were still left on the site of the Prophet's mosque; these included the broken trunk of the palm-tree against which he had leaned when he preached, and the bench that had then been built for him. To indicate the direction of Mecca, an 'Omayyad innovation was introduced, in the form of a stone slab with a niche in it. This was placed at the exact spot where Muhammad had been wont to pray. It will be remembered that the Apostle would use any object that came to hand—a stone or frequently a lance—to indicate the direction of Mecca, and this was known as the *mihrab*, where in the words of Muhammad, one attempted " the greatest struggle, the one against one's own inclination to evil," through prayer. In the Mediterranean civilisation to which the Arabs belonged, the niche was well

76. A Persian *mihrab* made in tiles, from Kashan, c. 1300 A.D. It bears an inscription from the Qoran – CXII, 1-4. 60 × 40 cm.

known. It existed in pre-Islamic Arabian architecture and is mentioned in a religious context both in a history of the beginning of Islam and in the Qoran. The circumstances in which the niche was adapted for a *mihrab* remain obscure, however. A coin of the 'Omayyad period shows the lance and the niche together, thus indicating that both were in use at once. As well as the Apostle's mosque, the first house of Moslem worship at Quba was also enlarged.

In 64 A. H. a pietist uprising occurred in Mecca, led by the grandson of Abu Bakr, 'Abd-Allah, son of Zubair. He was encouraged in this by his mother Asma, a centenarian now but still a valiant woman. After she had helped her father and Muhammad to escape from Mecca, Asma had crossed the desert herself to Madinah, alone and bearing the unborn 'Abd-Allah in her womb. He was the first Moslem child born in Madinah, and was blessed by the Apostle at his birth. 'Abd-Allah ("Servant of God") as Muhammad named him, grew to be a man of many parts; he was a memoriser of the Qoran, a poet of some ability, and a soldier who had fought in Egypt and Khorassan. He belonged to the pietist group who went robed in black, as a sign of permanent mourning.

The 'Omayyad cohorts sent to quell the rebellion opened their attack by hurling projectiles at the Ka'bah with huge catapults. This sacrilegious onslaught raised such violent indignation in the Meccans that all of them, pietist and non-pietist alike, rallied round 'Abd-Allah, ready to defend Abraham's monument, single-handed if need be. Indeed, in one terrible night, a Nubian woman chased the enemy unaided out of the city, by throwing a blazing torch into their midst. During the siege a fire occurred in a shelter where the wounded were being tended. It spread to the Ka'bah, burning the curtains and the wooden structure. The temple was so badly damaged that, as 'Abd-Allah said, "The flight of one of its doves would be enough to make it crumble." The Black Stone had been broken in three pieces, presumably by the 'Omayyad catapults.

'Abd-Allah now devoted himself with fervour to rebuilding "God's House," neglecting all other considerations. By so doing, he missed a great opportunity. The caliph Yazid had just died. Public opinion had risen so strongly against the 'Omayyad, not only in the Hijaz but in other parts of the Moslem world, that 'Abd-Allah was regarded as the rightful successor to the dignity of the caliphate. But he believed that his first duty was to rebuild the symbol of Islamic monotheism, and, immersed in his task, would not leave it to ride at the head of his adherents to crush the few remaining 'Omayyad sympathisers.

Traditional Yemenite techniques were used to reconstruct the seriously damaged building. As before, Abraham's Cyclopean green stones were left in place to serve as the foundation. Above them were set stones from the mountains near Mecca, cut into two-ell cubes and bound with mortar made of Yemenite clay. In accordance with a wish once expressed by Muhammad, the site of Ishmael's dwelling which had been left out of the Qorashi building, was now included within the Ka'bah. Incidentally, a green slab was discovered, under which Ishmael was believed to be buried.

The Ka'bah was now larger, and was made proportionately higher, the walls being raised to 27 ells. Again following the Apostle's wishes, the interior of the building was made more easily accessible by means of two doors set at ground level, one for the entrance and one for the exit. Two window panes of Yemenite alabaster were also placed in the walls, so that people entering the Ka'bah would no longer be in darkness.

The three fragments of the Black Gem were set into silver and replaced in their usual position at the eastern corner of the building. The walls of the Ka'bah were polished inside and outside with musk, and curtains were hung all round; for the first time, these were of Coptic cloth, brought from the recently conquered land of Egypt. The pathway for the circuit of the Ka'bah was paved with stones that had been washed in water from the Zamzam well. The enclosure surrounding the building was enlarged and made into a square shape, the walls were repaired, and new pillared porticoes were built, roofed with plane wood. 'Abd-Allah's restoration of the Ka'bah was finished on the 27th of Rajab, 65 A. H., a date which for the next five hundred years became an occasion for popular rejoicing.

While 'Abd-Allah was occupied with rebuilding, the 'Omayyad pretender had gathered partisans and sent an expedition to Mecca, under the leadership of the ferocious al-Hajjaj. The city was besieged for so long that the inhabitants became ravaged by famine and epidemic, and when their endurance began to fail, al-Hajjaj bombarded the Ka'bah. Rather than see " God's House " lying again in ruins, 'Abd-Allah decided to open the city to the enemy and to sacrifice his own life. When the 'Omayyad legions entered the holy precincts, they found no one there except 'Abd-Allah, who was praying in front of the Ka'bah. He finished his devotions, then calmly turned to face the enemy troops and drew his sword. Blows were rained on him and he fell to his knees. The heroic son of Asma was exclaiming: " My wounds will not be in my heels but in front," when a soldier struck off his head.

Al-Hajjaj had 'Abd-Allah's body crucified, upside down. One of the Prophet's companions, now old and blind, came to mourn beneath the cross, personifying the despair of all pietists. Seeing this violent end to all their hopes for Islam's future, another pietist said:—" The young men... who were in the full bloom of youth yet averted their eyes from evil and their feet were heavy when invited to the ways of vanity. God saw them in the depths of the night, worn out by ascetic practices, exhausted by vigil, their spines bent over the Qoranic folios. The earth had gnawed their knees and the hands which supported their prostrated bodies, but they thought this but a minor service to God. When the arrows were notched, the lances aimed, the sabres unsheathed and the squadron hurled its thunderbolt, the young man walked towards it until his feet knocked against each other and his noble features were bathed in blood. And now the wild beasts of the earth are running towards them, and the birds of the air are pouncing upon them. Many a human eye that once, in the heart of the night, would brim in awe of God, is now in the beak of a bird of prey! And many hands upon which their owners had rested in prostration before God are now severed from their wrists. Alas, alas! "[52]

Asma, now more than a hundred years old, took her son down from the cross and carried the body to Madinah. Secretly she buried him near Muhammad, for whose blessing she had offered him at his birth.

In Mecca, the 'Omayyad immediately destroyed 'Abd-Allah's work on the Ka'bah. They walled up one doorway and raised the other four ells off the ground, so that it could only be reached by the privileged few who had permission to enter. The building was embellished with a splendour which Muhammad would have condemned, had he been alive to see it. The façades were divided horizontally into two registers; the lower was eighteen ells high, with the real door and three false ones set under the cornice, one on each side of the building. On the higher register, or entablature, which was two ells high, there were four alabaster windows. Under the roof was a separate ceiling, at the level of the division between the registers. This was composed of aligned logs, the ends of which contained iron rings protruding beyond the Ka'bah's walls, on which to hang the curtain. The roof was decorated with shells, to begin with, but these did not stand up to the weather and had to be replaced by marble slabs. Inside the building the log ceiling was supported by three red marble columns. The windows in the entablature were framed with shells, arranged to imitate arches. The shells of the Arabian Gulf became a favourite element of decoration, not only in the Hijaz, but also in 'Omayyad Transjordania and in Spain. The fluted conch shell, said to echo the waves of the Red Sea, was too fragile to be used in this way, but it was often copied in stone and other materials.

Everything in the Ka'bah, including the porticoes round the courtyard, was covered with gold and silver slabs. The gold was said to have been obtained from Solomon's " credence," which was allegedly taken from the temple in Jerusalem by the Romans and later removed to Spain by the Visigoths, where the Arabs had found it.

In 80 and 84 A. H. the Ka'bah's basin was flooded again and new dykes had to be built, but the 'Omayyad did not confine their building activities to the temple. The descendants of the Qorashi princes were happy to make occasional visits to the valley which had been their ancestral home, and tried to install there some of the amenities they had known at the court of Damascus. To their palates, accustomed to the sweetmeats of Damascus, the Zamzam water tasted bitter, so they tapped a spring far away in the Sarat mountains, bringing it down to a gushing fountain in the heart of Mecca. The Meccans regarded this as a symbol of 'Omayyad self-indulgence and refused to touch a drop from the spring.

Mu'awiyah bought Qusayy's senate house for his own use, and also built several new mansions, in brick and stucco, or decorated with designs in coloured stone mosaic. One house had ornaments of multi-coloured glass, a great luxury at that time. Lamps burned all night in front of the princes' dwellings, illuminating the Ka'bah's courtyard which they overlooked.

The house where Muhammad had lived with Khadijah was made into a mosque. Relatives of the Governor al-Hajjaj lived in Aminah's house, where Muhammad had been born. Foreign princes came to live in Mecca, among them the Barmakids, a dynasty who formerly had been Buddhist high priests, from Balkh in Central Asia, and who no doubt brought with them the elements of their own art and culture.

The houses of the noblemen, both Arab and " Barbarian " ('Ajam—that is, non-Arab), were filled with poets, musicians, painters and craftsmen. The profligate caliph Yazid had introduced secular music into the Hijaz, and now stringed instruments played gay melodies in the holy cities where once only the call to prayer had been heard. A Madinese singer girl, Jamila, who went to Mecca on a pilgrimage of repentance, found a triumphant reception awaiting her there from those who had come to enjoy light music. Manners became so lax that for the circumambulation round the Ka'bah it become necessary to separate the men and the women into two processions.

The pietists in the holy cities continued to show their silent disapproval of the 'Omayyad excesses. In the offensively gilded precincts of the Ka'bah, they looked only at the lance which stood in Abraham's station, to indicate the congregation's gathering place, as in the days of the Prophet. To them, it now more than ever symbolised man's struggle against the worldly temptations which now surrounded it.

In spite of the 'Omayyad extravagance, a gradual transformation was taking place in Mecca. Slowly, Islamic ideology was beginning to prevail. The houses overlooking the Ka'bah were not always reserved for the nobility; former slaves, to whom under Islam the highest offices were open, now lived there also. Bathhouses were built, for the Islamic purification rites. Charitable institutions, such as hospices and a hospital, were set up in Mecca, and the 'Omayyad themselves gave freely to pious causes.[52]

Martyrdom struck the 'Omayyad dynasty just as they were settling into a more orthodox mode of life. In the Hijaz silent indignation still prevailed against them, but elsewhere in the Islamic world their implacable enemies the Khariji, the most

77. A Syrian mosque lamp in glass, dating from the Mameluk period, and said to have come from a convent near Damascus. It bears a Qoranic inscription and a dedication to an arm-bearer who died in 1313 A. H. in the service of the Mameluk Sultan of Egypt, Al-Nasr Muhammad. Height about 30 cm.

78. Saudi guards in front of the " Salutation Gate ", the ceremonial gate on the western façade of the Apostle's mosque. The Turkish ceramic tiles, covered with flowers and inscriptions, bear the name of the Sultan-caliph Suleyman, and must therefore date from the renovations made in 940 A. H. (1534 A. D.).

extreme pietists, had never abandoned their apparently desperate struggle against the " godless " caliphs. Revolt was also brewing in Khorassan, where the 'Alids and the descendents of 'Abbas, one of Muhammad's uncles, had found support among the " Barbarians." In 132 A. H. Marwan II, the last of the Damascus 'Omayyads, suffered final defeat, and one of the 'Abbassid family, Abu al-'Abbas, assumed the caliphate.

He was installed at al-Hira, once the capital of the Lakhmid princes. Around him were his kinsmen, sitting on chairs. The 'Omayyads were allotted two cushions each, instead of the thrones they had been accustomed to use during the period of their rule. The Chamberlain made an unexpected announcement: " Prince of the Believers, there stands at thy gate, seeking entrance, a man riding upon a thoroughbred camel. He comes from the Hijaz, he is a negro, his face is veiled. He will not vouchsafe his name, nor lift his veil, unless it be in thy presence." The veiled man came in, looked with deliberation at the caliph, his surroundings and particularly at the 'Omayyads sitting on their cushions. Then he spoke these verses:

> Lo, our state is now based on solid ground...
> O thou who commands the blameless hosts, O leader of leaders!
> Beware of an error... cut the accursed tree at its root and branches!
> Mow them, O Caliph, let thy sword save thee from this impure stock!
> O think of the prostrate Husain, think of Zayd!

These words stirred the fires of traditional Arab tribal revenge, even though this was forbidden by Islam. The 'Abbassid caliph was " suddenly wan and trembling. One of the 'Omayyads turned to the others and said: ' By my faith, this slave has spelt our doom.' Abu al-'Abbas was already crying: ' Criminal brood! I now see before me the images of all my kindred whom you have murdered in the past. That you should still breathe and enjoy life...! Fall upon them!' The Khorassanis did fall upon them, and beat them to death one by one with their clubs." Abu al-'Abbas asked for a carpet to be spread over the still quivering corpes, and ate a meal upon it with every sign of enjoyment. Then the 'Omayyad bodies were tossed into the street. The narrator of this episode adds: " Methinks I still can see the dogs dragging them by their brocade-clad legs." [53]

The second period of the " dark night " prophesied by Muhammad had fallen upon Islam.

THE DEVELOPMENT OF MOSLEM CULTURE

As belief in Islam spread across the world Muhammad's humanistic faith came into contact with the doctrines of older religions. The 'Omayyad caliphs had lived in Palestine and Syria, the countries of Judaism and of Eastern Christianity. When the 'Abbassids came to power, the centre of the Moslem world shifted to the ancient ground of Zoroastrianism. Like the 'Alids, the 'Abbassids also had found eager supporters in Khorassan, the region between Iran and Turkestan, inhabited by a mixed Iranian and Turkish population. From there, Islam began to extend towards the borders of Europe, along the Volga to the Slavonic lands and to the Turks who lived there. At the other end of Asia, the Turkish mystics took Islam as far as China. On the way, Islam came into contact not only with Buddhism in Central Asia, but also with Taoism on the confines of China.[54]

After the fourth century A. H. the Near East recovered its lost hold over the Moslems, when Islamic teachers discovered Alexandrian Neoplatonism. Moslem philosophers hailed Socrates as the prophet of his time. In this maelstrom of intellectual currents, Muhammad's views were challenged. Heretical Moslem sects revived the religions of Zoroaster, Manes and Mazdak, endangering Islamic monotheism. It was also menaced equally by the extremism of formalists, who insisted that the Qoran should be interpreted literally, and by the insidious incredulity of the sceptics. The essentially liberal nature of Muhammad's teaching, however, allowed Islam to survive all these dangers.

Near the ruins of the Sassanid capital Ctesiphon, in a setting where successive cultures had previously flourished, the 'Abbassid caliphs founded a new city, Baghdad. It was designed according to a cosmographic plan by Central Asian astrologers who had formerly belonged to the Buddhist faith. The centre of this artificial universe was the "Green Dome," as the caliph's residence was called. Here sat "the Prince of the Believers," surrounded by a cosmopolitan court. No doubt he gave little thought to the arid valley which had been the home of his Qorashi ancestors. For his devotions he contented himself with a model of the Ka'bah constructed in the nearby city of Samarra. This second great 'Abbassid city had been built, somewhat paradoxically, largely by the pagan Turks belonging to the Caliph's retinue. Great care was taken to isolate them, however, adds the Arab historian Ya'qubi, so that they should not contaminate the Moslems.[55]

In 305 A. H. (917 A. D.), during the reign of Muqtadir Billah, two ambassadors came to Baghdad from the Byzantine emperor Constantine VII. The magnificence of the reception that awaited them gives some idea of life at the Baghdad court

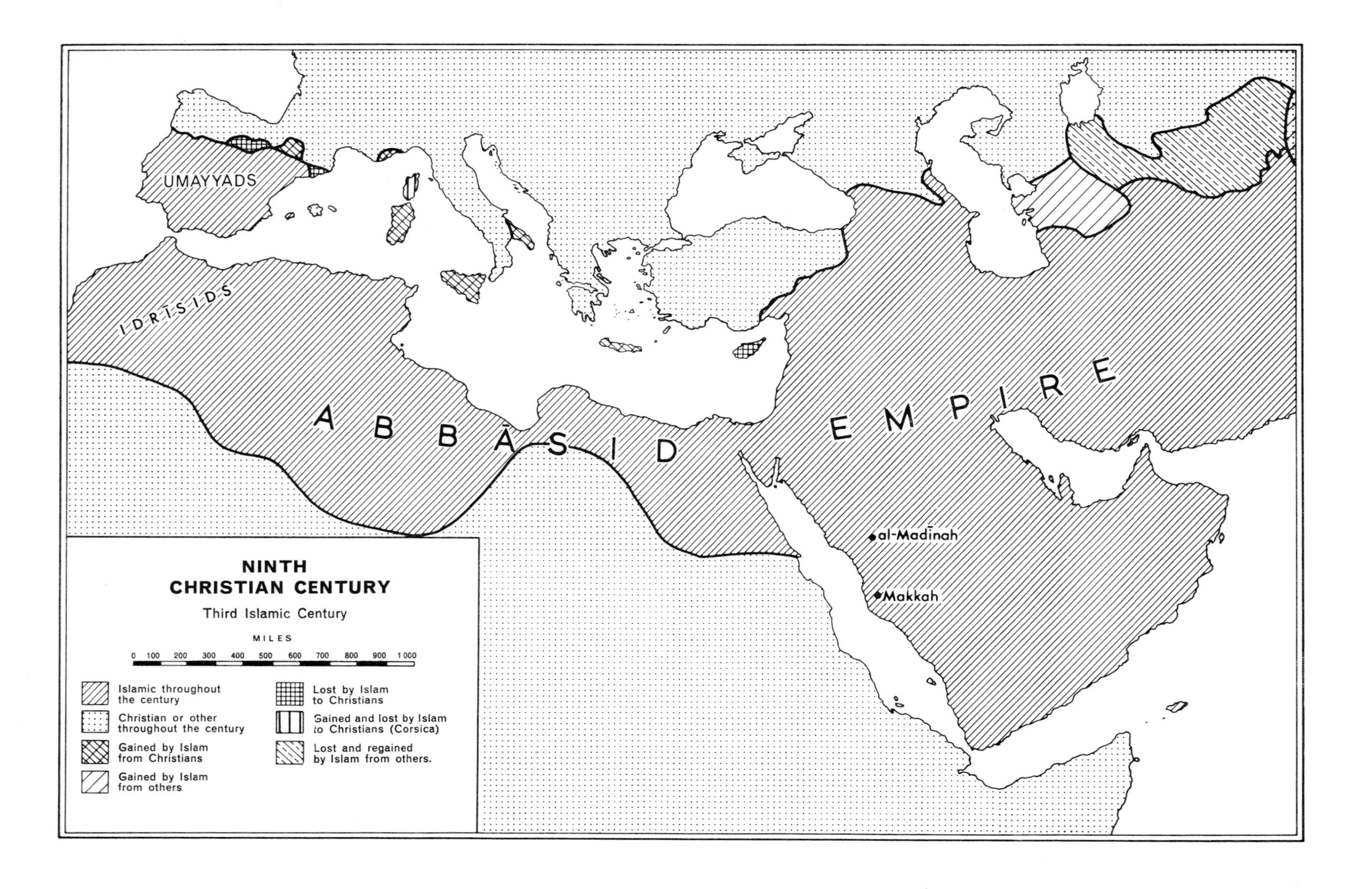
UMAYYADS
IDRĪSIDS
ABBĀSID EMPIRE
al-Madīnah
Makkah
NINTH
CHRISTIAN CENTURY
Third Islamic Century
MILES
0 100 200 300 400 500 600 700 800 900 1 000
Islamic throughout the century
Christian or other throughout the century
Gained by Islam from Christians
Gained by Islam from others
Lost by Islam to Christians
Gained and lost by Islam to Christians (Corsica)
Lost and regained by Islam from others.

during the time of the "Arabian Nights" caliphs. On leaving their residence, the ambassadors went to fetch their horses, which were housed in the Caliph's stables. They found " a large hall with porticoes, and marble columns. Here were, on one side, five hundred horses, wearing saddles decorated in gold and silver... On the opposite side were another five hundred steeds, all wearing cloths of patterned silk. Each horse had its groom. Then the ambassadors were conducted, on horseback, to an enclosure which was reserved for tamed beasts. Animals of many species drew near and ate out of people's hands. After that, they were taken to a house where eight elephants and their grooms lived, together with two giraffes, the sight of which caused the two envoys to take fright. Next they rode to an enclosure where there were about a hundred ravenous and ferocious beasts, held by their tamers on iron chains round their necks... Then they came to a pavilion set among orchards, where there was a pond, lined with lead that gleamed more perfectly than polished silver. Beyond this, there was another garden where there grew four hundred date-palms, all of equal height." Each one had a teakwood frame round its trunk, to protect it. " Various species of dates hung in abundant clusters from the trees. Round the edge of the garden stood tall citron-trees, all bearing fruit.

" Leaving this garden, they entered the... ' Edenic Palace.'

" Here there were collections of curios and vast quantities of patterned fabrics... bearing designs of cups, and figures of animals such as camels, elephants and beasts of prey; there were curtains of Chinese silk, and tissues from Armenia and Wasit, woven with bands of inscriptions." Through the long corridors of the Palace the ambassadors walked between two rows of black eunuchs, two thousand in all. On the walls were " five thousand suits of golden armour... a thousand shields, helmets, coats of mail, cuirasses, ornate quivers, and bows... After passing through thirteen successive mansions, they came to a courtyard... where there were pages, clad either in armour or in handsome garments, holding clubs and hatchets in their hands. The envoys passed in review a detachment of soldiers in black uniform...

" They entered the 'Abode of Peace '... Here also there were numerous soldiers originating from Slavonic regions. They served water and fruit juices." The ambassadors were now constantly attended by eunuchs, who walked beside them carrying refreshments. " They had to sit and rest at seven different places on the way... The chamberlains ushered them through many passages and courtyards, all crowded with eunuchs and soldiers, until they arrived at the ' Crown Palace,' situated on the banks of the Tigris, where the caliph was enthroned...

" The monarch was dressed in gold brocade tissue... He wore a tall brimless hat. Nine necklaces, resembling rosaries, were hung on the right of the throne. Another nine ornaments, with even larger and more brilliant gems, the splendour of which eclipsed the moon and the sun, hung on the left. The officers of the bodyguard were present, aligned according to their rank... The vizier faced the caliph, while the chief eunuch ... and the subordinate eunuchs stood beside the monarch. When the two envoys came in, they kissed the ground, greeted the caliph, and stood in the places indicated by the head chamberlain. The caliph ordered that the cupola should be unveiled and the artificial tree set going; by various devices, the tree was made to emerge from the ground until it filled the whole of the cupola, gushing streams of rose-and-musk water. The artificial birds on the tree began to twitter." [56]

Oriental tales relate that some time at the end of the third century A. H., the eminent Turkish philosopher and musician Muhammad Farabi came to the caliph's audience-hall. On the strings of an instrument, as yet unknown in Baghdad, the psaltery (*qanun*), the Moslem Orpheus played with such virtuosity that he made the caliph and his courtiers smile, weep or dream, at will. Farabi had written a treatise in emulation of Plato's *Republic*, in which he had set out the Islamic ideal of a Virtuous City, comparing it to the human soul. In his music there was no doubt a nostalgic echo of Madinah, the Apostle's city.

Each year the pilgrims of Baghdad formed a caravan, sometimes led by the caliph, and set off across the Tigris, southwards to the Hijaz, along the road built by the 'Abbassid princess Zubaidah in the second century A. H. This charming and cultured woman, the grand-daughter of the caliph Mansur, was married to her handsome cousin the Caliph Harun al-Rashid. In spite of her upbringing amid the extravagance of the 'Abbassid court, where dancing, drinking, and other forbidden pleasures were commonplace, Zubaidah's devotion to Islam caused her to render great service to the Hijaz. According to legend this came about in a dramatic way: Zubaidah was once holding a cup of wine, when from the minarets of the caliph's metropolis on the Tigris there rose the Muhammadan call to prayer. Suddenly the princess was touched by faith, and the glass fell from her hands.

When the caravans arrived in Madinah, the pilgrims found very little had changed since the time of the 'Omayyad. The second century caliph al-Mahdi had enlarged the area of the sanctuary by an addition of fifteen pillars on the north-east side. The mother of Harun al-Rashid had presented red and violet silk covers, embroidered with pearls, to the Prophet's grave, and a lady-in-waiting had the permanent task of renewing the aromatic herbs in the casket that stood at his head.

The 'Abbassids felt ill at ease in Madinah, where the descendants of 'Ali continued to live, for it was still thought by many that the 'Alids had been tricked out of their rightful claim to the caliphate. In 145 A. H. there had been an 'Alid uprising in Madinah, supported by two of the most eminent canonists, the Imam Malik ibn Anas (90-178 A. H.) and the Imam Abu Hanifah (80-150 A. H.). The first of these had always lived in Madinah. He taught that in disputed matters, the Prophet's example always outweighed the uncertainty of personal judgment. Students came to him from all over the Islamic world, and particularly from North Africa and Andalusia. Abu Hanifah was probably a Persian. His view was that the dictates of conscience were of paramount importance, even coming before Islamic tradition. It is said that Abu Hanifah had foretold the Turks' gradual rise to power in the Islamic states; he had a great following in Turkestan, and in Khorassan and Iraq also. Both imams had been ill-treated by the 'Omayyads because they had refused to accept offices conferred on them by these rulers, whom they considered tyrants. The 'Abbassids persecuted them also; it is thought, in fact, that Abu Hanifah died in prison as the result of a flogging.

Led by dignitaries clad in black, their dynastic colour, the 'Abbassid caravan entered Mecca a few days before the annual celebration of Abraham's sacrifice. Caravans also came from Egypt and Khorassan, but not from Andalusia, which was still under 'Omayyad rule. The leaders of the processions brought alms to the needy of the Hijaz and presents to the Ka'bah from the kings who reigned in their regions. Among other gifts the caliph sent the curtain for the Ka'bah, which was changed at least once a year.

Some of the presents brought by the foreigners were seen by the watching crowd of Meccans. In 197 A. H. Baghdad sent a trophy, the throne that had belonged to the King of Kabul, a Turkish Buddhist who had succeeded the Kushan emperors. The following year, another rich gift was set up in one of the squares in Mecca: a statue of gold, seated on a square silver throne upon a silk carpet decorated with small gold and silver bells. A herald stood beside this effigy, proclaiming that as God had guided the King of Tibet to embrace the Islamic faith, the sovereign had sent the idol he had formerly worshipped as an offering to the Ka'bah.[57]

The population of the holy city had become cosmopolitan, for many pious Moslems from remote countries had come to settle, or at least to stay for long periods, in the country of Muhammad. Fervent believers would walk all the way to the Hijaz, across mountains, plains and deserts.

In the 'Abbassid period, it became possible to determine the origin or social conditions of various people by the style of their clothes or the colours they wore. The 'Abbassids themselves and their adherents wore the black garments that had once been the pietists' sign of protest against the 'Omayyads. As the 'Abbassids had adopted this dress, it was withdrawn from the 'Alids, who were made to wear green coats and turbans. Ordinary Moslems wore white. The canonists had large turbans, wide sleeves to their coats and scarves (*taylasan*) across their shoulders.

Among this last-mentioned group were some of the most distinguished authors of their time. This was the age of the two Azraqis (" The Blue-Eyed "), grandfather and grandson, descendants of the Ghassanid princes and chroniclers of Mecca, and of the Central Asian Imam Bukhari, all of whom have frequently been quoted in the preceding pages. At this time, too, Ahmad ibn Hanbal, an elderly and timid scholar, could be found in Mecca; born in Baghdad, of Arab stock, this teacher put his greatest trust, above Prophetic tradition and personal conscience, in the Qoranic text. He maintained that the Qoran, as a manifestation of the Divine Word, must have been in existence for all time, and for this an 'Abbassid caliph, who held contrary beliefs, had him prosecuted.

Towards the end of the second century A. H. the pillared halls of the Ka'bah sheltered the Qorashi Imam Muhammad ibn Idris Shafi'i. As a child in Mecca, he had proved himself an infant prodigy in learning, and thereafter had hardly ever left the holy precincts. His doctrine was that the Moslem should be guided by the combination of Qoranic revelation, Prophetic example and personal judgment. This truly Muhammadan moderation earned him great admiration among his own countrymen and in Khorassan.

There were also many great mystics in the holy city during the second and third centuries after the Hegira. Those who were not natives of the Hijaz often took years to accomplish their pilgrimage, alternating steps with prostrations all the way. They came, not so much in search of formal instruction, as of " knowledge through the heart " and the spiritual illumination of the " Radiant Lustre," as the Qoran calls Muhammad. Like the Apostle, they insisted on meditating completely in the abstract, free from all worldly sensation. They were usually of a retiring nature and it was difficult to recognise them. A carpenter at work in the darkness of a hospice cell might well be Ibrahim Adham, the prince of Khorassan who had suddenly been touched by divine grace while on a hunting party, and had thereupon chosen to become a hermit. Another Khorassani, Bayazid of Bistam, the grandson of a Magi, called " the splendid beggar" because of his haughty disposition, was a monist. At his first visit to Mecca, after undertaking a long pilgrimage, he had felt himself to be unworthy to enter Muhammad's birthplace and dared to come no further than the outskirts of the city. Another monist, Mansur, who adopted the humble trade of carder and wandered the streets with his crescent-shaped comb, was executed in 261 A. H. for having uttered a major heresy: " I am the Truth." But the saints did not only come from Asia; in the third century A. H. a great African mystic, the Nubian Dhu al-Nun, walked from the sources of the Nile to the Hijaz.

79. The interior of the Apostle's mosque in Madinah. The arcades in the foreground are modern, and those in the background are Ottoman. The " Green Dome " and the " Head Minaret " are seen at the south-eastern corner.

Among the long-robed and veiled women who came to the Ka'bah was Rab'iah al-'Adawiyah, the poetess of divine love. She had been born in a poor family of Basrah and sold as a slave, but when her master noticed her assiduous devotions he set her free. She chose to live as a vegetarian hermit amongst the wild creatures

80 81

of the desert. To God, the constant friend of the "solitary old woman," as she called herself, she said:

> In two ways have I loved Thee, selfishly,
> And with a love that is worthy of Thee.
> In selfish love my joy in Thee I find.
> While to all else and other, I am blind.
> But in that love which seeks Thee worthily,
> The veil is raised that I may look on Thee.

To "raise the veil" separating humanity from Divinity, Rabi'ah dragged herself along the ground from 'Arafat to Mecca, but God admonished her for her excessive saintly ambition.[58]

The road she followed between 'Arafat and Mecca had been repaired by the 'Abbassids. A mosque was built at Mina, and another in the clearing near 'Aqabah (*ill.* 47) where Muhammad had pledged himself to the Madinese. ('Abbas, the ancestor of the caliphs, had been present at this momentous ceremony.) Just outside the Mina gorge, a mosque was built at al-Khaif, where the Apostle was said to have camped once in a tent (*ill.* 110).

One of the great benefits brought to Mecca by Zubaidah had been the construction of a water course from Hunain, a considerable distance away on the road towards Taif, to the Meccan valley. The hated urn installed by the 'Omayyad had been removed, and in its stead the city had a large number of troughs and fountains.

Many charitable institutions had been built for pilgrims from Iraq, Khorassan and India, designed in the styles native to these regions.

Two of the city's most venerated monuments—the house where Muhammad had been born, and the building containing the cellar in which the first Moslems had held their secret religious services—were turned into mosques. The cost of this work was borne by Harun al-Rashid's mother.

Harun al-Rashid himself had a palace overlooking the Ka'bah, which was called the "Crystal House."

Another famous building, a centre of cultural life at that time, was the Barmakids' mansion. This had been bought by Zubaidah after the last of the Barmakid dynasty had been murdered, on the orders of Harun al-Rashid, because he was secretly married to the caliph's sister.

The house where Qusayy had lived, to the north of the Ka'bah, had at last been demolished and rebuilt. It was now a splendid edifice, 65 × 84 ells in area, and consisting of sumptuous colonnaded halls, with a gilded ceiling. Lamps hung on chains along its façade, lighting up the mosque's courtyard at night.

The wall round the Ka'bah was built up to about 22 ells in height, and embellished with bartizans. There were five minarets, perhaps in the spiral shape of the minaret constructed on the Samarra mosque. Twenty-three arched gates and descending flights of steps led into the courtyard, which had now been enlarged, on the orders of successive caliphs, to an area of 407 × 208 ells. The caliph who had taken the closest interest in this work was al-Mahdi, who reigned from 158 to 169 A. H. He had come to Mecca and superintended the proceedings himself, going to the top of Mount Abu Qubais to ensure that the Ka'bah was at the exact centre of the courtyard. To effect the enlargements, further expropriations had had to be made—notably the house which had belonged to 'Ali's sister, where Qusayy was buried.

Three rows of covered arcades surrounded the court, built on marble or stone columns. In 222, some yellow stone columns were put there which had come

80. Northern façade of the Apostle's mosque, at dawn-prayer, when the minarets are still lighted.

81. A bastion which has survived from the chain of forts that surrounded Madinah until quite recently.

from Samarra, given by the victorious commander of the Moslem expedition against Babak the Heretic in Armenia. The walls and paths were inlaid with polychrome marbles, and green marble was used to pave the area to the east of the Ka'bah where Ishmael's arbour had stood. The stone which bore the imprint of Abraham's feet was gilded and placed under a wooden cupola, to protect it from the weather. Round the Ka'bah, wooden pillars were erected and lamps were suspended from them.

More changes had also been made in the Ka'bah itself, necessitated by the perennial flooding and other accidents. The top of the " House " was covered with green marble. The silver gate was plated with gold, and a key was made

Eighteenth century Turkish compass showing the direction of the Ka'bah.

for it, bearing a Qoranic verse in gold inlay work. A decorative band of gold embossing, about an ell wide, ran round the inside walls, and the same embossing was used to replace the shells round the entablature windows. A red silk curtain was hung round the building, painted with pious inscriptions in gold.

The Baghdad branch of the 'Abbassids, ever devoted to the pursuit of pleasure, declined steadily in power until their end came in 656 A. H. A courtier of al-Wathiq, who reigned from 227 to 232 A. H., has told a story which illustrates

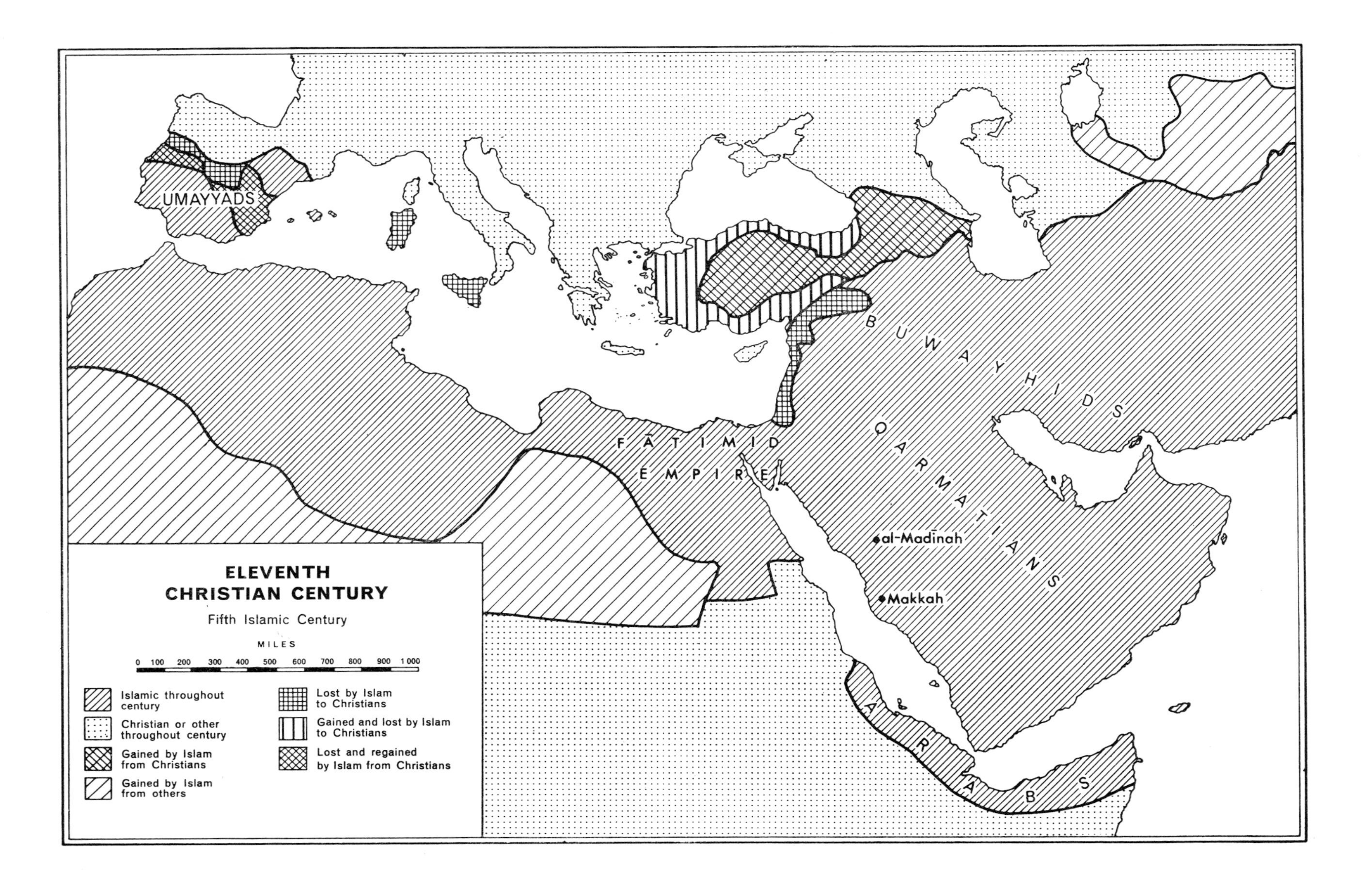
UMAYYADS
FĀTIMID EMPIRE
BUWAYHIDS
QARMATIANS
al-Madīnah
Makkah
ARABS
ELEVENTH CHRISTIAN CENTURY
Fifth Islamic Century
MILES
0 100 200 300 400 500 600 700 800 900 1 000
Islamic throughout century
Christian or other throughout century
Gained by Islam from Christians
Gained by Islam from others
Lost by Islam to Christians
Gained and lost by Islam to Christians
Lost and regained by Islam from Christians

how effete their society had become, and how powerless to resist the onrushing tide of events that eventually swept them to their doom. The narrator had been called to al-Wathiq's presence, late in the night. " The eunuchs showed me to a loggia where a carpet had been spread on the floor and where the walls were decorated with draperies in gold brocade... Al-Wathiq was there, seated on a throne inlaid with gems. He was wearing a robe of gold brocade. Beside him sat his slave-girl, Faridah the singer; she was dressed like him and held a lute in her lap. When he saw me, the Caliph exclaimed: ' By my faith, it is good of you to have come... Approach! ' I kissed the ground. He told me to sit and ordered for me a measure of wine in a cup. Faridah began to sing:

> ' I dread you, imbued with reverence, yet you have no power over me,
> My soul flees not from you, O Lailah, nor does it belittle you,
> Although it has received but little of your favour.'

She sang bewitchingly... Quit unexpectedly, the Caliph stretched out his foot and hit Faridah on the breast with such violence that she fell from the throne and her lute was broken in pieces. She ran away weeping, and I sat there aghast, afraid that he had noticed I admired her... He paused, as if in doubt, his eyes fixed to the floor, then he called me. ' My lord,' I said, ' I am in great anxiety.' He replied: ' No, no, I only thought that Ja'far (his brother and later his successor) will also sit in this alcove one day and that she will sit beside him... I could not bear this idea.' I interposed: ' God will surely kill Ja'far and my lord will live for ever.' He sent a eunuch to Faridah and she came after a while, carrying a new lute, and having changed her gown... They both wept and he repeated to her what he had told me... The Caliph made a sign... They brought a jewel-case. He opened it and took out a necklace with a pendant the like of which I have never seen. He put it round Faridah's neck.

" Then destiny struck at al-Wathiq (he was murdered, at the age of thirty-three) and his brother became the caliph al-Mutawwakil...Again I was called and, by God, I was ushered into the same apartment. Al-Mutawakkil sat on the same throne, with the same Faridah beside him. When he saw me he exclaimed: ' My dear man, you cannot know how she vexes me! I have been insisting all the morning that she should sing, but she refuses! ' ' Faridah,' I said, trying to reason with her, ' you are contradicting your lord, my lord, the lord of the world.' Thereupon she sang:

> ' Leave me not, for every youth will encounter death,
> Perchance on a night, perchance on a morn.'

" Then she shattered her lute and fled in tears. ' Confound her,' said the Caliph, ' what does this mean? ' ' I know not, my lord,' I replied." [59]

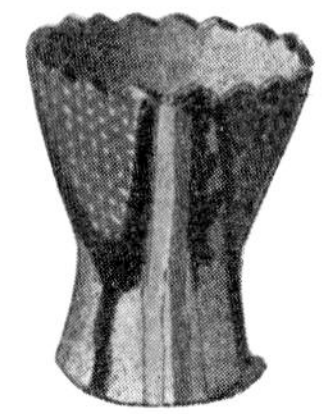

83

84

ISLAM IN CONFLAGRATION

Four centuries after the death of Muhammad, the Islamic world was in the throes of internal sectarian dissension and external warfare. After the Council of Clermont in 1095 A. D. (486 A. H.), European Christianity took up arms for the long battle to redeem the sepulchre of Christ. The Franks invaded the Near East. In 408 A. H., the Cathayans (Kara-Khitay) had attacked the Kara-hanli Turkish ruler, newly converted to Islam, in his capital of Balasagun, in the hope that with the help of the pagan, Buddhist and Manichean Turks, they would be able to recover Central Asia from the power of Islam. By 531 A. H., their dominion extended as far as Khorassan. Behind them, a century later, came a more redoubtable conqueror, Jenghiz Khan, with his Mongol hordes. The once flourishing centres of Moslem civilisation in Turkestan and Khorassan became smoking ruins. Those who managed to escape the wholesale massacres fled across the desert southwards and westwards, as the Mongols moved on to capture the seat of the caliphate, Baghdad.

In the fifth century A. H., some Moslem Turkish tribes left Turkestan and settled in large colonies in the Islamic lands. Successive Turkish immigrations produced great changes in the ethnical composition of vast areas of the Near East, including the Anatolian province of the Near Eastern Roman Empire, in Azerbaijan and in northern Iraq. Culturally and politically, these immigrations had very far-reaching consequences.

The cultural influences that through the ages had trickled from Western Asia now came in a great tide. As in Parthian times, the vigorous artistic genius of the Eurasian nomad appeared again on the Near Eastern scene, and meeting the inspiration of Islamic tradition, evolved new concepts of art. A new form of architecture grew up, transforming the appearance of Baghdad and Cairo, and, to judge from historical reports, those of Mecca and Madinah also. It was introduced by builders such as Karakush (in Turkish, " the Eagle"), who rose to fame in the sixth century A. H. Everywhere theological schools appeared, with cloisters and cells like the Buddhist monasteries of Central Asia, and cupolas shaped like the calices of lotus-blossoms, as on stupas. The ogival Buddhist arch, already introduced in the 'Omayyad period, now came into common use, and stalactite decoration, also imported from the Kara-hanli regions of Central Asia, appeared on Near Eastern cupolas. Round and polygonal minarets were built, fluted and decorated with leaf-patterns rather like Central Asian stupas, but in the tall and slender form of the date-palm trunk against which Muhammad had leaned in the

82. The interior of the Apostle's mosque.

83. A gold casket for the Apostle's mantle, decorated with inscriptions in black enamel repeating the credo of Islam. It is Turkish, and dates from about the sixteenth century. 70 × 70 × 97 cm.

84. A painting representing Muhammad's footprint, and the emblems of the Ottoman dynasty.

mosque. The brickwork on the walls of sacred buildings formed designs as in the Prophet's mosque, but was worked into elaborate pious quadrangular inscriptions somewhat in the style of the square seals made in China and Eastern Turkestan. Figures also began to be seen on the walls of Islamic buildings—seated, Buddha-like personages, angels reminiscent of Buddhist apsaras, warriors wearing the pointed helmets and horizontally woven coats of mail of the Turks, and the heraldic animal emblems of the Eurasian nomads. Those representations, so incongruous in Islamic lands, never reached the hallowed region of the Hijaz.[60]

The principal " arts of the pagan Cathayans "—that is, painting in general and book-painting in particular—did not penetrate these regions either, but they flourished at the courts of the Turkish princes. Another " Cathayan " art, at which the Uygur Turks were expert, was calligraphy; this, however, was easily adapted to orthodox use and was widely practised in Islam with Arabic characters that sometimes looked rather like Uygur letters, as for instance in tenth century Samarkand plates.

People no longer wore the loose draperies of the East, but the tight-fitting tunics, breeches and boots of colder climes. The " moon-faced " beauties of Cathay were much admired. Everyone drank China tea, and ate rice like the Chinese and the Turks. The Indian game of chess, introduced during the 'Abbassid period by the Turk al-Suli, became extremely fashionable.[61]

The immigrant Turks were an asset for the Islamic world in its struggles against the Crusaders and the Mongols. Near-Easterners looked with astonishment at their phenomenal physical vitality: " The Turk," said the third century Arabian historian al-Jahiz, " can drive his galloping horse up the slope of a mountain or down a precipice... If the Turkish rider seems to be fleeing, it means certain death for his opponent. He can aim his bow and arrow behind him as accurately as before him. He is also to be dreaded when he uses his lasso to overpower the adversary's horse and capture its rider... The Turk has two pairs of eyes, one at the front and one at the back." [62]

The Turks succeeded in establishing in 430 A. H. an empire bearing the name of Selçuk, one of their chiefs, and united Khorassan, Azerbaijan, Iran, Anatolia and Iraq under their aegis. In almost all the Islamic states Turkish praetorians managed to take the real power into their hands. The caliph of Baghdad, who had already lost his temporal powers to other princes, was placed under Selçuk protection. Egypt had already fallen under Turkish domination with the successive dynasties of the Tulunids (254-292 A. H.) and the Ikhshids (326-358 A. H.). These Turks then gave way to the Shiite dynasty of the Fatimids, who had taken the name of the Prophet's daughter in order to underline the legitimacy of their descent from 'Ali and Fatimah and thereby their claim to the caliphate. But the Fatimids were under the sway of their Turkish praetorians. It is said that in 444 A. H. (1052 A. D.), the Basileus Michael sent to the Caliph al-Mustansir " white partridges, white peacocks, white storks, white crows, white starlings... and Turkish slaves, all the same age, including Turkish girls." [63] In 567 A. H. the Fatimids at last collapsed under the pressure of the Turks and were succeeded by the Kurdish dynasty of the Ayyubids, whose greatest glory was Salah al-Din, or Saladin, so renowned in the Crusades.

In 648 A. H., Egypt and Syria came under the domination of a succession of Turks who had all been " Mameluks," or slaves, and had risen to power through merit and the opportunities afforded by the democratic structure of the Islamic social order. After 658 A. H., the Mameluks became the protectors of the 'Abbassid caliphs. The Turkish Mameluks were evicted in their turn by another group of ex-slaves, this time Circassians, but whose culture was nonetheless Turkish.

Taking advantage of the rivalry between the caliph of Baghdad and the Fatimid

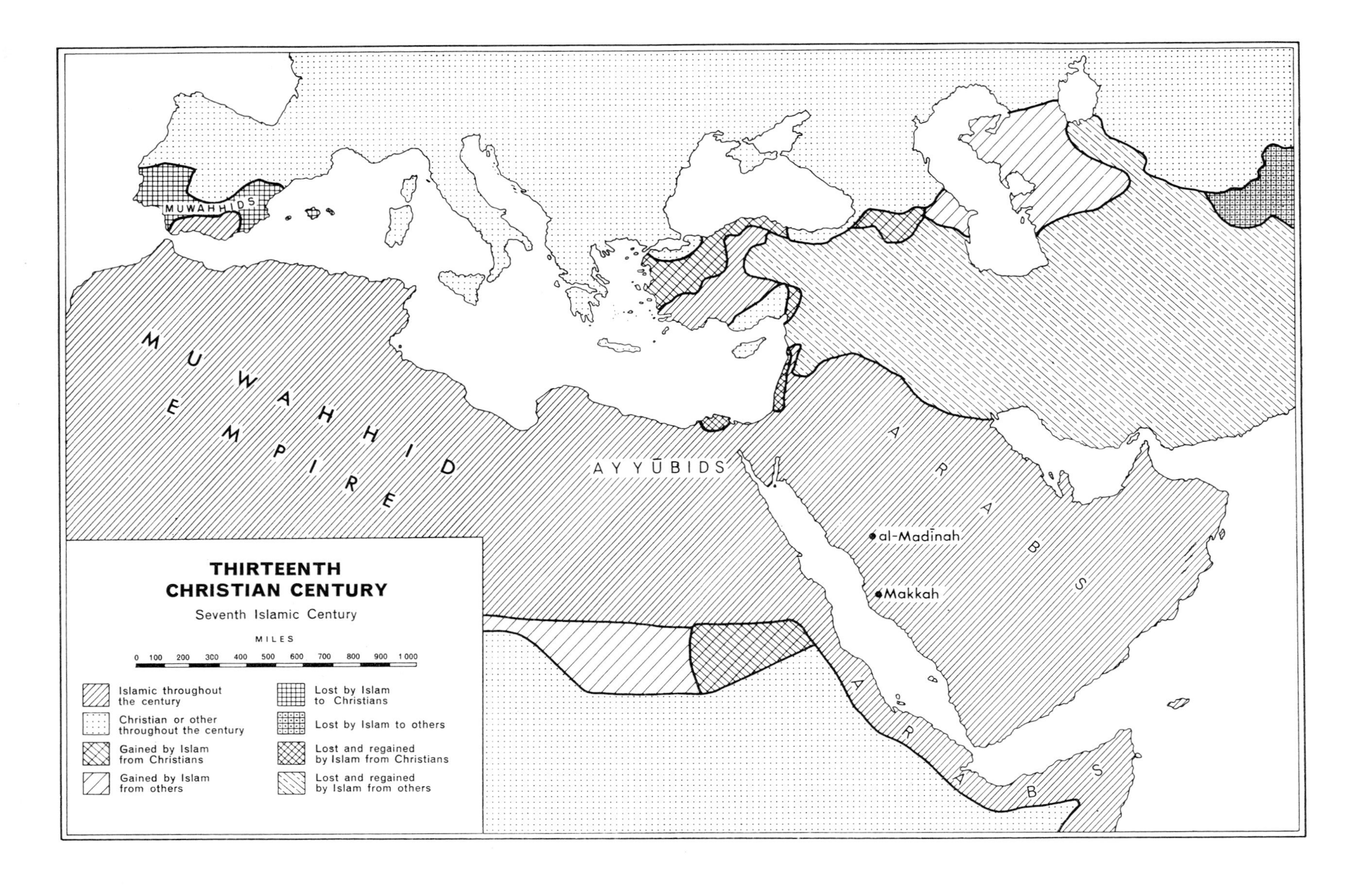
THIRTEENTH
CHRISTIAN CENTURY
Seventh Islamic Century
MILES
0 100 200 300 400 500 600 700 800 900 1 000
Islamic throughout the century
Christian or other throughout the century
Gained by Islam from Christians
Gained by Islam from others
Lost by Islam to Christians
Lost by Islam to others
Lost and regained by Islam from Christians
Lost and regained by Islam from others
MUWAHHIDS
MUWAHHID EMPIRE
AYYŪBIDS
ARABS
al-Madīnah
Makkah
ARABS

anti-caliph in Cairo, the 'Alids in the Hijaz had set themselves up in the fourth century A. H. as temporal rulers in the holy cities and the Yemen.

In 411 A. H., the Fatimids sent a Shiite teacher to the Prophet's mosque in Madinah. Sectarianism had never been introduced there, but now the Shiites gained the ascendancy and began to chase away the adherents of other sects. They took to holding a separate service within the Apostle's mausoleum, and it must have been this which gave rise to the idea of transporting Muhammad's body to a land where the Shiites were securely settled, such as Egypt. Such intentions were voiced more than once, in the Fatimid period and under the 'Alid claimant to the caliphate Abu al-Futuh (384-430 A. H.). Tradition relates that the would-be perpetrators of this sacrilege never achieved their aim because they either met a violent death or were too overcome with awe to make the attempt.

An endeavour to carry away the Prophet's remains was however made in 557 A. H. (1162 A. D.) by the Franks. The plot was discovered through Nur al-din Zengi, a Turkish prince who had won fame in the wars against the Crusaders. He was in Aleppo, keeping a vigil, when he saw a vision in which Muhammad showed him two tall, red-faced men, and said to him: " Help, Nur al-Din! ". The pious knight immediately rode to Madinah, where he found the two tall men. Under the pretext of being pilgrims, they had settled there and excavated an underground tunnel to Muhammad's grave. They had very nearly reached their goal, as Nur al-Din discovered when he went along the tunnel with a lamp. After this alarm, a deep moat was dug round the Prophet's grave and filled with lead. One of Nur al-Din's retinue built a lattice of ebony and sandalwood round the double walls of the funeral chamber. The prince appointed twelve old men to guard the sepulchre day and night. Probably chosen from among his palace eunuchs, they had memorised the Qoran and were well known for their piety. They came from non-Moslem lands, where mutilation was not forbidden, such as Anatolia, India or Ethiopia.

Madinah was not very far from the scene of battle between the Saracens, as the Moslems were called, and the Crusaders. It was for that reason that Nur al-Din, and other princes before him, had taken care to raise the fortifications around the Prophet's city, until it had taken on the aspect of other mediaeval towns. In spite of these defences, the Crusaders did prepare to attack Madinah in 578 A. H. The Frankish knight Raynald of Chatillon and his soldiers landed at Yanbu', the sea port for Madinah, and began to advance inland, but a nephew of Saladin managed to repel the invasion.

In 654 A. H. (1256 A. D.), the Madinese thought that Doomsday had arrived. The clear sky darkened ominously and a terrifying roar was heard, like the crashing of a thousand thunderbolts. The noise continued until the evening and the ground began to shake. As the livid sun set and a pallid moon rose, a blinding yellow flash appeared in the east. In the sky the Madinese saw a vision of a glowing red city, complete even to the battlements of the castles. Then the city seemed to melt into a stream of fire, a stream which flowed for months, consuming and carrying with it the trees and rocks which were in its path. The Madinese, who had gathered in the mosque and clutched in fear and supplication the railings of the Prophet's mausoleum, thought that this must be the " fire in the Hijaz " that Muhammad had predicted. Gradually the earthquakes ceased and after some months the lava, which luckily had flowed to the east and north, away from Madinah, cooled into rock.

In that same year, the mosque was damaged by fire. Candles were lit on the balconies of the minarets to celebrate the month of fasting, and by some mischance the wooden parts of the building caught light. Everything which remained from the time of Muhammad, as well as from the periods of the first four caliphs and the 'Omayyads, was reduced to rubble. The Apostle's bench, a venerated relic, was completely consumed. The only part of the mosque that miraculously remained intact was a small domed pavilion in the centre of the sandy courtyard, built by the last caliph of Baghdad, where 'Othman's Qoran, other precious objects and the mosque candles were kept.

Child dressed as angel, carrying a taper to the Prophet's Mosque in mediaeval Madinah.

The Madinese regarded the earthquake followed by the fire as dreadful precursors of Islam's downfall. Indeed, only two years later the capital of the 'Abbassids was left in flaming ruins by the Mongol invasion. There seemed to be nothing to stop them from advancing as far as the holy land of Islam.

In 658 the unexpected miracle happened. The Turkish Mameluks, some of whom had been sold into slavery by the Mongols themselves, managed to halt the invaders in Syria.

Once the danger was averted, it was time for the Moslems to put their own house in order again. The Prophet's mosque in Madinah had remained unrepaired for twenty years; a wooden ceiling and five layers of waxed cloth had been placed over Muhammad's tomb, but that was all. Renovations were at last begun in 668 by Baypars (in Turkish, " the Lord Panther "), the Sultan of Egypt, who had fought in the victorious engagement against the Mongols. It was not until 678, however, in the time of the Mameluk Kalaun, that a wooden dome on an octagonal drum was built over the burial chamber.

Considerable repair work was again effected in 896 and 897, under the Circassian Sultan of Egypt, Qayit Bay, who sent his architect Shams al-Zaman to Madinah. The double walls round the Prophet's mausoleum had been so badly damaged that they had to be demolished. For the first time since the 'Omayyad reconstructions, the place where Muhammad had died and been buried lay open to view. Again the sweet odour of saintliness pervaded the air. One of the authors to whom we owe much of our information about Madinah, Nur al-Din al-Samhudi, an 'Alid born in Egypt, was there at the time. He had implored the architect not to destroy the original interior wall of the mosque, but in vain. Samhudi fulfilled an official function in the mosque, and in this capacity he had to witness the repairs that were made. He entered the burial chamber with his eyes closed, and only opened them after he had mentally asked the Prophet's forgiveness. He looked around but saw no sign of a mound; evidently the sand had subsided with time. From tradition, however, Samhudi knew that Muhammad's grave was close to the southern wall, and with this knowledge three new mounds were made for the Apostle and his two companions.

The old walls were restored, but the chamber was shortened on the northern side, so that it was now square. Upon this base, and covering the former ceiling, a high dome was built. As it was plated with polished lead, it shone in the sun and the mausoleum was thereafter known as the White Dome, or the Blue Dome. While the work was in progress, a grave was found under the floor of Fatimah's room. This was presumed to be the tomb of the Prophet's daughter herself, and a railing of iron and copper was set round this spot and the mausoleum of Muhammad. Arcades, glazed with stained glass, were also added to the eastern side, to enclose the mausoleum within the area of the mosque.

The rest of the building was made in black stone, with white stone for the columns. The walls were coated with stucco and painted with decorative motifs. The columns were ornamented with reliefs. Some of the floors and the roof terraces were flagged with polychrome marble. The *mihrab* was renewed.

The minarets were now square but tall, in the style of the Cairo Mameluk period. They had gradually been renovated and raised, until now they varied in height between fifty and ninety ells. Qayit Bay added a fifth minaret, over the western side of the mosque. After the year 700 A. H., it became the custom to end the call to prayer with salutations to the Apostle from all five minarets.

Near the mosque, Qayit Bay built a theological school, with lodgings for the students in the surrounding cloisters. The libraries of Madinah were filled with new manuscripts, to replace those lost in the fire. New hospices were also built, and presented with giant cauldrons in which to cook meals for the pilgrims. The Sultan had a watermill constructed, too, and a bath house with a hypocaust.

In order to diminish the sway of the Shiites in Madinah, the Mameluk appointed teachers from the orthodox sects to work there. With patience and forbearance they at length succeeded in re-establishing the orthodox creed in the Apostle's City.[64]

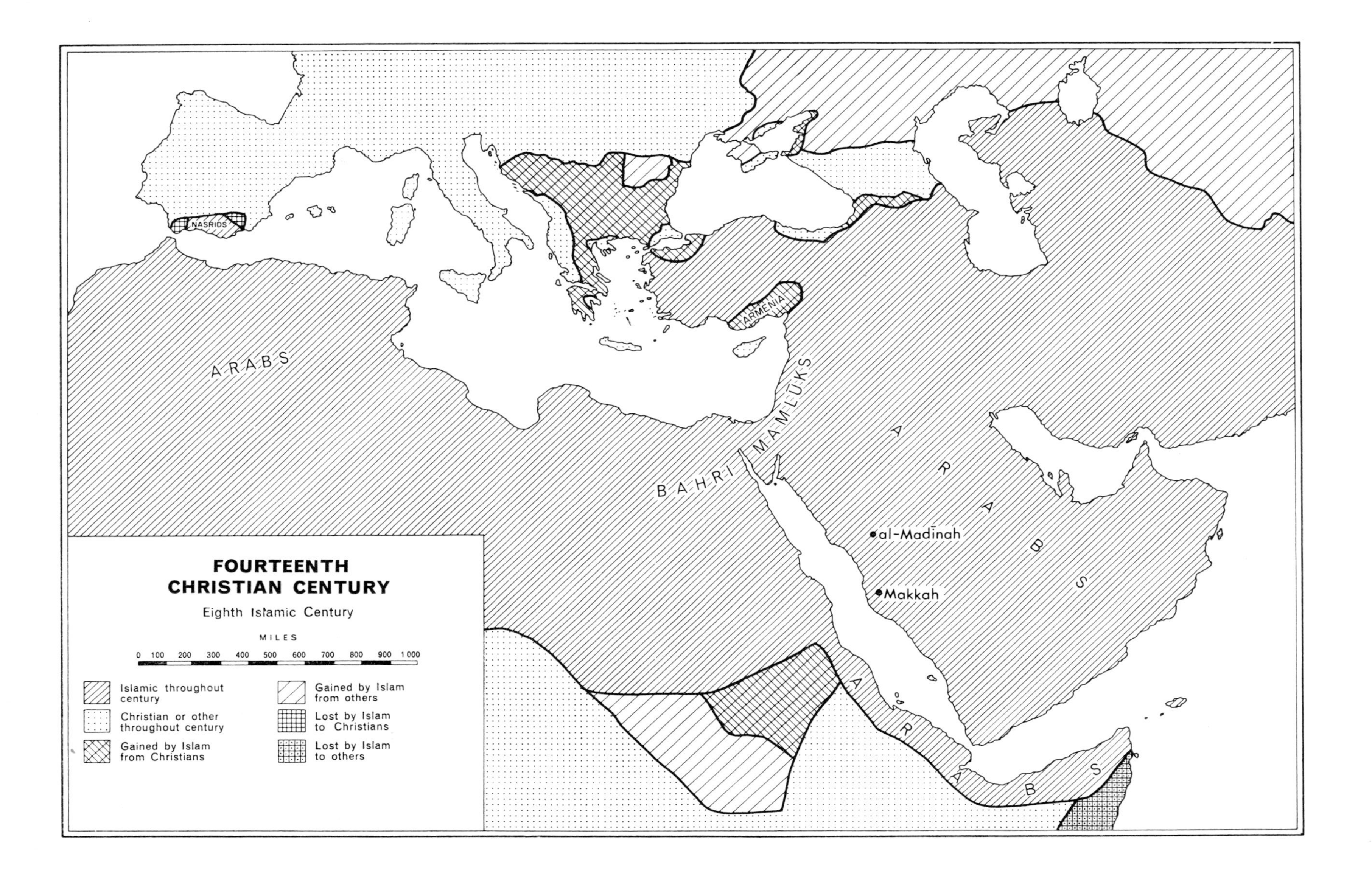
FOURTEENTH
CHRISTIAN CENTURY
Eighth Islamic Century
MILES
0 100 200 300 400 500 600 700 800 900 1 000
Islamic throughout century
Christian or other throughout century
Gained by Islam from Christians
Gained by Islam from others
Lost by Islam to Christians
Lost by Islam to others
NASRIDS
ARABS
ARMENIA
BAHRI MAMLUKS
ARABS
al-Madīnah
Makkah
ARABS

MECCA IN MEDIAEVAL TIMES

MECCA IS FURTHER south than Madinah and the sounds of warfare against the Crusaders and the Mongols did not penetrate there. But the quarrels of the " seventy-two sects," ruefully prophesied by Muhammad, raged through Mecca at the time of the annual pilgrimages.

As the moon of Dhu al-hijjah appeared in the Hijaz sky, the caravans of pilgrims would begin to arrive from every direction. At the various entrances to the holy territories they would stop to take their vows of pilgrimage and change into their penitential garb. Before the same dress was adopted by all Moslem pilgrims, the inhabitants of the Hijaz were able to see the varied splendour of costumes from India, Turkestan, Iran, Syria, Anatolia, Egypt and Africa.

A highly respected group were the 'Alids, in their green coats and turbans. They had formed a hereditary knighthood among themselves, based on the association of public-spirited citizens which Muhammad had joined as a young man. They took their knightly vows by dipping their fingers into a cup, and this vessel was emblazoned on their costume. The headquarters of their order was in Cairo.

Similar orders had grown up among the Turks of Anatolia. The Turkish knights, known as *Ahi*—" the Brethren," were not noblemen but ordinary people, mostly artisans, who had banded together to protect the oppressed against the tyranny of princes. These guilds, semi-religious in character, formed a network that challenged the authority of local lords. In the seventh and eighth centuries A. H., when Islamic principles were seriously endangered by the ideologies brought by the Mongol invasion, the Brethren founded a republic, modelled on Muhammad's ideal state of Madinah, in the ancient fortified city of Ankara. These modest men must have passed unnoticed in the crowd of pilgrims. Yet among them were men who were to leave their mark on Islamic culture, such as Bektash Veli, the eighth century A. H. Khorassani saint who founded a large religious sect in Anatolia, and became the patron of the Janissary corps. Bayram Veli, the saintly poet of Ankara, was also in the Brethren's group.

85. Turkish gold ewer for Zamzam water. The blue enamel inlay is studded with diamonds and rubies. Length 31 cm.

86. A pair of Turkish iron keys to the Ka'bah, inlaid with gold inscriptions from Qoran III, 195-6, and a dedication: " O God, Opener of gates, let us enter the gate of virtue. Presented in 910 A. H. (1504 A.D.) by the humble slave, the Sultan Bayezid Han, son of Mehmed Han ". Length 26 cm.

In contrast to their unobtrusive compatriots, the Turkish princes who now made their homes in all the lands of Islam remained faithful to the pomp of their warlike ancestors. Wherever they went, they were preceded by a fanfare, a sign of dignity conferred on their forefathers by the Emperor of China. Their banners and the ceremonial parasols which were held above their heads bore their heraldic symbols. These pictures, of lions, dragons, panthers, or falcons, represented the tribal or personal names of the princes who used them. The racial characteristics of the Turks

85 86

بسم الله الرحمن الرحيم فيه ايات بينات مقام ابرهيم ومن دخله كان امنا
محمد رسول الله

set them clearly apart from the Semite Arabs, the Africans and the dark-skinned, aquiline-nosed, hairy Iranians. At that time the " sons of Japhet," as the Turks were called, had the features of a mixed Mongolo-Caucasian race. They were sturdily built, large-faced and slant-eyed, but their skins were ruddy like the Caucasians, their eyes were sometimes blue and their hair blond. They wore boots and riding-breeches, and their Islamic turbans were occasionally decorated with horns, a token of the cult of animal-genii in their Northern Asian ancestry.[65]

Princesses also came on pilgrimage, dispensing largesse to the members of their caravan, to the desert Beduin and the Meccans. A Hamadan princess belonging to an Arab dynasty arrived in a file of four hundred camels, all the same colour and all bearing palanquins, so that it was impossible to know in which carriage she was concealed. Later it was said that she had thrown herself into the Tigris to escape the attentions of an unwelcome bridegroom. No matter how elegant the ladies who came on pilgrimage, the Meccans thought none could compare with their own 'Alid princess, the Lady Jumanah.

When the pilgrims had taken their vows, the caravans would enter the valley and pitch camp outside Mecca. The tents would be set out in rows, like streets. They were not only used for temporary dwelling-places: there would also be an oratory, a hospital, shops, restaurants, even a prison for possible delinquents. The " streets " were lit with torches. Beating a drum to attract attention, a crier would announce news of public interest. An embroidered cloth would be hung all the way round the encampment, in guise of a wall. When the camp had been pitched at each stopping-place along the way to Mecca, guards patrolled it all the time in case of attack by bandits, foraging Beduins or hostile Crusaders.

As the pilgrims entered Mecca, they would notice that the birth-place of Muhammad had acquired the look of a typical mediaeval town. On Abu Qubais there rose the castle of the Sharif. There were new hospices, built in the architectural styles of India and Anatolia, where Islam had started to spread. But, as in Madinah, most of the new buildings followed the contemporary Egyptian pattern, for the Mameluk Sultans of Egypt, being the Sharifs' overlords and the protectors of the 'Abbassid caliphs, had erected a great many monuments in the holy cities. One outstanding example was the Hanafi school of theology, with its cloistered lodges for students, built under the supervision of the Turk Sungur al-Jamali.

The house where Muhammad had been born, made into a mosque during the 'Abbassid period, had been destroyed and rebuilt. To indicate the exact spot where the birth had taken place, there was a square green marble basin, with a silver arch above it. It is not known whether special ceremonies took place here to mark the Apostle's birthday. In Fatimid Egypt, for instance, there were public processions on the anniversary of Muhammad's birth; the caliph would take part in these, as the Prophet's successor, wearing a veil over his face. The Anatolian Turks also celebrated the nativity with torchlight or candlelight processions, at least after the composition of Suleyman Çelebi's famous birthday hymn in the eighth century A. H.

In the Qoran, Muhammad is called " the Radiant Lustre," and since the third century A. H. all sources of light, from the moon and stars to a humble candle, seem to have been used in literature as symbols of the Apostle, and of his disciples who were consumed by the same flame of divine love. In art, the motif of the lamp appeared on sixth century Khorassani *mihrabs*. An eighth century Anatolian tombstone carries the image of a candle, and this emblem spread later to *mihrabs* and prayer carpets, mainly in Turkey but also in Mameluk Egypt. In the seventh century, the treatise by Abu al-Khattab ibn Dihyah entitled *The Book of Illumination on the Birth of the Radiant Lustre* confirmed the use of the candle in religious pro-

87. A Persian lustre tile from a mosque at Khonsar, near Kashan dating from about the fourteenth century, and inscribed: " Surely the believers enter..." 45×60 cm.

cessions. In Mecca, during Ramadan, children dressed as angels and with their eyes rimmed with kohl carried tall candelabra to the courtyard of the Ka'bah.

It is possible that the nativity ceremonies were introduced into the Hijaz in mediaeval times. The lord of Irbil Muzaffar al-Din Kökburi, a Turkish prince, as stated by his historian Ibn Khallikan, whose name means in Turkish "Celestial Wolf" (549-630 A. H.), was a frequent visitor to the region and had contributed to the project of bringing water to 'Arafat. Certainly he celebrated the anniversary at home in his city of Irbil, in Mesopotamia. Ibn Khallikan described the festival in these terms:—"Every year there came to Irbil an immense council of canonic scholars, mystics, preachers, Qoranic reciters and poets... The prince caused a score of wooden pavilions to be built... These four-and-five-storied pavilions were in a row, starting at the entrance to the castle and ending at the hippodrome, beside the gateway of the mystics' hospice... They were splendidly decked. Each had a company of vocalists and musicians, and a troop of illusionists to give puppet-shows... On the night of the nativity, after evening prayer, he (Kökburi) came out of the castle, preceded by a procession carrying countless tapers. Tree-shaped candelabra holding three or four candles were borne on the backs of mules, each of which was accompanied by its groom... He went thus to the gate of the mystics' hospice and attended religious performances (perhaps including sacred dances) to the sound of music. The next day the prince went to the hippodrome, where the lords, the white people (the notables), the army, the preachers were all gathered... A pulpit had been set up for the preacher and a wooden tower for Kökburi, with many windows which enabled him to see the crowds in the hippodrome. The lords took their places in the other wooden pavilions. A great banquet was served to the poor and clothing was distributed." That night the prince went again to the mystics' hospices, where there were more religious performances accompanied by music.[66]

In mediaeval times, the surroundings of the Ka'bah were also renovated. When the Hanafi school was built nearby, a sixth minaret was added to the mosque. The site of Ishmael's bower on the north-western façade was paved with lilac marble; only the funeral slabs of Ishmael and Hagar were left in green marble.

The various Islamic sects were separated in the temple, each one praying on a different side of the Ka'bah behind their own teacher, who would sit on a dais in front of a lamp which was coloured according to the sect. The Station of Abraham on the north-eastern side was reserved to the followers of the Qorashi Imam, Shafi'i. His congregation included the Sharif and the inhabitants of Mecca. The Mameluks had placed a seat facing Ishmael's arbour for the sect of Abu Hanifah, "the Turks' Imam."

When the pilgrimage rites began, the Sharif of Mecca, wearing white robes and a sword hanging from his neck as a token of submission to God, would make the circuit of the Ka'bah. A herald belonging to the Shafi'ites was posted on the roof of the mosque and every time the prince completed one circumambulation on the black marble path, the crier and the Sharif would both lift their right hands and magnify the Lord. Then the other pilgrims would make the ritual circuits.

At the time of pilgrimage, the curtains of the Ka'bah would be raised and the gateway would be opened to visitors. The interior of the temple was illuminated with candles. The pilgrims would vie with each other to pray on the slab of red marble that marked the spot where Muhammad himself had prayed. A traveller in the year 442 A. H. described the interior of the Ka'bah as follows: The arrangement remained as in the 'Omayyad period, with the three columns. The alabaster panes of the entablature windows had been replaced with glass. At each of the four corners there was a high recess in which lay a Qoran. The walls were inlaid with gold slabs. On the north-eastern wall there were six silver *mihrabs*. Pieces

88. A street in the south-eastern corner of the mosque square in Madinah. On the far right is a house which is built on the site of Abu Ayyub Khalid's dwelling, where Muhammad stayed at the time of the Hegira.

of wood which were said to come from Noah's Ark had been set in silver and hung on the walls.

The pilgrims proceeded to 'Arafat and the other stations in groups, gathered round the banners of their regions. On their return to Mecca after completing the devotions at each of the pilgrimage stations, the Ka'bah's white over-curtain and some of the under-curtains were changed for new ones. Before the Mongol invasion of Baghdad, when the rivalry between the 'Abbassid caliphs and the Fatimid anti-caliphs was at its height, the renewal of the Ka'bah's curtains had been the signal for riots. The official representatives of the rulers, who led the caravans, would each insist that his own curtain should be the one to be used. The problem would be solved by hanging several curtains at once on the building. One superbly embroidered yellow silk cloth, sent by the Sultan Mahmud of Gaznah, had attracted particular attention. White covers were sent by the 'Alids of Cairo and Yemen. During the Mameluk period, the emblematic black of the 'Abbassid caliphs gradually became the usual colour for the curtain.

It was a sign of the troubled age that the sanctuary where no unkind word should be spoken became the scene of brawls and battles. On one occasion the Turks closed the gates of the temple and would let no one in. At other times, the leaders of the caravans, and even the 'Alids themselves, began to pillage each other's encampments and the houses of the Meccans. The 'Alids and the Turks both ransacked the Ka'bah's treasury. A maniac once attempted to attack the House of God with a stick and a sword.

Worst of all was the Carmathian invasion. The Carmathians were a fanatical Shiite sect who had established in Bahrain a state run according to an ideology resembling communism. During the pilgrimage season of 317 A. H., the Carmathians invaded Mecca. When their leader entered the Ka'bah, he was drunk, thereby showing his contempt for the Qoranic injunction to avoid wine. He jeered at the verse which was quoted to him concerning the immunity of those who took refuge in the temple, and said: " If He created you, I will kill you." The Carmathians thereupon murdered two thousand pilgrims, and took the women and children captive. If any of the Meccans dared to express pity at the sight of the heaped corpses, they were promptly killed. The invaders plundered the Ka'bah's treasury and carried away the Black Stone. It was not until twenty-two years later, after the Meccans had threatened or offered money repeatedly and to no avail, and the Carmathian chief had died of leprosy, that they decided to send the Stone back where it belonged. It was brought on the back of a camel, broken into more pieces than when it had been hit by the 'Omayyads' catapults.

As a result of constant inter-tribal strife, it was difficult to bring food into Mecca and prices rose continually. Many people starved and epidemics were rife. The valley was still flooded from time to time. Once when the Ka'bah was partly submerged, the Meccans were astonished to see a mystic from Baghdad, 'Abd al-Qadir Gilani (470-561 A. H.), making the ritual circuits by swimming.[67]

Many other saintly persons lived in the Hijaz at this time, " hidden under the folds of God's mantle," as Muhammad had said. The great Andalusian mystic Muhi al-Din ibn al-Arabi (560-638 A. H.) wrote his major work there in 598—*The Meccan Inspirations*. Jalal al-Din Rumi, one of the most illustrious mystic poets of Islam, spent some time there as a youth; he was probably inspired to write his famous invocation to Muhammad in the Hijaz. This poem was set to music in the eleventh century A. H. by the Turkish composer Itri, and is chanted each year to the sound of reed flutes at a ceremony on the anniversary of Jalal al-Din's death, in Konya, where he lived.

In 488 A. H., when Moslem culture seemed to be in decline, Muhammad al-Ghazali came to Mecca on pilgrimage. Born in Khorassan in 450 A. H., he had

89. A veiled lady among the crowd in Madinah.

taught theology at Baghdad, where his wide knowledge and brilliant intelligence brought him all the success that was open to a canonist. Yet Ghazali found the formalism of theologians and the scepticism of philosophers empty and disappointing, and devoted himself to mystic contemplation. One day he was sitting in a cell of a Meccan hospice when he saw a man come into the courtyard of the mosque and make his devotions. But the man's prayers were distorted by fetishist ritual and Ghazali thought: " How sad for the Apostle is this return to heathen ways." Suddenly a vision came to him. He saw Muhammad sitting among the teachers of preceding generations, discussing with them the treatises they had written. Then all the doctors went away and Ghazali realised that, in the fifth century after Muhammad, there were no great teachers left in Islam. For a while the Apostle sat alone, and Ghazali wondered whether he might dare to approach him. At last Muhammad asked: " Where is Ghazali? ". The Khorassani hesitantly held out to the Prophet a book that had appeared in his hands: it was *The Revivification of Religious Sapiences*, a work that attempted to return to the sources of Muhammad's faith, and was to earn for Ghazali the title of " the Justifier of Islam." [68]

THE TURKISH CALIPHS

THE ANATOLIAN colonies of the Eastern Roman Empire were opened to Turkish immigrants in 463 A. H. (1071 A. D.), when the Turkish Sultan Alp Arslan defeated the Emperor Romanus Diogenes at Malazgird, in Eastern Anatolia. Several Turkish principalities were established in Anatolia during the following century, and a state which bore the paradoxical name of the Sultanate of Rome. Pilgrims began to plod the long roads from Anatolia to the Hijaz. (The Turkish miniatures in this book, incidentally, are reproduced from tenth and twelfth century A. H. manuscript copies of a celebrated work written on Muhammad's life, the *Sirat al-Nabi*, in 770 A. H. by a blind Turkish pilgrim, Mustafa Dariri Erzeni, " the blind man from Erzerum.") [69]

Among the many Anatolian Turks who followed the road to the holy land of Islam in the fourteenth century A. D. was perhaps the great poet and saint Yunus (Jonas) Emre. No doubt he walked to the Hijaz along the caravan route with his head bowed and his arms crossed on his breast, in the position commonly adopted by the Anatolian mystics in token of humility. The pilgrimage is described in a poem attributed to Jonas which is still sung in Turkey as a hymn:

> I left the Roman land apace,
> A candle I became that melted.
> Blessed be God that I could there bow my head,
> Lord Apostle, how fair were the ways of the Ka'bah.
> The moon rose as I started on the road,
> I chanted benedictions.
> Oh come with me, let us wander together,
> Lord Apostle, how fair were the ways of the Ka'bah.
> The peaks came close;
> Fain would one drink a drop, for it is hot.
> The man who dies on the wayside has no mourner,
> Lord Apostle, how fair were the ways of the Ka'bah.
> The mountains tower over the Ka'bah,
> The spring that saw the Epiphany ever flows.
> Jonas the loving remembers and weeps,
> Lord Apostle, how fair were the ways of the Ka'bah.[70]

While the Turkish people of Anatolia gave their heart to Muhammad, their princely dynasties were establishing an empire. The House of Osman, which had succeeded the Selçuks, extended their territories to Europe.

Their glances turned towards Constantinople, the last stronghold left to the Basileus. Muhammad had prophesied: " Verily, the gates of Constantinople shall be opened," and more than once since the 'Omayyad period Moslem expeditions had attempted to overthrow the imperial city. At last in 856 A. H. (1453 A. D.), the Turkish Sultan Mehmed II achieved the long-awaited aim. The fall of the Eastern Roman Empire was an event of world-wide importance, and the beginning of a new age.

On the shores of the Sea of Marmara, round the Byzantine church of Saint Sophia, rose the cupolas and incredibly slender minarets of six hundred mosques. The lance of Muhammad was now firmly planted in the Byzantine city.

It was the grandson of Mehmed II, Selim the Valiant (875-926 A. H.), who was to raise the Ottomans to the supreme throne of Islam. The descendent of legendary Asian heroes, the Sultan " who had mounted his ancestors' throne with grandeur and honour " was made of sterner stuff than the Arab caliphs. His short reign and his boundless energies were devoted to the glory of Islam, identified in his mind with his military victories. He sacrificed his nearest kin to the interests of the Ottoman state, as he thought, and obtained the Sultanate for himself. Then he turned to Turkey's neighbours. He defeated the Shiite Safawid dynasty of Iran in 920, thus making himself the champion of orthodox Islam. The only rivals now left to him were the Mameluks of Egypt and their puppet the 'Abbassid caliph. The Ottoman historian Sadeddin Efendi, who wrote a biography of Selim, says that the Sultan then began to hope that some divine sign might direct him towards the Hijaz. Impatiently he asked the pious members of his court whether they had seen any vision connected with the holy land of Islam. When they said no, he reproached them with sleeping brutishly throughout the night instead of devoting themselves to contemplation. At last one of the courtiers did have a significant dream, and the Sultan felt able to launch his attack on Cairo. In 923 A. H. he overpowered the " city of Mars," as the Egyptian capital is called, and the last 'Abbassid Caliph surrendered his title to Selim.

The 'Alid Sharif of Mecca sent his thirteen-year-old son to Selim with the Prophet's mantle, his banner, early Qorans written by 'Othman and 'Ali, the hood of the Yemenite saint Uwais al-Qarani, and other relics. The new caliph received these gifts with great humility, and placed them in the most beautiful pavilion of his palace. The Ottoman caliphs were laid beside the window of the pavilion containing Muhammad's mantle when they died (*ill.* 71). The sultans had new caskets made, inlaid with gold and precious metals, in which to keep the relics (*ill.* 83, 90). An outline of the Prophet's footprint was placed on a wall of the Ottoman palace (*ill.* 84), and the Sultan Ahmed I (998-1026 A. H.), the builder of the famous Blue Mosque, wore the same image on his turban. These relics are still preserved in the pavilion of the caliph's Topkapu Palace, which is now a museum.

The Turkish caliphs bore the title of " the Servant of the Two Sanctuaries," thus defining their reverent devotion to the Hijaz. None of them attempted to make a pilgrimage to Mecca, as they feared the troubles that might arise during a prolonged absence, but they all tried to serve Muhammad's country faithfully.

It might even have been possible for the Ottoman caliphs to have healed the long-standing breach between orthodox Islam and the Shiites, if they had chosen to heed a proposal made by the Shah of Persia. In 1116 A. H. Nadir Shah, who was himself a Shiite and of Turkish origin, offered to recognise the Ottoman caliph, whom he considered " the glory of the Turkish race," if the caliph would grant the Shiites equal standing with the other sects in the holy cities of Islam.

90. A silver Qoran-cabinet, inlaid with gold, presented to the Ka'bah by the Turkish Sultan-caliph Ahmed I – 999-1027 A.H. (1590-1617 A. D.). 42 × 42 × 145 cm.

91. A Turkish gold crescent, set with rubies, emeralds and rock-crystal, which once hung in one of the Hijazi sanctuaries. 30 × 25 cm.

92. A gold Qoran casket, embossed and studded with rubies and emeralds, dating from about the seventeenth century. As stated on the golden plaque attached to the casket, it was presented to the Apostle's mosque in Madinah by " Enver Pasha, Minister for War and Servant of Islam ", when he visited the city in March 1916.

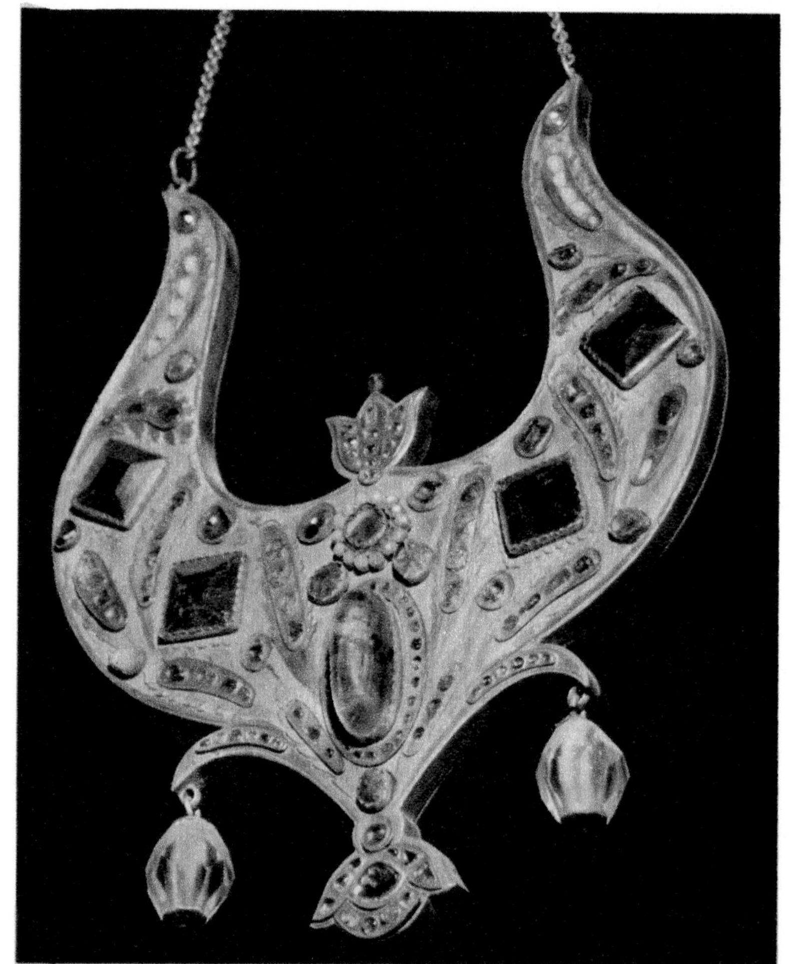

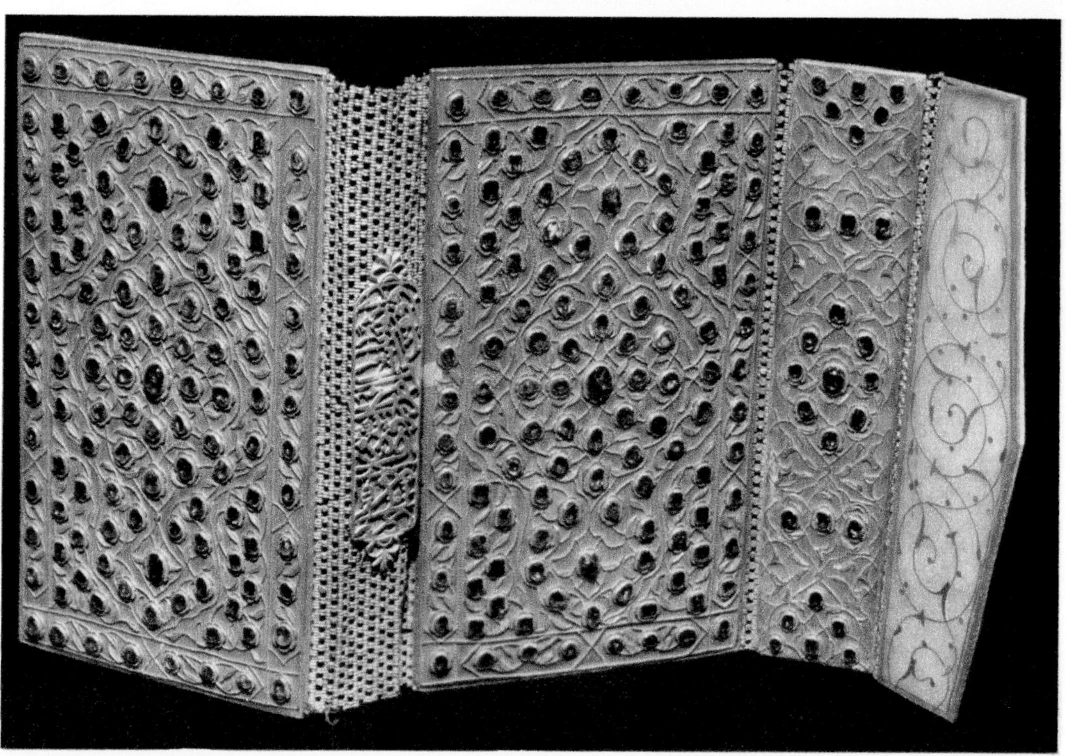

91
92

But the Ottomans feared the Shiite tendencies among their own Turkish subjects, and refused this offer, which might have brought unity to Islam after centuries of tragic dissension.

The 'Alid Sharifs and the inhabitants of the Hijaz received pensions, which relieved them at least of the worry of finding means to exist in that barren area. Every year the court of Constantinople went down to the Asian shore with the pilgrim caravan, which took with it a camel bearing a chest filled with gold to be distributed in the Hijaz. From the revenues of the imperial treasury and of the province of Egypt, large sums and a provision of grain were set aside for the needs of the Moslem holy land.

The Turks found it impossible, however, to govern the Beduin. They fortified the holy places and sent guards with caravans in case of attack by the desert

Street scene in Mecca.

raiders. Even so, many pilgrims preferred to take the sea route via the Arabian Gulf, risking the hazards of coral banks rather than those of the bandits.

An account of pilgrimage in Ottoman times was given by Nabi, who was hailed at the Sultan's court as the "king of poets." He was already over fifty when in 1089 A. H. (1677 A. D.) he set out from Scutari. The caravan rode for some miles along the shore of the Marmara Sea until they reached Kartal, where they crossed the Gulf of Izmit. They rode through Anatolia, stopping in various towns and particularly in Konya, at the shrine of Jalal al-Din Rumi. Then they continued via Damascus and Jerusalem to Gaza, where they embarked for Egypt. They visited Cairo, then followed the route of the Egyptian pilgrims across Sinai. The poet describes the journey in the precious phraseology which was fashionable at that time in the court of Constantinople, as elsewhere:

"At dawn, as the caravan of torch-bearing stars began to move their trappings

93. Another view of the street shown in *ill.* 88. On the far left is the wall of a library founded in 1279 A. H. (1862 A. D.) by the Turkish Shaikh al-Islam (the senior teacher of Islam), Arif Hikmet Efendi.

away from the leaden cupola of the ancient celestial hospice, the joyful cavalcade at once started happily out, chanting litanies, and left the emerald fields of Scutari behind... On the next day, as it was observed by those who rushed to the coast that the expanse of sea round Constantinople, famous for its troubled moods, was momentarily disinclined to daunt the heart by sending up sky-high waves, it was decided that we should embark immediately." After many months, and many adventures, they arrived at a " most distressing desert," known as " 'Aqabah of Egypt." They rode into a narrow ravine, where " the peaks of the mountains on both sides rose to higher altitudes then the nests of birds of prey... The path coiled like a snake, and ended at the sea coast. Now the ocean kissed the folds of the tents' long trains." The travellers were roused by " the assembling drum and the iron-tongued bell, admonishing them to observe the exact minute of departure... The scissor-like legs of the steeds cut a narrow margin along the turquoise-coloured page of the sea, the translucent symbol of pure thoughts... The land of Madian was reached... The crescent manifested itself as the fair ornament of the celestial dome, as the tragic plain of Badr became the tents' splendid resting-place. The purple earth, where lay those who drained the cup of martyrdom's red wine, was venerated by the travellers... Two days later, as the meeting-place with the Egyptian pilgrims was reached, the open plain called Rabik was to be the land of the canvas shelters. Here all those who followed the way to the Deity's House cast away their worldly garments, and after purifying their bodies they adorned their backs and waists with the garment of eternal life, consisting of two pieces of sanctified white cloth, saying: ' When alive my vestment and when dead my shroud.'... As they stood at the station of divine love and took their vows, their clamour rose to the highest heavens... The half-naked pilgrim, his head exposed to the sun, now prepared to enter the path of procession of the mystic firmament... When they arrived at the place yet two hours' walk from Mecca the Glorious and saw the two stone pillars on each side of the road, then blown by a tempest of passion, the pilgrims fell prostrate, as autumn leaves."

The holy cities, guarded by fortresses where the banner of the Sultan-Caliphs flew in the sunshine, knew four hundred years of almost uninterrupted peace. They became a religious haven for mystics, theologians, scholars—for all who wished to retire from the harsh struggle of the world outside. " The guests of God," as those who lived in Mecca were called, and " the Prophet's neighbours," the Madinese, lived on the threshold of eternity. It was the hope of many pilgrims to die and be buried in Mecca or Madinah, as the first Moslems had been. Such was the lot of the Turkish musician Hamami Zade Ismail (1192-1261 A. H.), known as Dede Efendi, who when he died was buried at the feet of Khadijah.

Four theological schools were founded in Mecca for the orthodox sects. The professors were the leaders of the congregations in the mosque, and the curriculum included the study of the Qoran, the Prophet's life, and medicine.

In cloisters and hospices, the mystics pursued their spiritual flights into abstract realms. There were now many Anatolians among them, often belonging to the school of the Turkestani saint Ahmad of Yasi (died 562 A. H.,) who were wont to meditate in absolute darkness, either in an artificial grave or beneath a black mantle.

The best architects and decorators of Turkey were sent to work in the Hijaz. Mecca and Madinah began to take on the appearance of Ottoman cities, with plain classical façades, an abundance of cupolas and tall, delicate minarets. The Egyptian marbles were replaced with flower-patterned Turkish ceramics. Turkish ladies embroidered silken palls for the holy graves with floral designs in rose or blue. Gardens were made to flourish in the arid valley. Wooden lattices appeared on houses, " in the fashion of Istanbul."

94. The courtyard of the Ka'bah, showing the kiosk containing the stone on which Abraham is said to have stood as he summoned mankind to the Meccan pilgrimage.

95. A plaque in one of the Hijazi monuments, commemorating a donation of the Saudi Sultan ' Abd al-Aziz, made in 1345 A.H. (1926 A.D.).

94
95

With the aid of donations made by the Turkish caliphs and Indian princes, the old benevolent foundations of the holy land were kept in repair and new ones built. There were now many schools, both elementary and advanced in their teaching, there were libraries endowed with precious manuscripts, hospices, hospitals, and kitchens where the needy could obtain food. As Zubaidah's gift to Mecca, the water supply from Hunain, had dried up, the Princess Mihrimah, daughter of Suleyman the Magnificent, had the installation repaired and extended. In 923 A. H. a special corps of African workers was appointed to keep the supply in good order, and the result was that Mecca had the use of many fountains.

Mosques and mausoleums were the objects of special care, being extensively decorated and furnished with carpets. The temples on the way to 'Arafat (*ill.* 112), at al-Khaif (*ill.* 110, 111) and the oratories built over the houses of the first Moslems were repaired. In 1257 A. H. new mosques were erected on Mount Abu Qubais, the supposed site of Adam's grave, and on Hira, where Muhammad had his first vision. In Madinah the various mosques were renovated, and at Quba the first house of Islamic worship was entirely rebuilt, in its original shape, during the reign of Mahmud II (1199-1255 A. H.).

The mosque of the Nativity had been reconstructed in 954 A. H. Beneath the cupola which indicated the place where Muhammad came into the world was a casket, covered with gold-embroidered taffeta hangings from Turkey and surrounded by a railing. Here, day and night, sat reciters chanting passages from the Qoran.

In 1113 A. H. an edict was issued, introducing the celebration of Muhammad's birth to his own country. After the evening prayer a procession would form in the courtyard of the Ka'bah, and would walk to the Mosque of the Nativity bearing candles and banners. There the eighth century Turkish poem by Suleyman Çelebi would be recited by a solo voice. For the pious Moslem, it was a great experience to stand near the place where Muhammad was born and hear the well-known words:

> On that night of the twelfth Rabi' al-Awwal,
> The Lady Aminah, Mother of Muhammad....

When the singer reached the description of the hour in which the infant was born, the congregation rose and took up the chant in chorus:

> Hail to Thee, O Moon of Splendour, hail to Thee!
> Hail to Thee, O Helper of the Forsaken!
> God bless our Lord Muhammad, the Prophet of the Portionless.

Suleyman the Magnificent (926-973 A. H.) sent the celebrated architect Sinan, who built the Suleymaniye Mosque in Istanbul, to Mecca, to make plans for an eventual reconstruction of the Ka'bah, but they did not come to fruition in his lifetime. Later, in 990 A. H., the architect Mehmed Aga used the same plans when he renovated the courtyard of the Ka'bah, extending it to measure 537 × 550 feet. The nineteen gates were renewed, but kept in the same places. In the porticoes which surrounded the court, the 892 existing columns were replaced with marble and yellow stone columns were set between them, to help support the stuccoed stone arches and cupolas that had been substituted for the old wooden ones. Instead of a flat roof over the porticoes, five hundred little bulbous domes now appeared there, according to the Ottoman style (*ill.* 113).

One of the two Turkish artists who painted the illustrations of Muhammad's life which appear in this book, Abdullah Lutfi, was sent to Mecca in 994 A. H.

96. The market in Mecca—approximately where Abu Bakr had his shop.

He decorated the interior of the cupolas with gold motifs and calligraphic compositions, for which he received a fee of 1050 florins. No doubt he also made sketches of the holy land of Islam at the same time; his illustrations for Mustafa Erzeni's book show that he had made acute observations of the Hijaz landscape.

During the renovations in 994 A. H., the floors of the porticoes and the path round the Ka'bah were repaved with polychrome marbles. In addition to the lamps which hung on the columns, candelabra in the shape of date-palms were placed in the courtyard. The four teachers' seats were replaced with new ones in the graceful shapes of Turkish kiosks. There were now seven minarets on the holy building, of which the last built, the tallest and most slender, was in Ottoman style. It was circular, had three balconies, and rose to a point at the top. The new minaret in fact formed part of the theological school built by the Sultan Suleyman, which adjoined the Ka'bah. The call to prayer now began from the " Caliph's minaret " and was echoed by the reciters on the six others. Forty learned and elderly eunuchs were put in charge of the Ka'bah's service.

Since the beginning of the tenth century A. H. a major problem had arisen: the " House of God," the Ka'bah itself, was in need of reconstruction. The three Meccan teachers of the orthodox sects and the Shaikh al-Islam (Senior Teacher of Islam), who resided in Constantinople, believed that the work should be done forthwith, but the Shafi'ite Imam of Mecca held to the more conservative view that it would not be lawful to demolish the temple; it must fall down of its own accord. It was only in 1039, after the Meccan valley had had one of its frequent floods and two corner stones collapsed that the Shafi'ite Imam agreed that the work of rebuilding could begin. The people of Mecca were also consulted, and they too felt that the task was necessary.

The reconstruction began under the supervision of one of the Sultan's chamberlains, a Circassian. Fearing that the Meccans would be critical of his efforts, he prayed daily for guidance before he gave his orders. Architects came from Istanbul, Ankara, and other Turkish cities. The Black Stone was under the especial care of an Indian architect. The four Imams, the judges, the administrative officials of Mecca, and the inhabitants themselves, all helped to carry stones, as Muhammad had done during the Qorashi rebuilding. One of the carpenters saw a vision of Muhammad among the Ottoman workmen. The Qoran was recited all the time the reconstruction went on.

The demolition was stopped when the huge green stones believed to be Abraham's foundations were reached. The new Ka'bah was built upon these, in its previous form and incorporating much of the old masonry. Inside the Ka'bah the old columns were coated with a preservative solution of saffron and gum arabic. The gate, plated in gold and silver, which had been given by the Sultan Suleyman, was put back. Indian potentates presented two portable silver staircases, to give access to the gateway. A new golden gargoyle, with an inlaid inscription set in blue enamel, came from Istanbul and was placed on the roof of the Ka'bah; the old one went to the Caliph's treasury. The two curtains—red underneath and black on top—were hung round the Ka'bah. Another gift from Sultan Suleyman, a pulpit in elaborate woodwork, was set in its place. Finally, the sand in the courtyard was washed.

Once again, " God's House " stood complete, perhaps for another thousand years, as the symbol of the faith of Abraham and Muhammad.[71]

97.* Mecca in Ottoman times. The inscription within the cypress outline is the text of the Islamic pilgrimage vow. 20 × 11 cm.

اوزرينه
اوچ كره
قويوب
قالديروب
يوزينه
وگوزلرينه
سوره رك
هر كره سنده
بوني اوقيه
لبيك اللهم
لبيك لبيك
لا شريك لك
لبيك ان الحمد
والنعمة لك
والملك لا شريك لك

98

99

THE ROSE-HUED MOSQUE

In Madinah, as in Mecca, an important task awaited the Turkish caliphs and their architects. The Apostle's mosque was in need of complete overhaul. Since the reconstruction in 868 A. H., in the time of the Egyptian Mameluks, the shrine had only been partially repaired. The Sultan Suleyman had made various changes in 940, by rebuilding the north-western minaret (*ill.* 51) and the ceremonial entrance at the south-western corner known as the " Salutation Gate," which still has the ceramic tiles upon it bearing the name and genealogy of the Sultan (*ill.* 78). Within the mosque, an important addition had been made in the southern hall, the site of the original mosque. For the first time a *mihrab* had been erected for the Hanafi congregation, to which the caliph and many other Turks belonged. The Sultan Suleyman also presented a new pulpit, which was set in the place where Muhammad's bench had stood and therefore became the chief pulpit of Islam.

In 994 and 1127 A. H., other changes were made and gradually the Apostle's Mosque began to take on a new aspect. In 1196 a new Ottoman *mihrab* was built on the site of 'Othman's *mihrab*, on the southern wall. It was surmounted by a cupola which is still in existence and can be seen from outside the mosque (*ill.* 80).

The caliphs, the princes and princesses of the Ottoman house, and others had over the years presented many sumptuous gifts to the mosque. These included precious manuscript Qorans, gem-embossed Qoran caskets (*ill.* 90), containers for Zamzam water (*ill.* 85), incense burners, reliquaries, carpets, brocades, gold-embroidered palls, baldaquins and lamps. Finally the Sultan Ahmed I, who reigned from 998 to 1026 A. H., presented to the mosque a number of gold pendants in the shapes of crescents (*ill.* 91) and stars, set with fabulous diamonds, rubies and emeralds of hundreds of carats. These were hung in the Prophet's mausoleum, while the other precious objects were arranged behind the railing which surrounded the graves of Muhammad, Abu Bakr, 'Omar, and the site of Fatimah's hut.

In 1266 A. H., after long hesitation, the Madinese citizens at last consented to allow extensive alterations in the Prophet's Mosque. The caliph sent the architect, Halim, the headmason, Ibrahim, the calligrapher Shukrullah, and all the skilled workmen from Istanbul, and, helped by the Madinese, they set to work.

Only the most devout were allowed to penetrate within the railing of the mausoleum. One of those so honoured was Eyub Sabri Pasha, an officer in the Turkish navy and the author of a comprehensive history of the two Hijazi sanctuaries.

98. The sign on the road from Jiddah to Mecca beyond which only Moslems may go.

99. The plain of 'Arafat at the time of pilgrimage, showing the rows of tents for pilgrims from various countries.

Much of the information given in the present work has been gained from Sabri's exhaustive researches. Eyub Sabri was entrusted with the task of laying the ceramic tiles in the space beyond the railing. Complete silence was observed while the renovations were carried out.

The outer dome of the mausoleum was in a precarious state, so the repairs were started there. A temporary roof was put up first, over the inner cupola, so that no rubble would fall and no one would be able to look into the funeral chamber while the work was proceeding above. The double walls were not demolished, but were shored up with a third wall upon which the new dome was built. The Mameluk-style dome was rebuilt in the same shape as before, but this time the lead cover was painted green. Muhammad's mausoleum has thereafter been called " the Green Dome " (*ill.* 74).

Very little was altered in the arcades surrounding the courtyard, except that most of the old columns and the wooden cupolas were replaced by stuccoed stone ones. Great care was taken not to change the position of any of the historical elements of the building, as for instance in the southern gallery, where every column indicated the site of a memorable event. As in Mecca, a large number of small domes were added to the roof, all covered with lead. The interiors of the cupolas and the pediments of the gateways were ornamented with gold suns and stars, the emblems of the Ottoman caliphs, and many calligraphic inscriptions.

The small pavilion in the centre of the courtyard where the mosque lamps were kept was now removed, so that camels bringing supplies of oil no longer had to come right into the mosque. As another means of achieving tranquillity for the worshippers, a nursery and school was erected at the north-western corner of the mosque, and mothers who wished to attend the service could leave their children there in safety.

Remembering that Muhammad had said: " Between my grave and my pulpit lies one of the Gardens of Paradise," the Turks built the whole of the mosque in a rose-coloured stone cut from the hills above the 'Aqiq valley, near Madinah. Seen from the palm-groves, the mosque, with its multitude of rounded cupolas, arcades and columns, all in pale red stone, looked like a gigantic rose, the unearthly flower of Muhammad's garden.

The Sultan who had set the reconstruction in motion, 'Abd al-Mejid, was not cast in the heroic mould of his ancestors. He was a constitutional monarch, in keeping with the already comparatively westernised atmosphere of Turkey. Imbued, like his predecessors, with strong religious principles, 'Abd al-Mejid took care to see that donations used for the Madinah reconstructions were untainted by any worldly gain, such as excessive interest on capital investment for example. In 1277 A. H. (1860 A. D.) the Sultan, already dying of consumption at the age of thirty-nine, rose from his sick-bed to hear the report that the rose-red mosque was about to be finished.

* * *

Life in the Apostle's City centred round the mosque. Each year during the three months especially devoted to piety in the Moslem world, Rajab, Shaban and Ramadan, many ceremonies took place in Madinah. The desert Beduins would open the proceedings by coming to the mosque to sing to the Apostle the ancient cantilena that commemorated his Hegira:

> Welcome, welcome, Muhammad!
> O Crescent that rises over the vale of Quba
> Who taught us our religion.

The women of Madinah would gather to prepare the aromatic herbs and the incense which were changed once a year in the mosque.

During Ramadan, as choirs of reciters chanted their way through the Qoran, each day, at the close of evening prayers, the imams, scholars and elderly citizens would assemble beside the Apostle's mausoleum. The tall eunuchs, wearing their great turbans and blue coats with long sleeves lined with red, would join the gathering. Facing the mausoleum, a reciter would speak an invocation. Then the dignitaries would move in procession beyond the railing surrounding the Prophet's intoning their salutations to him. Each of them would take one of the lamps tomb, which were set within the enclosure on ceremonial occasions, and carry it out of the mausoleum. Outside in the courtyard, beside the cluster of palm-trees and the well of Fatimah's garden, waited the children of Madinah. They took charge of the lamps and carried them, in procession, back to the pavilion where they were kept.

Each day, some hours before dawn, the balconies on the five minarets were lit with candles. From the balustrade of the highest minaret, a herald proclaimed: " There is none to worship but God." In the sandy courtyard below the watchman keeping vigil answered: " Muhammad is God's Apostle." At this signal, the sixteen gates of the sanctuary were opened. Early worshippers would hurry along the narrow streets, each muffled in his *kafiyah* against the coolness of the night, and carrying a lantern to light his way through the city, still shrouded in night.

Inside the mosque, the rose-red colonnades of the southern nave were faintly illumined by candles. In the dim south-eastern corner of the galleries appeared the outline of the Apostle's mausoleum, like a great cage covered with a baldaquin; inside it, a shimmer reflected from the " Resplendent Star," a jewel that was considered the symbol of a Qoranic allegory (XXIV, 35) and of Muhammad's soul.

At the corner of the southern colonnade, on the raised dais where the infirm and aged companions of the Apostle had spent their lives, were now the teachers of the four sects and the elderly eunuchs who acted as the servants of the sanctuary. Beyond the dais and to the east of the mausoleum was a recess where the walls were entirely panelled with floral ceramics; this indicated the place where more than once the Spirit had appeared to Muhammad in the shape of the Archangel. On the white background of the ceramic, blue hyacinths, tulips, carnations and delicate fern leaves evoked the immortal blooms of beatitude.

Towards the end of the night, a magnificat was sung from all five minarets by a choir composed of treble, tenor and bass voices. Then followed litanies, a Benedictus to the Apostle, and finally the call to pre-dawn prayer.

During the day, five services were held, each sect gathered behind its own teacher. Between services, mothers would bring their babies to the mosque, handing them over to a eunuch who would hold them beneath the railing of the mausoleum for Muhammad's blessing.

At mid-day prayer, the dead were carried as far as the entrance to the mosque, so that the congregation could invoke God's mercy and the Apostle's intercession upon them.

It was long after midnight when the mosque was at last empty and the lights were extinguished. The eighty eunuchs would close all the gates and gather in the courtyard. Turning towards the Apostle's grave, they would greet him in chorus: " Peace be upon Thee, O Apostle of God." Then they would pitch their small tents and hang their turbans on top; some would keep watch while the others retired to sleep. From a distance the turbans above the little tents made it look as if the eunuchs were still standing. But they were lying down, turned towards Muhammad's tomb—faithful servants, even in sleep.[72]

THE END OF THE CALIPHATE

In 1301 A. H. (1885 A. D.), the Hijaz was startled out of its four-centuries-long calm. The former Grand Vizier of the Ottoman state, Midhat Pasha, now a political prisoner in the citadel of Taif, had been strangled, presumably on the orders of the Sultan-Caliph 'Abd ul-Hamid II. The conflict that had arisen between the monarch and his prime minister was suddenly seen to symbolise the crisis in the Moslem world. For too long the Islamic intellectuals had been content to discuss the subtle nuances of a culture that seemed to be the apogee of liberal humanism, while neglecting the true essence of Islam, reducing it to a series of ritualistic rules. The priestly class which Muhammad had dreaded was now in existence, objecting even to the translation of the Qoran for the benefit of non-Arab Moslems. There can be no denying the profound attachment which these ultra-conservatives had for Islam, but it was their rigidity which led to the indifference now felt by many Moslems for their religion. This in turn caused their culture to collapse in ruins, and material downfall followed.

In Europe, the age of research had begun. Unsuspected fields of knowledge were being opened up, bringing wealth and power to the west and leaving the backward eastern countries at the mercy of colonialist ambitions. " Wake up to the modern world," warned Midhat Pasha and his adherents. Such bluntness seemed impious to the conservatives of the Moslem world. To complicate matters further, waves of nationalism began to undermine the heteroclite structure of the Ottoman state.

The long-established isolation of the Hijaz was ending. The Sharifs now represented their country in the Ottoman Parliament, where they absorbed new ideas and discussed the possibility of eventual autonomy for the Arab states. European converts to Islam came to the Hijaz, and even some non-Moslems who disguised themselves as pilgrims in order to satisfy their curiosity.

It was in these circumstances that the Ottoman Empire entered the First World War on the side of Germany. The Sultan-Caliph proclaimed to all Moslems that Islam was in danger and that conditions permitting a holy war of resistance were therefore in existence. Outside Turkey itself, there was little response to this announcement. The era of the caliphate was clearly over.

When the authorities in Istanbul nominated Prince Husain as Sharif of Mecca, they unwittingly chose the man who was to deal the final blow at the Ottoman caliphs and indeed to the caliphate as a whole. Many conflicting opinions have been expressed about this famous Sharif. To his followers, he was an ardent Arab

100. Pilgrims preparing for ritual ablutions before prayer.

إن أول بيت وضع للناس للذي ببكة مباركا وهدى للعالمين
فيه آيات بينات مقام إبراهيم ومن دخله كان آمنا ولله على الناس
حج البيت من استطاع إليه سبيلا ومن كفر فإن الله غني عن العالمين

nationalist, fully justified in trying to shake off the Turkish yoke. The Ottoman government, on the other hand, engaged in a desperate struggle for existence, regarded expressions of independence in time of war as treasonable. It was reported to the Turkish Governor-General of the Hijaz that the Hanafi Imam of Mecca had been heard advising the Sharif to come to terms with Britain in order to end the blockade of the Red Sea, and to bring his hungry people the relief of food imports. The Governor-General believed that the Sharif was being tempted to cause dissension in Islam for the sake of his own vanity, but, hoping to avoid trouble, contented himself with saying to the prince: " My lord, Your Highness could not hold the Hijaz without the support of the Ottoman forces." (It later seemed that this remark had some truth in it, for the princes of Najd occupied the Hijaz and brought the reign of Husain to an end). Husain assured the Governor-General of his loyalty, and went to the Ka'bah to make public declaration of his allegiance to the Caliph. Even so, the prince could not fail to see that the Turks' power was fast disappearing, and that at long last he might have an opportunity to substantiate the claim of his 'Alid race to the caliphate. The people of the Hijaz might be induced to support him; they had become alienated from the Turks when the Damascus-Madinah railway was built in 1908, for it meant a reduction in the income they derived from guiding pilgrim caravans. The desert Beduins would gather beside the track, uttering curses as the little train ground its way slowly through the Hijaz. The Arabs also resented the hardships thrust upon them by Turkey's entry into the war and the resulting blockade set up by the British in the Red Sea. Another provocation was the teaching of Turkish in schools, in addition to Arabic.

The British authorities, represented by Sir Henry McMahon, the High Commissioner in Cairo, and his Secretary, Storrs, tried to persuade Prince Husain to make the final break with Turkey, but according to T. E. Lawrence they finally grew impatient with his procrastination. Husain's son, Prince 'Abdullah, was apparently an easier man to deal with. " 'Abdullah on a white mare came to us softly," wrote Lawrence, " with a bevy of richly armed slaves on foot about him... His eye had a confirmed twinkle, and though only thirty-five, he was putting on flesh... When we fell into serious talk, the veil of humour seemed to fade away, and he chose his words and argued shrewdly." 'Abdullah had come to ask for extra military help, but it was difficult to give it because non-Moslem British troops could not enter the sanctified territory, and Moslem Egyptians and Indians were unwilling to fight against the Turks.

In 1916, Husain and his son succeeded in raising Taif and Mecca in revolt against the Turks. Prince 'Abdullah went to Taif with his troops, ostensibly to pay a visit to the Turkish Governor-General at his summer residence. Because of this, the Arabs themselves were under the impression that the Sharif's expedition was directed merely against some recalcitrant Beduins. Yet the same day, Husain's forces launched their attack on the Turkish garrisons at Taif and Mecca, and hostilities were irremediably engaged.

While the Governor-General was suffering defeat in Taif, a young Turkish officer gathered his garrison to the fort in Mecca and began to bombard the Sharif's palace. A stray shell landed in the courtyard of the Ka'bah, and the curtain of the temple caught fire. The Turks rushed out of the fort and managed to extinguish the fire, but the Meccans believed that this had been a deliberate attempt at sacrilege and set upon them. The entire Turkish garrison was massacred and the body of the young lieutenant was dragged through the streets.

Writing of the Arab victory, Lawrence tells of Husain's joy at having captured the Turkish Governor-General's brass band. The Ottoman military band had been a symbol of the Sultan's power, and when the Sharif captured it he tele-

101. A tile, c. 1077 A.H. (1666 A.D.), bearing an inscription from the Qoran (III, 195-6) and a plan of the Ka'bah's precincts, with the names of the principal monuments written in Turkish. 70 × 45 cm.

phoned Storrs and made him listen to it. " That evening," says Lawrence, " 'Abdullah came to dine... We received him in the courtyard of the house steps. Behind him were his brilliant household servants and behind them a pale crew of bearded, emaciated men with woebegone faces, wearing tatters of military uniforms and carrying tarnished brass instruments of music... They played heart-broken Turkish airs. Our ears ached with noise... We got tired of Turkish music and asked for German... They played *Deutschland über alles* and *Ein' feste Burg*."

On the second Friday in April 1918, after divine service at the Apostle's mosque in Madinah, a Turkish officer slowly ascended the steps of the pulpit, draped in his country's purple flag. Omer Fahruddin Pasha was the general commanding the Turkish forces in Madinah. Halfway up the steps, the general turned to face the congregation, which included many officers and men. To them he was known as " Fahri—the Glorious," because of his heroic temperament, and his stringent severity which was tempered by a paternal friendliness that inspired affection. A witness described the scene like this:—" Stillness reigned in the Mosque. Waves of amber and musk rose from the silver censers behind the railing surrounding the Apostle's grave. For a moment, the General's eyes seemed absorbed in the contemplation of the candles burning beside the mausoleum. Then he raised his right hand and declared: 'Apostle of God, I will not abandon you.' Turning to the uniformed men before him, he addressed them: ' Soldiers, I appeal to you in the presence of that Apostle who lies in his grave but hears the words spoken here. I invite you to engage yourselves to defend him, to our last cartridge and our last breath, no matter how strong our enemies may be. God help us, and may the Apostle's spiritual aid be with us! You officers of the heroic Turkish army and you little Muhammads (this is a familiar appellation for Turkish soldiers) who are used to paying your debt to your faith with your lives, come, take with me this engagement before our Lord.' " Immediately the mosque echoed to the response, as the Turkish soldiers rushed towards the Prophet's grave to make their pledge.

Not only were the Turks struggling to hold off the Anglo-Arab armies; they were under pressure from home as well. Already in February 1916, there had been deliberations at the headquarters of the Fourth Army at Damascus. It had become exceedingly difficult to defend the six hundred kilometres of the railway to Madinah, the defenders' only supply line. Fahruddin Pasha nonetheless refused to evacuate Madinah, so Jamal Pasha, the commander of the Fourth Army, summoned a young general, already celebrated for his defence of Gallipoli, with the intention of entrusting the dangerous task to him. This was Mustafa Kemal Pasha, the future first President of the Turkish Republic. A witness relates that, as they talked, the electric lights failed. " In the darkness, Jamal Pasha said in a tremulous voice: 'Or do you think we should defend Madinah at all costs?' Mustafa Kemal replied quietly in words implying that he did not wish to go down in history as the man who had abandoned Madinah." The city was defended against all odds. In token of this determination, Jamal Pasha and the Minister for War Enver Pasha visited Madinah in March 1916, and Enver Pasha presented a Qoran cover to the Mosque (*ill.* 92).

The last pensions were sent from the Ottoman capital to the people of Madinah, together with a written invocation from the caliph to the Apostle: " Let me not be the last caliph," begged Mehmed V. His prayer seemed to be answered, for he died suddenly in July 1918, three months before Turkey signed the Armistice. His successor, Mehmed VI, waged civil war on the nationalist forces that tried and eventually succeeded in saving Turkey from the consequences of her utter defeat and was forced to flee from the wrath of his own people. Later he went to Mecca, and the Sharif Husain II, who had become the King of the Hijaz in

102. A balcony, with lattice and jalousies in Turkish style, on the front of a house in Mecca.

103. Houses in the east of Mecca, where Muhammad and Khadijah lived.

I

1916, asked Mehmed to relinquish the caliphate to him. It was not to be, however. Mehmed VI died, poverty-stricken, in San Remo, in 1926. His body was taken to a nameless grave in Damascus, in a coffin borrowed from a charitable institution. In the same year, the Saudi princes of Najd assumed power in the Hijaz and Husain went into exile.

The handful of Turks who had held out in Madinah throughout the war continued to do so for three months after Turkey had capitulated. They were so short of food that they ate locusts. Fahruddin Pasha still led them, fully determined to die in Madinah. He was living in the elementary school which adjoined the mosque. In March 1918 all non-combatants, the women and children, had been evacuated, together with some of the Ottomans' presents to the mosque and to the libraries of the city. The houses adjoining the mosque were filled with ammunition; machine-guns were placed on the minarets. Having refused point-blank to obey the surrender orders given by Mehmed VI, Fahruddin Pasha seemed care-free, and devoted his time to improving the city as well as to defending it. He made expropriations in order to enlarge the square round the mosque, and laid out a straight road to Quba.

He was in the habit of keeping long vigils, and one night he heard the sound of steps and a scuffle outside his room; his comrades in arms had been overpowered. A group of officers came in and knelt before their general, imploring him to remember that Turkey had signed an armistice including the provision that the Turkish troops in Madinah would surrender, that the Sultan himself had ordered them to give up this senseless resistance, and that Husain had been proclaimed King of the Hijaz. They did not want to die in Madinah when they could all go home safely, simply by surrendering to the Anglo-Arabs, who, however, were insisting that Fahruddin Pasha must be in their hands before they entered Madinah. The general remained adamant. The officers thereupon dragged him bodily from the room, intending to force him into a car that would take him to the Sharifian headquarters.

Fahruddin Pasha managed to shake them off, however, and made one last attempt to stay in the city. He ran towards the Apostle's grave and laid down his sword, thus claiming sanctuary. But he had the misfortune to live in an age when knightly behaviour could be mistaken for lack of judgment. The broken-hearted and now silent man was taken away to captivity and exile, watched by the crowd of Madinese who shouted their farewells to him.[73]

The last Turkish knight was relieved of his watch in the Apostle's mosque.

THE HOLY COUNTENANCE

WITH THE DECLINE of Islamic culture, the vision of the Apostle's ideal city had been lost and the world had become a lonely place for the Moslems. They sought for new hopes, but these sometimes proved to be mere palliatives. In Punjab, the philosopher and poet Iqbal (1876-1938) surveyed the horizons around him, the ancient heritage of his native India, and asked:

> Where can a friend be found for the son of Adam?
> . . . .
> This world is but earth and water; who can say that it has a heart?
> The sea, the desert, the mountain and the sheaf of grass are deaf and dumb,
> Deaf and dumb also the sun and the moon.
> Hosts of stars move isolated in different spheres.

Iqbal saw in his mind a modern image of the Apostle's City, in the form of an international Moslem community:

> We are neither Afghans, nor Turk, nor Tartars,
> But the inmates of the same garden, raised from a single stem;
> It is forbidden to us to make discrimination between colour or essence.[74]

Eleven years after his death, Iqbal's hope was realised, with the foundation of the Islamic State of Pakistan.

The new rulers of the Hijaz, called Wahabites after the puritan sect founded by Muhammad ibn 'Abd al-Wahhab (1115-1201 A. H.), thought it an advantage that the secular accumulation of traditions, often alien to Islam, had at last collapsed. They considered, for instance, that the reverence paid to the tomb of the early Moslems contradicted the Islamic principle of monotheism. Now they destroyed these funerary monuments in order to stop such practices, making exception only of the Prophet's mausoleum.

At the same time, the Saudi authorities devoted themselves also to works of reconstruction. They had large funds at their disposal, for the barren deserts of Arabia had yielded up their source of fabulous wealth—oil. The enclosures of both the Mecca and Madinah sanctuaries were pulled down and rebuilt over larger areas. However, in both mosques the holiest parts were left intact as Islamic tradition does not allow their destruction until the ravages of time make rebuild-

104. Turkish prayer rug, of the Kula type, dating from the seventeenth century. 120 × 160 cm.

105. A woman pilgrim who walked to the Hijaz from Central Asia.

106. Pilgrims facing the Ka'bah, dressed in the traditional two lengths of cloth.

107
108

ing unavoidable. In Mecca, therefore, the Ka'bah itself remained as it was when restored by the Turks three hundred years earlier, while in Madinah the southern hall of the rose-hued mosque, the site of the original temple, was also untouched.[75]

The Saudis also built hospitals, schools, a theological institute in Madinah, and many roads. Most important of all, they brought the Hijaz a security hitherto unknown. People were able to sleep with their doors ajar, and tradesmen left their shops open and unguarded at night. These utopian conditions were apparently achieved by the application of Qoranic law, though with a severity that transcends the context of the holy verses.

With the aid of the efficient organisation which now exists in the Hijaz, ever-increasing numbers of Moslems have been enabled to make the pilgrimage from foreign lands. Let us follow the progress of one such traveller, who comes on pilgrimage by one of the modern means of communication now open to him.

* * *

The pilgrim starts on his solemn journey full of expectation and apprehension. As night ends, the aircraft that carries him flies swiftly towards the dark blue tropical skies, girded with the sombre red hue of sunrise. At daybreak the traveller sees below him the turquoise waters of the Arabian Gulf, deepening in concentric circles round its coral banks. Muhammad's desert appears, with the rocky chains of Sarat radiating in every direction. The Apostle himself must have wandered along these sandy gullies and desolate tracks.

Now the plane circles over the petrified lava streams which surround Muhammad's adopted country. As the traveller sets foot on the Madinese plain, he is greeted by bright sunshine and the warm caress of the restless Hijaz breeze. Along with a group of other pilgrims, he sets off to explore the countryside that Muhammad found mild and hospitable. Fields of reddish clay, " the alkaline earth," and palm-groves surround them on every side. On their right rises a purplish mass of rocks. This is Mount Ohod, where the first Moslems met defeat and death. But on this morning, under the radiance of the new-risen sun, the mountain's eastern flank shines with gem-like brilliancy—the " gateway to Paradise," as Muhammad had called it.

A negress, draped in black cotton, comes from behind a hedge of wild cypresses and invites the pilgrims to rest for a while. They follow her into a shrubbery where a prattling white parakeet pecks at the luscious fruits which hang from the trees, and huge flowers give off rare and pungent scents. Beyond the rose-garden, filled with the vivid pink emblems of Madinah, the pilgrims arrive at the marble terraces of a large house. Here they are separated into two groups: the men are taken to a pink marble loggia, where they are seated on gilded thrones upholstered in green velvet, while the women go to a higher terrace, beside a marble pond filled with floating rose petals. This is perhaps a symbol of the Kawthar, the Paradisian source of Islam. Beside it stands a woman, dressed in the long green gown worn by angels in Islamic book-painting. The lower part of her face is veiled, so that only her slanting green eyes are visible. She is the owner of the estate, which she has planned according to instructions vouchsafed to her in dreams, as a " garden for the initiated." She points to Mount Ohod, rising like a giant amethyst above the waving green treetops, and says: " On the south-west are the peaks of Paradise." From the southern corner of the terrace, the pilgrims can look down a long straight path through the palm-grove and see the graceful minarets and the dome of the Apostle's mosque shimmering on the horizon.

The travellers leave the garden and continue round the base of Mount Ohod. Now it is no longer beautiful but a bleak mass of dark volcanic rock. Before the

107. A street on the outskirts of Upper Mecca.

108. A street in Mecca, in the quarter of the Sons of Hashim, where Muhammad was born and spent part of his life.

pilgrims stretches the desolate plain where the mutilated dead were buried after the battle of Ohod, a row of flints marking their common grave. A group of Beduin girls sits on the crumbling walls of Hamzah's tomb, flapping their black veils and chattering eerily, like the echoing Soul-birds of ancient Arab tradition. The battlefield looks tragic, as if its dead had just been buried.

The pilgrims now turn to the east, and pass a series of white-washed enclosures built to indicate the exact places where Muhammad received revelations (*ill.* 67). Here they take the southward track, towards the first mosque of Islam at Quba. From afar they hear the ceaseless complaint of water-wheels which irrigate the many gardens of this region. Canals run among the plantations, where grow pomegranates, citrons, and the many-hued Madinese dates. In these fields, under tumuli and even on the surface of the ground, lie the ruins of the ancient fortified houses of Madinah. The people who live here still occasionally use the earthen oil-lamps which they find in the soil. As the pilgrims walk along a shady path, the heady perfume of mimosa is borne to them on the breeze, and they find the thorny bush, covered with fluffy, amber-yellow balls, growing at the edge of the plantation where Salman had once worked as a slave.

At the next corner, they come within sight of the Quba Mosque (*ill.* 60), a simple white-washed enclosure with a tapering Turkish minaret. They pray in the sandy courtyard where Muhammad had first set foot on Madinese ground. Opposite the mosque stands a monument, probably dating from the Mameluk period, indicating one of the places where Fatimah rested on her journey from Mecca to Madinah (*ill.* 59).

The straight road from Quba to Madinah, laid by Fahri Pasha and his soldiers, takes the pilgrims northwards through country untouched by modern life. A nomad shepherd goes by, leading a herd of humped Indian cows. Beduins perched on camels sway along to the slow rhythm that is said to have accompanied the earliest Arab poetry. The strange-looking beasts bend their swan-like necks down to the ground, to browse among the thistles, and stare at the pilgrims, baring their teeth and whining plaintively.

At the entrance to the Apostle's city, only a splendid inner castle remains of the mediaeval walls which once defended it. The pilgrims come to streets of stucco houses, ornamented with intricately worked wooden lattices (*ill.* 89). Street sellers, carrying their wares in baskets on their heads, walk slowly along the winding, shaded lanes. Ladies hurry past, wearing the long skirt, the cape and the veil over the face after the fashion of Turkish women in the late nineteenth century. A mother holds up her child to watch the travellers pass, revealing her ungloved hand and nails tinted with henna. Another female form slips through a great porchway into a cloister; a sign hangs on the gate, saying that this is a hospice, founded in 1291 A. H. by the Ottoman Princess Adile, daughter of Mahmud II, for single ladies. The hospice is now poverty-stricken, and the women live in dark cells, reduced to emaciation by their ascetic life. The more learned amongst them give lessons by candlelight to the children of the neighbourhood.

In Madinah, every corner has its little oratory, evoking the memory of the Prophet's companions. A scent of spices wafts from the bazaar, an area of large squares and paved paths lined with shops. Merchants, with faces resembling those of archaic Yemenite sculptures, and wearing brilliant turbans, sit in the little booths. They sell dates, perfumes, chaplets, silver rings and other jewellery set with the semi-precious stones which are so abundant in the soil of the Hijaz. Each shopkeeper has a servant in attendance who holds a gold-embroidered towel on one arm and a brass ewer in his hand, from which he pours for the customers the pale, scented Yemen coffee, brewed from the peel of the grains.

There are many refugees from Russian or Chinese Turkestan among the shop-

109. A group of people, including men, veiled women, children and invalids dragging themselves along the ground, making the ritual circuit of the Ka'bah.

110
111

keepers, and in the crowds, recognisable by their semi-Mongoloid features. In the tropical climate of the Hijaz, the exiles still wear the costumes of their native steppes: quilted or felt coats, riding breeches and boots, large-brimmed felt hats, sometimes lined with fur. They have introduced into the Hijaz a kind of stitched cap commonly worn in Central Asia, and manufacture it for the use of the Arabs in white cotton. One of these hard-working, good-humoured people, an old librarian with a white beard of phenomenal length, sits with his ankles crossed, like a Central Asian Buddha, reading a book of Islamic wisdom.

In a dark, narrow street, the pilgrim comes upon a library (*ill.* 88). Opposite, there is a mouldering ochre wall, built on the site of the house owned by Abu Ayyub Khalid, who harboured the Apostle at the time of the Hegira. He died on the shores of the Golden Horn in Constantinople, and became the patron saint of Istanbul. In his memory, the Turkish Shaikh al-Islam Arif Hikmet Efendi founded the library in 1271 A. H. (*ill.* 93). It contains precious manuscripts, many of them illuminated, dating from the earliest periods of Islamic history down to the most recent times (*ill.* 51, 97).

Our pilgrim comes to the paved square outside the Apostle's Mosque. Here it might still be the nineteenth century: looking round, he sees the rose-red Turkish mosque with its Ottoman minaret, Gabriel's Gate and the Ladies' Gate on the eastern side, still surmounted with the gold inscriptions set there by the Turkish calligraphers. The beautiful ceramics given by Suleyman the Magnificent still embellish the Salutation Gate (*ill.* 78). But on the northern side of the square the impression is quite different. Here the Mosque has been extended by one-third and entirely rebuilt in grey stone, in neo-Mameluk style (*ill.* 80). This was done during the reigns of the two successive Saudi kings, between 1368 and 1375 A. H. (1948-1955 A. D.). Some of the old houses have been left in place, but they are overshadowed by large modern hotels, with rows of cars parked outside.

Evening has fallen and the lights are lit on the minaret balconies as the pilgrim approaches the northern precincts of the Mosque (*ill.* 80). He removes his shoes and leaves them in a rack, so as to enter the holy enclosure barefoot, in penitential garb. Beneath the columns of the northern gallery he stops, surprised at what he sees beyond the courtyard. While the side colonnades in grey marble look cool and dim, the arcades of the southern hall are bathed in a rosy glow. Lights flicker inside, bringing the depths of the building to life; " this is indeed Muhammad's heart and temple," thinks the pilgrim.

The Mosque is divided down the centre; the western side is reserved for men and the eastern for women (*ill.* 82). The stranger, wondering how to proceed to the mausoleum at the south-eastern corner, accosts a tall elderly African eunuch, wearing the long-sleeved coat and voluminous turban of the eighteenth century Ottoman court. The old man's emaciated hand leans for support on the shoulder of a young page. But the eunuch looks at the visitor with a vacant expression and a sweet smile, mumbling incomprehensibly. So the pilgrim decides to walk across the courtyard, watched by the men awaiting the hour of worship, and the women with their prim little girls. The babies, left on the ground while their mothers pray, cry bitterly as he approaches.

A flock of doves flutter round him, apparently thinking that as he is coming across the sandy courtyard (*ill.* 79), normally their own domain, he must have come to feed them. He has hardly freed himself from the whirlwind of wings, when he is surrounded by old women and young boys who pour water from earthenware vessels into silver cups and offer them to him. Behind them come the beggars; wizened old women with trembling, rapacious hands, haggard old men, the sick and maimed dragging themselves along the ground. They ask for alms, not humbly, but as dignified instruments of providence, who give the

110. Courtyard of the mosque at al-Khaif, near Mecca. The kiosk in the middle indicates the spot where Muhammad once pitched his tent.

111. Exterior of the mosque at al-Khaif.

pilgrim an opportunity of exercising charity. The beggars ask the pilgrim his name and origin; it is one of their functions to go round the city and inform any compatriots of a visitor that one of their countrymen has arrived in Madinah. Unaware of this custom, the traveller becomes impatient and tries to wave them away. They withdraw, saddened by his unfriendliness. At once he feels the thrust of Muhammad's lance in his heart; he has hurt the friends of the "Apostle of the Portionless." He goes after them and asks their help. They forget their discontent and lead the way towards the mausoleum, tottering round him on their wooden legs, grimacing with deformed faces.

The pilgrim and his guides take their places in a long procession, murmuring litanies and moving slowly round the mausoleum. He sees that the green baldaquin which surmounts the iron palisade round the building is in tatters. The line of visitors winds round the eastern side, and a lamp casts a ray of light beyond the railing, revealing the wall of the funerary chamber; it is bare, save for a torn piece of cerise satin hanging in one corner. " So, Our Lord," muses the pilgrim, " you claim poverty in death also."

Suddenly, he finds himself standing before the brass railing of the burial chamber itself (*ill.* 73). This place is called " the holy countenance," because here the visitor stands before Muhammad as he lies in his grave, his face turned towards Mecca. A round brass disc indicates the site of the Prophet's head. A vague scent of aromata pervades the air. There are several rows of inscriptions on the railing, all repeating the same sentence: " There is none to worship but God, the Rightful and True Lord. Muhammad is God's Apostle, the faithful attester of the certain promise."

The pilgrim stands there, mute. " You must salute the Lord, salute the Lord! " whisper unknown voices behind him. But he has forgotten all that he had planned to say. Prompted by the others, he tries to repeat the ancient words of the salutation: " Peace be upon Thee, O Muhammad. I witness that Thou hast truly fulfilled Thy mission, invited to Thy Lord with wisdom and kind words... endeavoured rightfully, until death has come to Thee...." But no sound comes from his lips. He stands there dumb and transfixed, unaware of the tears rolling down his face.

The last day, the last hour, the last moment of the pilgrim's visit to the Radiant City comes at last. The aircraft bears him towards Jiddah, while he sits immersed in introspection. It seems as if, from the moment when he first stood dumbfounded before Muhammad's " holy countenance," his stay in Madinah had been a long vigil at that spot. Time might have been standing still, were it not for the melodious regularity of the call to prayer, repeated five times a day from all the minarets of the Apostle's Mosque. The words he had forgotten as he stood before the tomb now come back to him, but they seem insignificant. He wants to say: " Farewell, Muhammad!", yet he knows that there can be no farewell, no end, to an encounter that had taken place beyond time and space.

EPILOGUE

Now THE PILGRIM prepares for the supreme experience, to tread the hallowed ground that represents eternal life, " the House of God " in Mecca. When the aircraft comes down in Jiddah, he closes his eyes to the modern city, where the huge buildings have mercilessly driven out the charming old houses. Where can the tomb of Eve be found, amid this bustle of glittering shops and luxurious cars? Her monument, he is told, has fallen in ruins. " But Mecca," he thinks, " will not be like this. God could surely not allow the narrow street where Muhammad was born, or the hallowed rocks of Mount Hira, to be despoiled of their ancient simplicity."

In the anonymity of an hotel room, to the accompaniment of the rumbling of the air-conditioning apparatus, the pilgrim takes the vows of pilgrimage and puts on the traditional two lengths of cloth. Now he must try to avoid all worldly thoughts and conversations.

Before dawn, he starts on the eastward road to Mecca, in a car shared with other pilgrims. They leave behind them the gracious avenues of Jiddah, bordered with eucalyptus and hibiscus trees. The arid desert they have come so far to visit stretches away on both sides of the asphalt road. It is still not quite light, but the pilgrim tries to make out the landmarks he knows so well from Islamic literature. There is a figure walking along, staff in hand; it is perhaps one of the traditional wandering pilgrims.

The car stops at the pillars beyond which only Moslems may go. Now he is on holy ground, and the pilgrim begins to repeat in his heart the response to Abraham's call to pilgrimage. The road turns, and three mountains are seen against the eastern sky, rosy with the promise of dawn. These are Abu Qubais, Thabir and Hira, suddenly appearing as if Adam, Abraham and Muhammad had risen together. Mecca is in sight, and the pilgrim and his companions alight, to perform the morning prayer on the roadside.

They come into the holy valley from the western gorge. They pass the fortress, and other buildings put up by the Ottomans and the Saudi princes, and arrive in the narrow streets of old Mecca. Tall old houses, decorated with polychrome mosaic panels and wooden lattices, climb the side of Abu Qubais. Dark little streets come from the east and lead to the quarter of the Sons of Hashim, Muhammad's clan (*ill.* 103, 108). In the place where Muhammad was born stands a modern yellow house used as a library. The pilgrim enters, and sees nothing but a bare hall, giving on to study-rooms. He continues northwards. On his left, at the foot of Mount Qua'iqi'an, is the old cemetery, where Khadijah lies under a monument which is now in ruins.

At the northern end of the Meccan valley is the pass, eleven miles long, that leads to the plain of 'Arafat. This is the pilgrimage road, the symbol of the progress of life, going away from " God's House " to meet the problems of earthly life, then returning, slowly and painfully, to the source of existence. In a few days, the hour of pilgrimage will arrive and the pilgrim will follow this road himself, lost in an immense crowd (*ill.* 99). Perhaps he will explore it now, in solitude.

Going along the ancient track the pilgrim comes first to a place where the gully widens. This is the station of Mina, where the effigy of evil is stoned during the pilgrimage. On the left is Mount Thabir and the enclave of 'Aqabah at its foot. He enters the recess, screened by mimosa bushes, where Muhammad made his pact with the Madinese, and finds an oratory, apparently abandoned long ago (*ill.* 47).

To the north rises Mount Hira, its peak covered with golden dust. He walks towards the mountain where Muhammad received his first revelation, and as a gust of wind rushes through the desolate valley, it seems to the pilgrim that the boulders and plants are still faintly murmuring, still calling to Muhammad (*ill.* 35, 36).

He returns to the pilgrimage road and continues on his south-eastern course. On the right he sees the white-washed enclosure of the al-Khaif mosque, its stuccoed minaret decorated in green (*ill.* 111). There is an open pavilion in the centre of the large sandy courtyard; this is the place where the Apostle had once pitched his tent (*ill.* 110). Here the pilgrim prostrates himself, and feels for the first time the caress of warm sand on his brow.

Passing the white mosque at Muzdalifah (*ill.* 112), the pilgrim comes at last to the plain of 'Arafat. It is noon. He climbs the boulders of the Mount of Mercy and looks at the vast expanse of the plain, stretching away to the horizon and the Sarat range, more like bluish clouds at this distance than bleak mountains. Soon this plain will be filled with pilgrims, at the first station on their return to " God's House." As Adam and Muhammad before him, the pilgrim prays for the remission of human sins.

Night falls as he makes his way back to Mecca. The sky is intensely black above him, and the stars resplendent—" the sky of the Nocturnal Journey " thinks the pilgrim. The streets of Mecca are brightly lit and full of people who are enjoying the cool of the evening. The descendants of the Ishmaelite merchants, reserved men with thin lips and Semitic faces, sit in their little shops. Elegant Meccan ladies, swathed in black, walk delicately past on their high heels. Everywhere there are gaunt Beduin men and women, with tattooed brows, wearing hand-woven, gold-embroidered black mantles. Children play unheedingly among the passing cars.

The pilgrims go about in groups, the men wearing the two lengths of cloth (*ill.* 106), and the women in long white robes and double veils drawn over the head, leaving the face bare. They come from all over the world and from all walks of life. Some of them are Moslem statesmen, here as guests of the King of Saudi Arabia or of the Crown Prince, while their wives are entertained by the Saudi princesses. There are doctors, from various countries but all with the same aim in view—to care for the sick and poor among the pilgrims. A professor from Pakistan goes about making notes, preparing to write a learned work on the Prophet of Islam. A young woman from Istanbul, disfigured through an accident, who has hidden herself away ever since in a dark hospice cell, now slips timidly through the streets. She keeps one arm raised to hide the blank face, while the

112. A mosque on the way to the 'Arafat plain.

other rests on her breast in the traditional attitude of Turkish mystics. An old man from Indonesia is brought on a stretcher to make the circuit of the Ka'bah for the last time before he dies. An African who has walked all the way to Mecca from his home seeks out the places where Bilal endured torture for the sake of his faith.

In the throng, the pilgrim hurries to find his way to the Ka'bah. He reaches the depression, surrounded by a wall of grey stone, and enters through an ornate gateway, built in neo-Mameluk style and still not quite finished. He stands on the marble pavement within a huge enclosure, firstly of many-storied galleries and then of dark, towering mountains. In the midst of the wide podium stands the black-curtained Ka'bah, with a never-ending procession of people going round it (*ill.* 109). Even the circular pathway round the " ever-visited House "[76] seems to be revolving. " This is the world's axis," thinks the traveller.

Marble pathways radiate from the Ka'bah to the galleries. The pilgrim stands in awe, wondering whether he dares to do what everyone else is doing—the pilgrims, the veiled women, the invalids, little children, even the sanctuary's doves: to walk along one of the paths to the " House." At last he does so, and joins the procession round the building, beginning and ending each circuit at the eastern corner, where the Black Gem is set. As enjoined in the Qoran, he " remembers God " as he walks slowly round, his eyes fixed on the deep black silhouette of the Ka'bah against the night sky. At the end of each circuit he raises his arm and magnifies God.

When he has completed the seven circuits, he stands at the Station of Abraham, opposite the Ka'bah's silver gate. He reads the inscription which is embroidered in gold thread upon the dark drapery:

> *Verily, the first temple descended for mankind is that of Bakkah.*
> *It is blessed and a universal guidance.*
> *In it are manifestations....*
>
> (*Qoran:* III, 95-6).

He thinks with gratitude of those whose toil enabled him to stand here: those who last rebuilt " God's House " three centuries ago, then of the martyr 'Abd-Allah ibn Zubair. He thinks of the Apostle and Khadijah, and, finally, of Abraham and Hagar.

He must dedicate a special homage to her, the Egyptian maid. After so many centuries, the scene of her desperate search for water between Safa and Marwah has been reduced to two rocks, at each end of a covered gallery. The pilgrim is drinking from Hagar's fountain when the call to evening prayer echoes from seven minarets.

The pilgrim is uncertain: should he perform the prayer on one of the terraces above the porticoes, looking down upon the immense assemblage round the illuminated podium? (*ill.* 113). But the voice of Muhammad speaks in his heart and, avoiding the temptation of solitary worship, he takes his place in the thick of the crowd.

The service begins with a prolonged silence. It is so still that the pilgrims' garments can be heard fluttering in the warm breeze. Then comes the Imam's voice: " God is the Most High." His words are repeated, in long modulations, from every minaret and in every voice from bass to the crystal-clear soprano of a child. Then the pilgrim hears with astonishment a deafening roar, like an earth-quake, echoing and re-echoing from the mountains round the sacred valley. His own voice joins in, for this is the congregation of thousands of pilgrims, repeating the Gloria in unison.

113. The Ka'bah, just before evening service. The minarets and domes date from the period of the Turkish renovations in 994 A.H. (1585 A.D.). The unfinished building on the far left is the three-storied gallery set round the precincts after the Saudi extensions to the Ka'bah's courtyard.

EPILOGUE

The four periods of the service are over, and the pilgrim must now turn to his right and left to bless his companions in prayer. He sees first an African and then a slant-eyed Turkestani, who both smile at him as they bestow their blessings on him. Now he understands one of the "manifestations" of the Ka'bah: this is the union of humanity, bonded together since Adam in their aspirations towards the sublime word of God.

Street scene in Mecca.

NOTES

[1] The verse and chapter numbers of Qoranic quotations comply with the standard English translation of Muhammad 'Ali, Lahore, Pakistan 1951. The translations have however sometimes been modified, taking into consideration the interpretations given in an eighth century A. H. translation of the Qoran into Turkish, at the Topkapu Museum Library. In Qoranic as well as in all other translations from Arabic, I have been guided by the authoritative advice of Prof. Necati Lugal of the Faculty of Theology in Ankara.

[2] As mentioned by Prof. M. Hamidullah in *Le pèlerinage à La Mecque*, Paris 1960, p. 2, the Throne's description and the legends on Adam, Eve and their descendants, in the third century A. H. Islamic authors' texts, seem to follow the Hebraic cosmologic tradition. There are in these passages some other elements borrowed from Arabian paganism and Zoroastrian angelogy. Buddhist cosmologic concepts occur also, as in the successive reflections of the Throne, along the world's axis. For this concept, see S. Hummel, *Zum Buddhistischen Weltbild*, Leipzig 1948. The Buddhist contribution may be explained through the influence of the early Asian converts to Islam, as for instance the dynasty of the Barmakids, who were high priests of the Buddhist temple at Balkh. For the descriptions of the angels and of Adam's vision of the Throne, see the work of the Arabian chronicler of Mecca, the descendant of Ghassan princes, Muhammad ibn 'Abd Allah al-Azraqi, " The Blue-eyed" (died 244 A. H.), who recorded also his grandfather's reports on the legends and history of Mecca, ed. Wüstenfeld in Arabic, Leipzig 1858, p. 1-7.

[3] The symbolic character of angelic figures, as personified allegories of the current of emotions between the Creator and the created, becomes apparent in many of Muhammad's *hadith*, such as this: " Every time that a prayer is made, an angel is created..." Most Islamic authors have followed this opinion, in particular the great Andalusian Arab mystic Muhi al-Din ibn al-'Arabi (560-638 A. H.) in *Fusus al-hikam.*

[4] Muhammad's *hadith* " The believer's heart is God's throne " has been the accepted interpretation of most Islamic authors, as far as the " Throne " mentioned in the Qoran is concerned.

[5] The episodes on Adam and Noah have all been taken from the third century A. H. Islamic historian Abu Ja'far Muhammad ibn Jarir al-Tabari's work *Tarikh al-umam wa al-muluk* (*History of peoples and of kings*), Cairo ed. vol. I, p. 56-82. Some Qoranic quotations have also been added and are indicated where they occur.

[6] In Qoran XLII, 7, Mecca is called " Umm al-qura " (" The Mother of Agglomerations "), an expression which has been interpreted by historians to mean that the Meccan area is the core of the earth. The central part of the Meccan depression is sometimes designated as " Mecca's navel." The nineteenth century Turkish Scholar Eyyub Sabri Pasha, in his three-volume work dedicated to the Hijaz, to Mecca and to Madinah, published in Istanbul in 1304 A. H. (1886 A. D.) gives extensive information on bibliography, and on all other matters pertaining to the holy land of Islam. On the expression " Umm-al qura," see the volume entitled *Mir'at i-Mekke*, p. 37.

[7] The Qoranic passage XXIV, 35, where a lamp within an arch is described, has been interpreted by some mystics as the symbol of God in the human soul. The illustrious poet and mystic Jalal al-Din Rumi (604-672 A. H.) in his *Mathnawi* (Ismail Ankaravi ed., Istanbul 1257 A. H., vol. II, p. 130-31) has interpreted the Qoranic verse at length. Any source of light, from the modest candle to the moon, has been considered the emblem of Muhammad, whom the Qoran calls the " Nur " (Light) (V. 15-16) or the " Siraj al-Munir " (The Radiant Lustre) (XXXIII, 46). The word " *manarah* " (minaret) meaning " luminary," indicates the minaret's function in serving as a platform for the call to Islam. All believers are described in the Qoran (LVII, 12)

in these words: " *The believing men and the believing women, their lights advancing before them and on the right of them.*" The light within the niche, as described in the Qoranic parable XXIV, 35, made its appearance in tangible form, as a censer, in early Selçuk *mihrabs*. (For such an eleventh century Khorassan *mihrab* at the Teheran Museum, see *Turkistan Seyahatnamesi* by E. Esin, Ankara 1959, Introduction, *Selçuk period*.) Later, the censer motif became common on all Selçuk *mihrabs* in Iran and Turkey. It is on an Anatolian Selçuk tombstone that we see the first luminary in candle form (see M. Z. Oral, *Eshrefoglu Camiine ait bir kandil*, Ankara 1959. The candle motif either on tombstones or *mihrabs* (the Yesil Turbe in Bursa) is common in Anatolia and is seen also in Mameluk Egypt (Sultan Hasan's tomb, pulpit in Berkuk's mausoleum). Finally, Anatolian prayer-carpets show both the censer and the candle motifs (see M. Mostafa, *Turkish prayer rugs*, Cairo 1953). In the seventh century A. H., Abu al-Khattab ibn Bihyah's treatise on Muhammad's birth entitled *The Book of Illumination on the Nativity of the Radiant Lustre*, seems to have consecrated the appearance of luminaries in processions on the nativity night, and in all religious ceremonies. In the same century, Haji (" The Pilgrim ") Bektash Veli from Khorassan founded in Anatolia a mystic order (the Bektashi) where the candle played a symbolic part.

[8] This heap of boulders is called Jabal al-rahmah (" The Mount of Mercy ").

[9] According to the Qoran XI, 44, Noah's Ark landed on Mount Judi, in Asia Minor.

[10] The episodes concerning Abraham and Ishmael are either from Qoranic quotations or follow the related texts in Tabari, *op. cit.*, vol. I, p. 135; Azraqi, *op. cit.*, abridged edition in German by Wüstenfeld, p. 4; the *Al-jami' al-sahih* of the Central Asian Moslem traditionalist Abu 'Abd-Allah Muhammad Isma'il al-Bukhari (194-256 A. H.), Arabic-Turkish ed. A. Zebidi-K. Miras, Istanbul 1928, vol. IX, pp. 130, 142 and vol. VI, p. 120.

[11] The narrator of the quoted passage is Muhammad, as cited by Bukhari, vol. IX, pp. 135-146.

[12] Zamzam means " humming."

[13] Azraqi, Wüstenfeld abridg. pp. 7, 86, 135, Sabri, *Mir'at i-Mekke*, pp. 195, 249, 252.

[14] Bukhari, vol. VI, pp. 26-28, Azraqi, Wüstenfeld abridg., p. 9.

[15] For the period attributed to Abraham and Ishmael's life time in Islamic tradition, see E. Sabri, *Mir'at i-Mekke*, p. 190.

On the early records on the Arabs see: F. Hommel, *Arabia*, history, Encycl. Islam, Leyden 1913-17. Anon. *Al-'Arab*, Encycl. Isl. Loyden 1960; F. Buhl, *Das Leben Muhammads*, Heidelberg 1961, p. 1; Ameer 'Ali, *The Spirit of Islam*, London 1955, p. lxvi; Philipps, *Kataba und Saba*, Berlin 1955, p. 289; D. H. Muller, *Epigraphische Denkmaeler aus Arabien*, Vienna 1889; Ed. Glaser, *Skizze der Geschichte und Geographie Arabiens*, Berlin 1890.

On the origin of the names Yathrib and Madinah, see M. Hamidullah, *Le Prophète de l'Islam*, Paris 1959, p. 377.

[16] For the history of Madinah see the work of the Egyptian historian of 'Alid descent Nur al-Din 'Ali, ibn Ahmad al-Misri al-Samhudi (844-911 A. H.), *Wafa al-wafa*, Cairo 1955, vol. I, p. 156-173. Also E. Sabri, *Mir'at i-Medine*, Istanbul, 1304 A. H. p. 295. Tabari, vol. I, p. 106; F. Buhl, *Madina*, Encycl. Isl., 1313-27 ed.

[17] On the Ka'bah's isolated position in the valley of Bakkah, see Azraqi, Wüstenfeld abridg. pp. 10, 30. On the dwellings on the side of the mountains overlooking the Ka'bah, see Bukhari vol. XI, p. 354, and on the fact that they were cave dwellings, the description given in the year 442 A. H. by the Khorassani traveller Nasir Khusrav al-Marvazi, Turk. transl. A. Tarzi, Istanbul 1950. See Bukhari, vol. VI, p. 505, for the Ka'bah's outward decorations in the legendary 'Amalik period.

[18] On the ancient Arabian people called 'Ad, see Qoıan XXVI, 123-140, LXIX, 6-7. Also Tabari, vol. I, pp. 103, 106, 100-114. See the work of the Arabian historian and biographer of Muhammad, who used earlier sources also, 'Omar, Ibn 'Abd al-Malik, Ibn Hisham, Ibn Ayyub Al-Himyari Al-Basri (died 218 A. H.) *Al-Sirat al-Nabaw'yah*, Cairo 1936, vol. I, p. 121.

[19] For the episodes on the Jurhum and the Qatura, see Azraqi, Wüstenfeld abridg. pp. 10-13. Also Ibn Hisham, vol. I, pp. 116-119. The bronze horses of the Museum of the Ancient Orient in Istanbul are studied in H. Edhem, *Muze i-humayun rehberi*, sect. Asar i-himyariye, Istanbul 1315 A. H.

[20] On the ancient Arabic alphabet, see Philipps, *op. cit.*, p. 40-41. On the archaic Arabs' physical appearance, see *ibid.*, p. 240.

[21] On the eye-effigies, see L. Woolley, *Mesopotamia and the Middle East*, London 1961, p. 116-18.

[22] About the Arabian augurs, see A. Fischer, *Kahin*, Encycl. Isl., 1913-27 ed.

[23] For the Arabian idols see *Kitab al-asnam* (The Book of Idols) of the Arab historian Abu al-Mundhir Hisham al-Kalbi (died raound 206 A. H.), edit. A. Zaki, Cairo 1949. Also Wellhausen, *Reste Arabischen Heidentums* and F. Hommel, art. *Arabia, history*, Encycl. Isl. 1913-17 ed. See Philipps, pp. 200, 80, 103, 289. See Woolley, *op. cit.* A. Grohmann, *Arabien*, Munich 1963, abb. 30, 31.

[24] The altar with oxen relief in the Museum of the Ancient Orient in Istanbul is in room IX and bears the number 7665. See H. Edhem, *op. cit.*, for comments on the altar.

[25] Pre-Islamic Turkestan representations of the Buddhist motif of the bird of prey, a crea-

ture connected with the sun, carrying in its claws a snake, an animal connected with water, are reproduced in A. V. Le Coq, *Bilderatlas zur Kunst und Kunstgeschichte Mittelasiens*, Berlin 1925, figs. 237, 239.

[26] On the description of Southern Arabia and the itinerary of the caravans, see Babinger, arts. *Saba* and *Kataba*, Encycl. Isl. 1913-27 ed.; Philipps, pp. 151-183, 107, 114, 136, 235, 7-10 and a revised map of caravan routes at the end of the book. See also H. Lammens, *L'Arabie occidentale avant l'Hegire*, Beirut 1928, pp. 108, 230.

For Palmyra, see F. Buhl, *Palmyra*, Encycl. Isl., 1913-27 ed.

[27] On Nabateans, the Lihyan, the Thamud, see Tabari vol. I, p. 291; Woolley, *op. cit.*; E. Honigmann, *Nabateans*, Encycl. Isl., 1913-27 ed.; Bukhari, vol. IX, p. 250; C. Levi della Vida, *Lihyan*, Encycl. Isl.; J. Schleifer, *Al-Hidjr*, Encycl. Isl.; Glaser, *Thamud*, Encycl. Isl. Also Qoran VII, 73-9; XI, 67.

For the influence of the Nabatean alphabet on the historical Arabic alphabet, see B. Moritz, *Arabic Alphabet*, Encycl. Isl., 1913-27 ed.

For the architecture and the plastic works of the above-mentioned peoples, see Jausson et Savignac, *Mission archéologique en Arabie*, Paris 1909 and H. Edhem, *op. cit.*

[28] On the downfall of the Jurhum and on the Khuza'ah, see Azraqi, Wüstenfeld abridg. pp. 10-25, 31; Bukhari, vol. IX, p. 250; Sabri, *Mir'at i-Medine*, pp. 302-3; Lammens, *L'Arabie...*, p. 54; A. Grohmann, *Marib*, Encycl. Isl. Prof. Hamidullah kindly informed me that according to Ibn Habib (died 245 A. H.) in *Kitab al-muhabbar*, the final destruction of the Marib dam took place in the reign of Decius (249-51 A. D.). To try to determine the time of the Khuza'ah conquest of Mecca, one may take into consideration that the Khuza'ah's ally was the Ishmaelite B. Bakr ibn 'Abd Manat ibn Kinanah who lived thirteen generations before Muhammad and ten generations after 'Adnan, who is himself supposed to be a contemporary of Nebuchadnezzar. Mudad's poem is from Ibn Hisham vol. I, pp. 116-20.

[29] For the Meccan idols and the pagan pilgrimage, see Ibn Hisham, vol. I, pp. 78-93, 126-28, 211-15, Bukhari, vol. IX, pp. 245, 269-75, vol. VI, p. 173; Lammens, *L'Arabie...*, pp. 24, 30-37, 101-179, 185-236; *id.*, *Mecca*, Encycl. Isl.; Buhl, *Das Leben Muhammads*, pp. 76-80, 95; *id. Muzdalifa*, Encycl. Isl.; Brockelmann, *Arab literature*, Encycl. Isl.; Wensinck, *Khamr*, Encycl. Isl.; *id. 'Okaz*, Encycl. Isl.; Anon. *'Arabiyya*, Encycl. Isl., 1960 ed.; A. Guillaume, *The Life of Muhammad*, London 1955, p. 49, note 2; J. Schleifer, *Ghassan*, Encycl. Isl. and Qoran VIII, 35.

[30] On the Graeco-Roman period of Arabia, see Azraqi, Wüstenfeld abridg., p. 105; Philipps, p. 11; Lammens, *La Mecque...*, p. 114; *id.*, *Mecca*, Encycl. Isl.; J. H. Mordtmann, *Himyar*, Encycl. Isl.; E. Honigmann, *Nabateans*, Encycl. Isl.; Woolley, *op. cit.*; F. Buhl, *Das Leben Muhammaeds*, pp. 75, 90, 103.

For Graeco-Roman representations of al-Lat, see S. and A. Abdul-Hak, *Catalogue des antiquités greco-romaines du Musée de Damas*, Damascus, 1951, pl. XIII. For the stele of the South Arabian young woman, no. 130880 in the Syrian Room of the British Museum, see R. D. Barnett - D. J. Wiseman, *Fifty Masterpieces of Ancient Near-Eastern Art*, London 1960, pp. 74-5.

[31] The quotation of the pre-Islamic Arabian poem on the rider with the torch is after Guillaume, *op. cit.*, p. 174.

[32] On the Magians of Arabia see M. Hamidullah, *Le Prophète de l'Islam*, vol. I, pp. 240, 430; on Magians, Manicheans and followers of other cults in Arabia see the research made in Ameer 'Ali, *op. cit.*, pp. lviii-lxvii, xvii; F. Buhl, *Das Leben Muhammads*, p. 71; Lammens, *L'Arabie...*, p. 39; Brockelmann, *Arab Literature*, Encycl. Isl., ed. 1913; for the Meccans' angel worship, see Qoran XLIII, 19-20; XXVII, 53.

[33] One may try to determine the period in which As'ad Abu Karib lived, through the fact that in vol. I, p. 15-28, Ibn Hisham relates that As'ad Abu Karib's reign preceded that of Rabi'ah Ibn Nasr. The latter had dreamed, about seventy years before it occurred, of the first Ethiopian invasion of South Arabia, placed by historians between the second and the fourth century A. D. (see F. Babinger, *Saba*; J. H. Mordtmann, *Himyar*; F. Buhl, *Das Leben Muhammaeds*, p. 8).

According to Ibn Hisham, Abu Karib's successor was a contemporary of the Persian kings of the Shapur line. In the opinion of F. Buhl, in *Das Leben Muhammads*, p. 9, As'ad Abu Karib was the son of a king mentioned in an inscription dated 328 A. D.

[34] On the period of Judaic and Christian influences in and around the Hijaz, see Azraqi, Wüstenfeld abridgment, pp. 55-57; Ibn Hisham, vol. I, p. 32-37; Ameer 'Ali, p. lxiii; M. Hamidullah, *Le Prophète de l'Islam*, p. 109; Lammens, *L'Arabie...*, pp. 129, 24, 21-22, 146, 177, 41-44; Philipps, pp. 234-37; J. Schleifer, *Ghassan*, Encycl. Isl., 1913 ed.; the quotation of the Abrahah inscription is from J. H. Mordtmann, *Himyar*, Encycl. Isl., 1913 ed.

On the poets, see Brockelmann, *Arab literature*, Encycl. Isl.; M. Chemont, *Nabigha*, Encycl. Isl.; Ibn Qotaibah, *Kitab al-Shi'r* (De Goeje ed., p. 37); *id.*, *Kitab al-Ma'arif*, Cairo 1300 A. H., p. 212.

For the references to Turks in pre-Islamic Arab texts, see Ibn Hisham, vol. I, pp. 27, 294. I have also been privileged to use the compilation of sources in an unpubl. article by Prof. Z. V. Togan, *Turklere aid hadisler*.

[35] On Qoraish, on Qosayy and the foundation of a city in the Meccan vale, see Azraqi, Wüstenfeld abridg., pp. 43-63, 57-84; Ibn Hisham, vol. I, p. 123-4, 130-140.

[36] On the events preceding Muhammad's birth, see Ibn Hisham, vol. I, pp. 217-249, 339-340, 150-155, 164-168; the work on Muhammad and his followers by 'Abd-Allah Muhammad Ibn Sa'ad Al-Basri Al-Zuhri (168-230 A. H.), *Kitab al-tabaqat*, Beirut 1960, vol. I,

pp. 90-94, 95-104; M. Hamidullah, *Le Prophète de l'Islam*, vol. I, p. 33.
Some of the Biblical and Gospel texts, thought to be connected with the Comforter by Moslem theologians, are: Deut. XVIII, 15-18; Acts III, 21-22; John I, 22; XIV, 16; XV, 26; XVI, 5-15; Matthew XIII, 31; XXI, 33-45; Mark XII, 1-11; Luke XX, 9-18.

[37] This is part of an anonymous Turkish nativity hymn of mediaeval origin.

[38] I have given a slightly revised version of a translation by E. J. Gibb (*A History of Ottoman Poetry*, London 1958, vol. I, pp. 246-47), of a mediaeval Turkish hymn that Gibb attributes to Suleyman Çelebi of Bursa, the author of the famous nativity hymn of the fourteenth century A. D. It has been established through the publication of an early MS (see A. Ateş, *Vesiletu'n-necat*, *Mevlid*, Ankara 1954) that this passage is a later, though still mediaeval, addition to Suleyman Çelebi's hymn.

[39] The quotation on Halimah is from Ibn Hisham, vol. I, pp. 174-5. On the events of Muhammad's youth, see Ibn Hisham, vol. I, pp. 177-211, 316, vol. II, p. 42; Ibn Sa'ad, vol. I, pp. 112-13, 116-17, 410-25, 458-59; Bukhari, vol. IX, p. 302; Azraqi, Wüstenfeld abridg. pp. 71, 84-91.

[40] Bukhari, vol. VI, p. 505, describes traditions concerning painters in the time of the Prophet and of his companions.

[41] For the period of Muhammad's life at the beginning of the revelations, see Ibn Hisham, vol. I, pp. 316, 195-98, 211-15, 140, 145, 249, 256-58, 292; Bukhari, vol. VI, p. 123; vol. I, pp. 1-11; Azraqi, Wüstenfeld abridg., pp. 84-91, 54; Ibn Sa'ad, vol. I, pp. 160-194, 197; M. Hamidullah, *Le Prophète de l'Islam*, vol. I, pp. 47-49, 64-65, 67-68; E. Sabri, *Mir'at i-Mekke*, p. 1155; Guillaume, p. 81, note 2; T. Andrae, *Mohammed*, U. S. ed., 1960, p. 18.

[42] The forms of revelation received by Muhammad were described by his contemporaries, see Bukhari, vol. I, pp. 1-3.
For the identification of Islam with monotheism, see Qoran XXX, 30: "*So set thy face toward religion, as a 'hanif' (monotheist), in the nature originated by God, in which He has originated mankind. There is no change in what God created. This is the eternal religion, but most of mankind know not.*" Many other Qoranic verses, such as II, 62, II, 136, II, 213, clearly explain that the necessary and sufficient condition for salvation is defined as belief in the One God. In a *hadith*, (M. Arif, *Binbir hadis serh i-serifi*, Cairo 1319 A. H., p. 7), Muhammad makes the following comment on such Qoranic verses: "I announce and you must announce to the generations after you that whoever believes sincerely that there is none to worship except God, has entered Paradise."
On the contrast between the appearance of the world and its hidden significance, see, amongst other verses, Qoran, XXX, 7 and LII, 2-3.

[43] On the Meccan period of Muhammad's apostolate, see: Ibn Hisham, vol. I, pp. 257-389, vol. II, p. 110; Ibn Sa'ad, vol. I, p. 200, vol. VIII, pp. 14, 18, 36-8, 264; Bukhari, vol. IX, p. 33; Hamidullah, *Le Prophète de l'Islam*, vol. I, pp. 200, 90, 92, 78; Guillaume, pp. 118, 178, 190, 192; Arif, p. 64.
On the ascensional vision, see Bukhari, vol. X, p. 29; F. Buhl, *Mi'raj*, Encycl. Isl., 1913-27 ed.
The garden of Paradise, according to the Qoran is "a parable" (XLVII, 15) the significance of which "no soul knows" (XXXII, 17). The allegorical character of the garden image is apparent also in Muhammad's *hadith*: "Indeed Paradise is a flat expanse, a desert plain that is uncultivated. Sow the plants of paradise, while yet in this world" (M. Fazil Mevlevi, *Hakayik i Mevlana*, Istanbul, 1283 A. H.).

[44] On the Hegira, see Ibn Hisham, vol. II, pp. 52-96, 110; Ibn Sa'ad, vol. I, pp. 199, 213-34, 404; Hamidullah, *Le Prophète de l'Islam*, vol. I, pp. 74, 96-104; Lammens, *L'Arabie...*, p. 41, note 3.

[45] On Muhammad's apostolate in Madinah, see Ibn Sa'ad, vol. I, pp. 226, 233, 422, 246-56; vol. III, p. 31; Ibn Hisham, vol. I, p. 146, vol. II, pp. 42, 84 note 1; Bukhari, vol. IV, pp. 262-8, vol. VI, pp. 53, 127, 136, vol. X, pp. 93-5, 349, vol. XI, p. 91; Samhudi, vol. I, pp. 244 *ff*; Hamidullah, *The Battlefields of the Prophet Muhammad*, Woking, England, 1953, pp. 10, 19; Sabri, *Mir'at i-Medine*, pp. 911-21, 157, 364; Guillaume, p. 228.
For the *hadith* cited in connection with the Apostle's teaching at Madinah, see Arif, pp. 357, 119, 92, 97, 90. Muhammad also said: "The ways to God are as numerous as the number of creatures," thus confirming the importance he attached to personal conscience.
For the mediaeval mystics' comments on the broken palm-tree column at the Apostle's Mosque, see the passage entitled *Nalidan i-sutun i-hannanah*, in Jalal al-Din Rumi's *Mathnawi*, ed. 'Ala al-dawlah, 1299 A. H., vol. I, pp. 55-6.
On Muhammad's concept of Islam as a future world-wide religion, see Qoran XLVIII, 28; IX, 33; XLI, 53 and numerous *hadith* predicting the acceptance of Islam by peoples of various regions of the world. See also the interpretation given by Muhammad to the term "later Moslems" in Qoran LXII, 3.

[46] For details of Muhammad's personal life at Madinah, see Ibn Hisham, vol. IV, pp. 321-26; Ibn Sa'ad, vol. II, pp. 193, 185, vol. I, p. 422, 359, 364-73, 380-82, 400-10, 446-49; Bukhari, vol. VI, pp. 46, 293, vol. IV, p. 489, vol. VIII, p. 22, vol. IX, p. 445, vol. XII, pp. 204-6, 352, 166, 135.
For the quoted *hadith*, see Arif, pp. 98, 106, 119.

[47] On the religious wars, see Azraqi, Wüstenfeld abridg., pp. 94-116; Bukhari, vol. X, pp. 332-47, vol. VI, p. 137; Ibn Hisham, vol. III, pp. 64-177, vol. IV, pp. 26-81, 59-61; and M. Hamidullah, *The Battlefields of the Prophet Muhammad*.

The efforts made by Muhammad to encourage most of the first Moslems to take part in the battles is witnessed by Qoranic passages, such as VIII, 45-6, IX, 8, 13 and the many episodes related by Ibn Hisham and Ibn Sa'ad.

[48] For Muhammad's farewell pilgrimage and his death, see Ibn Sa'ad, vol. II, pp. 205-99; Bukhari, vol IV, pp. 291-92, 298-306, vol. X, pp. 16-29, vol. VI, p. 399; Ibn Hisham, vol. IV, pp. 298-317; Hamidullah, *Le Prophète de l'Islam*, pp. 689-96.

For the Apostle's itinerary on the Farewell Pilgrimage, see Ahmad ibn Yahya al-Baladhuri's (died 279 A. H.) *Ansab al-ashraf*, Cairo 1959, vol. I, p. 369.

For the symbolic character of cattle and hence also of the sacrificial animals as the symbols of worldly possessions, see many *hadith* and Qoran III, 13.

The history of Muhammad's death and burial mainly follows Ibn Sa'ad's account.

[49] On the events after the Prophet's death, see: Ibn Hisham, vol. IV, pp. 304-22; Ibn Sa'ad, vol. VIII, pp. 19-36, 58-86, 74-7, vol. II, pp. 265-71, 311-12, 351-57; Bukhari, vol. VI, pp. 280-81; Azraqi, Wüstenfeld abridg., pp. 12, 77, 117-24; Sabri *Mir'at i-Medine*, pp. 1153-54, 471-82.

For the descriptions of the first four orthodox caliphs and of the first 'Omayyad rulers, see Abu al-Hasan 'Ali ibn al-Husain al-Masu'udi (died 345 A. H.), *Kitab al-tanbih*, transl. Carra de Vaux, Paris 1897, pp. 379, 383, 387, 397.

For Salman's translation of part of the Qoran, see M. Hamidullah, *Sahifah Hamam Ibn Munabbih*, Hyderabad, India, 1961, p. 15.

The quotation on Uwais al-Qarani is from an Uygur Turkish memorial of saints, *Tezkerch i-evlia, MS ouigour de la Bibl. Nationale*, ed. Pavet de Courteille, Paris 1889, pp. 12-13.

[50] The quotation of the King of China's gift to the 'Omayyad caliph is from a manuscript of the Fatimid period, publ. by M. Hamidullah, *Qadi al-Rashid ibn al-Zubair's Kitab al-dhaka'ir wa al-tuhaf*, Kuwait 1959, narration no. 8. I think that this must be a king of a Central Asian land, because at the 'Omayyad period, the Arabs settled in Khorassan, Seistan, Transoxiana, Sind, all of which were open to the cultural influences of both China and India. In these lands, elephants were used, as in Kabul, in the army of the King (see Baladhuri, *Futuh al-buldan*, Turk. transl. Z. K. Ugan, Istanbul 1956, vol. II, p. 259). It is evident that for the Arabs, there was sometimes a confusion between Central Asia, China and India, for the King of India is also alluded to in similar terms (see the 'Omayyad report on India in the history of India of Ibn Fadl Allah al-'Omari's world history, publ. H. A. Faruq, Delhi 1961).

On 'Omayyad castles and their paintings and sculpture, see Hamilton-Grabar, *Khirbat al-Mafjar*, Oxford 1959; M. van Berchem, *Au pays de Moab et d'Edom, Journal des savants*, July-Sept. 1909; A. Musil, *Kusejr Amra und andere Schlosser östlich von Moab, Sitzungberichte der kaiserlichen Akademie der Wissenschaften*, LII, pp. 341 *ff.*; S. and A. Abdul Hak, *op. cit.* For illustrations of Qasr al-hair see R. Ettinghausen, *La peinture arabe*, Geneva, 1962.

[51] Baladhuri provides in *Futuh al-buldan*, Vol. II, pp. 260, 314, explanations of Central Asian influences on the 'Omayyad court which may be added to the documentation, on this subject previously gathered (see E. Esin, *Two Miniatures from the collections of Topkapu, Ars Orientalis*, V, note 7). The Turkish Emperor's son was taken prisoner and brought to the court of the builder of Mafjar, Hisham, and spent the rest of his life in the 'Omayyad retinue. Slaves from Kabul built in Basrah a mosque in the style of their country of origin.

The coin with the *mihrab* and the spear has been published by G. Miles, *Mihrab and 'Anazah, Archeolog. Orientalia*, in memor. E. Herzfeld, 1949.

[52] The quotations from the pietists are from Abu 'Abd Allah Muhammad ibn Muslim Ibn Qotaibah al-Kufi al-Marvazi (213-276 A. H.), *Kitab i-'uyun al-akhbar*, Cairo 1285 A. H., vol. IV, pp. 92-4.

[53] The quotation on the fate of the 'Omayyad is from Abu al-Faraj al-Isfahani (284-357), *Kitab al-aghani*, Cairo 1285 A. H., vol. IV, pp. 92-4. For the history of Mecca and Madinah in this period see Azraqi, pp. 124-57; Samhudi, vol. II, pp. 466-532; Sabri, *Mir'at i-Medine*, 482-534, 819.

[54] The acceptance of Islam by the Bulgar Turks living on the Volga in 310 A. H. (922 A. D.) is described by a member of the embassy sent by the 'Abbassid caliph al-Muqtadir, at the request of the King of the Bulgars. The narrator in Ahmad ibn Fadlan, whose *Rihlah* has been discovered and publ. by Prof. Z. V. Togan, *Ibn Fadlans Reisebericht*, Leipzig 1939.

Yusuf Khas Hajib's poetical mystery *Kutadgubilig* (Blissful Knowledge) written in 462 A. H. (1068 A. D.) in Turkish and dedicated to the Kara-hanli Emperor Hasan ibn Suleyman surnamed Arslan (" the Lion "), contains a well-known dialogue (parts LXXIII-LXXXI) between two brothers. The first represents the essential Moslem virtue of service to the community, according to Muhammad's *hadith*: " The best of mankind is one who is of most service to mankind." The other brother, although also Moslem, leads the solitary, ascetic life of a Buddhist or Taoist monk, dedicated to the contemplation of nature.

[55] The cosmographic plan of Baghdad is described in M. Mazaheri, *La vie quotidienne des musulmans au Moyen-age*, Paris, 1951, p. 95.

The construction of parts of Samarra by the pagan Turks and the splendour of the palace they made for their chief is related in Abu al-'Abbas Ahmad Ya'qubi's *Kitab al-buldan, Surra man raa.*

[56] The quotation concerning the reception of the Byzantine ambassadors is transl. from M. Hamidullah, *L'Europe et l'Orient musulman, Arabica VIII*, Sept. 1960, pp. 13-17.

[57] Muhammad Abu al-Nasir al-Farabi al-Turki's (257-339 A. H. — 870-950 A. D.) *Ara*

i-ahl al-Madinah al-fadilah (The Virtuous City) in which the ideal of Moslem existence, both in the community's organisation and in the discipline of the forces within the human soul, is stated at length, becomes thus not only an emulation of but also an opposition to Plato's *Republic*.

The information about the monuments of Mecca and Madinah in the 'Abbassid period is taken from Sabri, *Mir'at i-Medine*, pp. 507-62; *Mir'at i-Mekke*, p. 106; Azraqi, Wüstenfeld abridg., pp. 157-239; the narrations of the Khorassani traveller Abu Mu'in Nasir ibn Khusrav (394-453 A. H.), *Safarnamah*, Turk. transl. A. Tarzi, Istanbul 1950, pp. 111 *ff.*; M. Hamidullah, *The Battlefields...*, p. 8.

Baladhuri, *Futuh al-buldan*, vol. II, p. 95, states that when Mu'tasim Billah built the great Mosque of Samarra, he ordered that the minaret's height should be raised, so that the call to prayer might be heard within a larger radius. We might have here an explanation of the change in the form of the Samarra minaret.

[58] The information given on the subject of the canonists and the mystics is derived from: Muhammad al Sulami, *Kitab tabaqat al-sufiyya*, ed. J. Pedersen, Leyden 1960, p. 13; Farid al-din 'Attar, *Tadhkirat al-awlia*, sixteenth cent. A. D. anon. Turk. transl. Istanbul 1959, pp. 14, 18, 37, 80, 129, 135; also the work of the celebrated Khorassani mystic, pilgrim and author on the Hijaz, 'Abd al-Rahman al-Jami (807-848 A. H.) *Nafakhat al-uns*, Turk. transl. Lami'i Çelebi, Istanbul 1289 A. H., pp. 89, 95, 170, 315.

The quotation from Rabi'ah is transl. by Margaret Smith, *Rabi'ah al-'Adawiyah*, Encycl. Isl. 1936. Rabia' ah's vegetarian habits are described in Farid al-din 'Attar's *Ilahinamah* ed. H. Ritter, Istanbul 1940, p. 120.

[59] The quotation on al-Wathiq and the singer Faridah is from al-Isfahani, vol. III, p. 184.

[60] On the buildings attributed to the former slave Baha al-Din Karakush (died 598 A. H. - 1201 A. D.), see Ibn Khallikan, *Wafayat al-'ayan*, Bulak 1299 A. H., vol. I, p. 543. The same author mentions the introduction of the game of chess by the Turk al-Suli (see under that name), to the Near East.

[61] On the new art forms brought to the Near East by the Turkish migrations from Central Asia, between the eleventh and the fourteenth centuries, and by the Mongol invasion, amongst many works that may be recommended see for architectural forms E. Diez, *Die Kunst der islamischen Völker*, Wildpark-Potsdam 1927; *Das Erbe der Steppe in der turko-iranischen Baukunst*, Z. V. Togan'a Armagan, Istanbul 1950-55; *Masjid, its architecture, Manara, Mihrab*, Encycl. Isl. Leyden 1936. On development from the multiple niches common in Central Asian Buddhist architecture to stalactite decoration in regions under Karahanli rule, see *Architectural Monuments in Middle Asia from the VIII-XII Centuries, Proceedings of the first International Congress of Turkish Arts*, Ankara 1961, pp. 364-70. On the quadrangular, seal-shaped architectonic inscriptions in brickwork, see E. Esin, *Influences de l'art nomade et de l'art du Turkestan* from the above *Proceedings*, pp. 126-27. The Saraban minaret in Isfahan, dating from the Selçuk period, is an example of the palm-tree decoration in minarets that is reminiscent of Rumi's comments mentioned in note 45.

For the general aspects of the artistic influences brought by the Turks and Mongols to the Near East, see J. Strzygowski, *Turkler ve Orta Asya san'ati meselesi*, Turkiyat mecmuasi, Istanbul, vol. III, 1926-33; E. Diez, *Die Kunst der islamischen Völker*; E. Esin, *Turkish Miniature Painting, Influences de l'art nomade et de l'art du Turkestan, Two Miniatures...*

[62] The Turk's description is quoted from Abu 'Othman 'Amr ibn Bakr al-Jahiz (died 250 A. H.), *Risalah Abi al-Fath ibn Khaqan fi manaqib al-Turk*, Leyden 1903, pp. 28-31.

[63] The quotation on the gifts sent by the Byzantines to the Fatimid caliph is transl. from M. Hamidullah, *L'Europe et l'Orient musulman*, pp. 8-9.

As witnessed by the continuity in the architectural style and in other fields of art, the Circassian Mameluks became heir to the influences brought to Egypt and Syria by their Turkish predecessors. The numerous translations of classical Arabic works ordered by the Circassian Mameluks of Egypt (see Turkish MSS. catalogue at the Topkapu Library), show that they read Turkish and not Arabic or any other language.

[64] On the history of Madinah in the mediaeval period and the transformations then undergone by the Apostle's Mosque, see Sabri, *Mir'at i-Medine*, citing Samhudi and other sources, pp. 699-701, 283, 712-56, 588, 664, 494.

[65] On the 'Alid knights, see H. Fuchs, *Mawlid*, Encycl. Isl. 1913-27; on the physical types and the costumes of the Turks, I have used for sources, in early Islamic texts the extensive bibliography prepared by Prof. Z. V. Togan, in an unpubl. study, *Turk milli tipi*. See also Tabari, vol. I, pp. 102, 109, for the Turks' physical type. For ancient North-Asian costumes and particularly for the horns worn by *kams*, see A. O. Okladnikov, *Ancient Populations of Siberia and its Cultures*, Cambridge, Mass. 1959. The sculptures and paintings of the Selçuk period show us the Selçuk Turks wearing the costumes peculiar to the rider nomads of ancient Eurasia. One of the two statues of Selçuk warriors at the Metropolitan Museum, New York, represents a man wearing a head-dress with horns and thus provides an illustration of the " horns " attributed to the Mameluk Turkish warriors, in various histories of the time. See on the subject of Turkish helmets with horns, E. Esin, *Influences de l'art nomade et de l'art du Turkestan*, p. 114. On the drum presented as a sign of accession to Central Asian princes, by the Emperor of China, and the Western Turks' military music, see J. Mahler, *The Westerners among the Figurines of the T'ang Dynasty of China*, Rome 1959, p. 74.

[66] For the ceremonies on Muhammad's nativity, see Fuchs, *op. cit.* The quotations on the Irbil ceremonies are from the pen of a

native, Abu al-'Abbas Ahmad ibn Muhammad al-Barmaki al-Irbili Ibn Khallikan (608-681 A. H.), *Wafayat al-ayan*, Bulaq ed., vol. I, p. 550.

[67] For the descriptions of pilgrims and the history of Mecca and of its monuments in mediaeval times, see Wüstenfeld, *Geschichte der Stadt Mekka*, a compilation from the original sources, Leipzig 1861, pp. 210-300; Nasir i-Khusrav, pp. 119-22, the description of the Moroccan traveller Abu 'Abd Allah Muhammad Ibn Battutah who went to the Hijaz in 725 A. H. (1325 A. D.), ed. Defremery-Sanguinetti, vol. I, pp. 376, 379; the account of the Andalusian pilgrim Abu al-Husain Muhammad ibn Ahmad Ibn Jubair who visited Mecca in 579 A. H., *Rihlah*, Beirut 1959, pp. 128, 141, 59; Mazaheri, pp. 21-29; Sabri, *Mir'at i-Mekke*, pp. 95, 162, 686, 788, 847, 890, 1004, 1050, 982, 605, 838, 12.

[68] The episode concerning Ghazali is from Jami, *op. cit.*, p. 404.

[69] On Mustafa ibn Yusuf ibn Omer Erzeni Dariri who in the 14th century A. D. wrote for the Egyptian mameluk Sultan Berkuk a life of Muhammad in Turkish, see an old MS of his work at the Millet Kut. Istanbul and *Turkish Miniature Painting*, by E. Esin, p. 20. The illustrations from Erzeni's life of Muhammad which have been reproduced in this work are from three various sources: *a*) Detached miniatures in the Sharif Sabri collection in Cairo, of unknown origin and date, but attributed by Prof. F. Iz to the end of the 16th century A. D. and found stylistically akin to fifteenth and sixteenth century works by G. M. Meredith-Owens, in his work *Turkish Miniatures*, London 1963, p. 18. *b*) Paintings from the three vol. MS. of Topkapu no. H. 1221-23, a copy for Murad III by Ahmed Nur ibn Mustafa. The painter's name is not given but in the documents from the archives of Topkapu publ. by R. M. Meric, *Turk nakis san'ati tarihi arastirmalari*, Ankara 1953, pp. 70 and 57, it is mentioned that in 1003 A. H. a copy of Erzeni's work was made for Murad III by the court head-painter Lutfi and his pupils. On p. 57, it is also reported that "...in the same year (994 A. H. - 1585 A. D.) the head painter Master Lutfi has been sent to the honourable (city of) Mecca... and in 998 A. H. decorated with paintings a lamp-shaped revolving door in the honourable Sanctuary." Thus Lutfi stayed at least four years in the Hijaz and we are justified in finding in his works the mark of direct observation of the landscape. *c*) The remaining illustrations from Erzeni's work are reproduced from the one extant volume of a later MS. no. 1974 at the Turk ve Islam Eserleri Muzesi (see K. Cig, *Turk ve Islam eserleri Muzesindeki minyaturlu kitaplarin katalogu*, Istanbul 1959, p. 11). Here the "illuminator" and hence probably the painter is cited as Seyyid Suleyman Kasim Pasha. No date is given. Again consulting R. M. Meric, *op. cit.*, we find on p. 47 that in the list of court painters in a period corresponding to the date that might be ascribed to the MS. in 1207 and 1211 A. H., a Seyyid Suleyman ibn Osman is mentioned.

[70] The poem is attributed to Yunus Emre in an MS. book of hymns dated 1243 A. H. in my library. Also, in the last quatrain the author's name is given as Yunus. Yet other mediaeval poets have emulated Yunus and even adopted his name as his disciples.

[71] On the history of Selim I, see Sadeddin, *Taj al-tawarikh*, and *Selimnameh*, Istanbul 1280 A. H., vol. II, pp. 122 *ff*.

For the history of Mecca in Ottoman times, see Sabri, *Mir'at i-Mekke*, pp. 16-20, 119, 221, 513-37, 670-72, 711-88, 832-99, 904-17, 1004-78, 1112, 1130; Wüstenfeld, pp. 300-324.

On Sinan's plan for the reconstruction of the Ka'bah, see T. Oz, *Kabenin tamiri*, *Arkitekt*, Istanbul, 1947, no. 16.

On the relics at the Topkapu Museum, see T. Oz, *Emanat i-mukaddese*, Istanbul 1953.

The quotation on the pilgrimage journey is from Yusuf Nabi's *Tuhfat al-Haramain*, written in 1095 A. H. (1682 A. D.). The text transl. is in an MS. dated Edirne 1142 A. H. in my library, fols. 3 v., 29 r., v., 30.

[72] For the history of Madinah in Ottoman times, see Sabri, *Mir'at i-Medine*, pp. 57-75, 420, 552-86, 611-64, 716-97, 861, 887, 901-11, 1023-54, 1326.

For the mission of the calligrapher Shukrullah, commissioned after 'Abd ul-Mejid's death by the citizens of Istanbul to decorate the Apostle's Mosque, see M. K. Inal, *Son hattatlar*, Istanbul 1955, pp. 15-19.

[73] On the 1914-18 events in Mecca and Taif, see T. Ozmerd, unpubl, MS memoirs in the library of the Turk Tarih Kurumu, Ankara. The quotation from T. E. Lawrence is from *Revolt in the Desert*, p. 14-19, 171, 348. The Madinah events are from N. Kashif, *Hatiralar*, publ. in Tercuman i-hakikat, Istanbul, Feb.-May 1922. The quotation of Fahruddin Pasha's address is transl. from Anon. *Medine mudafaasi*, publ. Yakin Tarihimiz, Istanbul, March 1st 1962. The quotation on the meeting in the Damascus headquarters is from A. F. Erden, *Colde son Turk destanlari*, Dunya, Istanbul, Jan. 3, 8, 22-24, in 1955. Enver Pasha's visit to Madinah is described in H. Bayur, *Turk imkilabi tarihi*, vol. III, p. 555. I have also been allowed to consult Fahruddin Pasha's personal papers by kind permission of his daughter, Mrs. S. Turkkaan. On events in Madinah and for other information about the 1914-18 war in the Hijaz, I am indebted to Mr. Osman Saatci, formerly Fahruddin Pasha's interpreter and now professor at the Islamic Institute of Madinah.

[74] The first quotation from M. Iqbal (1873-1939 A. D.) is from *Jawidnameh*, verses 18,5-10; the second quotation is from his poem inscribed on his tombstone, in the courtyard of Padishahi Mosque, in Lahore.

[75] For the extensions in the Hijaz sanctuaries in the Saudi period, see, for Mecca, *Mashru' Jalalat al-Malik Su'ud al-Mu'azzam*, Jiddah 1377 A. H.; for Madinah, see *Al-masjid al-Nabawi al-Sharif*, Jiddah 1375 A. H.

[76] In Qoran LII, 4, the Ka'bah is called the "ever-visited House."

INDEX

صفا طرفندن آلنان رسمیدر